BANGKOK BOUND

BANGKOK BOUND

ELLEN BOCCUZZI

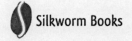
Silkworm Books

ISBN: 978-616-215-050-0

Silkworm Books
6 Sukkasem Road, T. Suthep
Chiang Mai 50200 Thailand
info@silkwormbooks.com
http://www.silkwormbooks.com

Typeset in Minion Pro 10 pt. by Silk Type

Printed and bound in China

5 4 3 2 1

For Joey

CONTENTS

CHAPTER 1

INTRODUCTION

BANGKOK BOUND

A hobby horse, a gift for me,
Hewn by my father's loving hands
From the stem of a banana tree,
And a gun to fire at hostile bands.

His words still ring in my ears:
A man must leave his home one day
To wander into the world for years,
In quest of destiny, not dismay.

With a leap we leave our humble home,
Heading for the woods and hilly heights,
For hundred days and thousand nights
Of sweet and bitter honeycomb.

    Thru brambles, o'er ponds and streams,
    The horizon in search of dreams!

A knotty tree stump for pillow,
A cloudless night sky as my shroud;
With only my lonely horse in tow,
To sustain courage e'er so proud.

    Thru brambles, o'er ponds and streams,
    The horizon in search of dreams!

Looking for bright civilization,
City of Angels under a veil
Of hazy smoke, the sleazy curtain
Hides my companion's dreamy trail.

The banana horse comes to a halt
On a jungle trail paved with asphalt,
'Neath rows and rows of concrete gables,
Jumbled wires and tangled cables.

Jingling and jangling sounds titillate,
Tinglingly tease my sad spirit,
As I search in vain for a mate
To find only my faithful steed.

> Man's tears wipe not defeat or shame,
> They only add a smear to our name!

Weak in face of many a demon,
Surrounded by ferocious foes,
Both my gun and horse, I reason,
Will wither ere anyone knows.

> Man's tears wipe not defeat or shame,
> They only add a smear to our name!

My father taught me by word and test,
That I should focus all our means
On unfolding dreams of conquest,
Now undone by urban machines.

With chest scars and a bleeding pain,
I must flee this chaos infernal,
And ride back o'er rice fields again
To beg for blessings paternal.

— *Paiwarin Khao-Ngam, "Banana Tree Horse 1"*
(Paiwarin 1995; translated by B. Kasemsri)

Paiwarin's hero, a young rural-urban migrant, is Bangkok bound. He rides to the city on a hobbyhorse crafted from a banana frond, a child's toy that is at once a symbol of his youth and of the natural world from which he comes. As this migrant leaves the countryside on his banana-tree horse, he appears wholly immersed in the rural world. His transportation (horse) and protection (gun) are both made from the leaves of a banana tree, and he rides across fields shrouded by the "cloudless night sky." As soon as the city appears up ahead, however, the hero's "banana horse comes to a halt" and his "dreamy trail" of migration is transformed. Bangkok appears before him as a "City of Angels under a veil / Of hazy smoke," where "rows and rows of concrete gables" obscure the natural environment, and "jingling and jangling sounds" confuse and mock him. The migrant is quickly enveloped by this seductive realm, but he finds himself estranged within it: he "search[es] in vain for a mate"—someone with whom to share a connection in the city—but finds only his "faithful steed," the bit of banana frond he brought with him from the village.

This migrant quickly understands that in the alienating urban space, "both [his] gun and horse" may "wither ere anyone knows." He and the rural sources of strength he has brought with him may atrophy and die in this environment without anyone to register the loss. His village-based "dreams of conquest" are quickly "undone by urban machines," and he tries to save what he can by "rid[ing] back o'er rice fields" to get in touch with his home and self once again.

As many of the migrant protagonists in this book find, true return to the village—and the remembered self—is impossible. The migrants who leave their homes bound for Bangkok with dreams of urban success soon learn that the experience of migration is much more complex than this. They may initially view the city ahead as a blank canvas on which they will make their mark, but they learn upon arrival that the city has the power to mark and transform *them* in ways they never could have imagined from their pre-migration standpoint. Bangkok-bound migrants are quickly bound *by* Bangkok, as the city forges ties that hold them to it, changing who they are and defining the bounds of a new identity, one that will always be both rural *and* urban.

Paiwarin Khao-Ngam's *Banana Tree Horse* explores several of the key themes found throughout the genre of Thai migration literature, including the transition from a rural to urban paradigm, nostalgia for "the way things used to be," the difficulty of evaluating the migrant's success in the urban realm, and the bittersweet moment of return when the migrant must face his family and define who he has become.[1] Paiwarin's collection of poetry

---

1. Paiwarin's collection is the best known and most widely read work of Thai literature about migration. It won the coveted S.E.A. Write Award in 1995 and since then has undergone twenty-four printings and an English translation.

is rooted in a centuries-old tradition of epic journey poems (Suchitra 2004), but the contemporary language and symbolism of the poetry locate the hero's journey firmly in the late twentieth century. *Banana Tree Horse* thus depicts an explicitly contemporary process—rural-urban migration to Bangkok—as a tale that has long been told, an epic journey. Through this particular combination of form, setting, and language, Paiwarin hints at the extent to which contemporary processes of migration have become both normalized and mythologized in the Thai collective consciousness.

Migration is common in contemporary Thailand, and any Thais who are not migrants themselves undoubtedly have friends, family members, and acquaintances who are. Representations of migration are widespread in the media: news programs, movies, songs, soap operas, documentaries, and print media all depict stories of migration with portrayals that range from alarmist to stereotypical to matter-of-fact. The sheer quantity of these representations speaks to the deep-seated place that "migration" holds as a social process and discourse in Thailand today.

Artistic and media representations of migration are so ubiquitous that writer Uthain Phromdaeng believes the Thai public has become desensitized to them. After seeing numerous television documentaries about elderly parents abandoned by their Bangkok-bound children, Uthain decided to re-present this story using magical realist literary techniques in order to create a "hyperreal" version of the story that would stand out and force his readers to take notice.

> I see this type of thing happening all of the time on TV: children leaving their parents behind and never coming back. There's even a common saying nowadays, "A mother can take care of ten children, but ten children can't take care of one mother." Children moving away to the city and abandoning their parents has become so prevalent that it no longer even has any effect on Thai people. The TV audience is so inured to it they don't even register it. So I decided to write a surreal version of this story to give it greater impact—to make the audience really take notice and analyze this phenomenon once again.[2]

---

2. Interview with Uthain Promdaeng, September 11, 2007. This and all excerpts from interviews, as well as all excerpts from material published in Thai, are the author's translation unless otherwise indicated.

The very pervasiveness of migration discourse in contemporary Thailand has paradoxically turned the subject into "background noise"—an invisible and unquestioned aspect of everyday life. Speaking about migration, writer Duanwad Pimwana notes, "It's all around us. Many people have lived with it for so long that they don't even notice it. They pass through Mo Chit,[3] which is filled with migrants coming and going, but they don't think about 'migration' per se."[4] This blindness to migration *per se* may explain why Thai literary critics have yet to remark on the large and growing corpus of Thai literature about migration. They, too, may be desensitized to frequent references to migration in contemporary literature. Or, it may be that these allusions are so common and the subject of migration so diffuse that it has not seemed like a germane organizing principle for scholarly analysis. Thai literary scholars have analyzed and canonized a number of contemporary works about migration, but almost always for reasons other than their migration themes. Critics have viewed such works as narratives about social and political transformation (Suvanna and Smith 1992; Mattani 1988; Anderson and Mendiones 1985; Sidaoruang 1994; Phillips 1987) or categorized them into existing rural and urban genres (Areeya 1996; Chitakasem 1995). Studies of social transformation in literature have focused on processes of industrialization, urbanization, and globalization, without addressing the migrant's central role as a driver and front-line negotiator of these processes. Criticism that has codified particular works of migration literature into categories such as "literature of the country" or "literature of the city" has effaced the ever closer connections between rural and urban realms in Thailand and the migrant's central role in bringing these worlds closer together. Literary scholarship has thus repeatedly addressed issues relating to migration without focusing specifically on the subject or probing the connections between migrant narratives.

The persistence of distinct rural and urban genres in Thai literature has strong historical roots. Literary production has long been an overwhelmingly urban phenomenon: the earliest works of Thai literature were created in the courts of Sukhothai and Ayutthaya, and the city has remained the center of literary production into the modern period. Martin Platt (2002,

---

3. The northern bus terminal in Bangkok.

4. Interview with Duanwad Pimwana, October 2, 2007.

51) notes that literature was highly regulated during the first half of the twentieth century and that any expression of regional sentiment would have been suppressed. It was not until the 1960s that a distinctly rural literature emerged with the work of Isan[5] writers such as Rom Ratiwan, Lao Khamhawm (Kamsingh Srinawk), and Kanchana Nakkhanan. These writers brought the countryside to the city, portraying the struggles of rural Thais for an urban audience. This body of work offered Bangkok readers a means of "returning to their roots"—to the village way of life understood as the basis of Thai society—whether or not these readers had any real connection to the village. Isan texts became enormously popular in the city, particularly in the context of rapid industrialization, when the traditional way of life seemed to be slipping ever further away. Kampoon Boonthawee's *A Child of the Northeast* was awarded the first S.E.A. Write Award in 1979, and this novel, along with many others about the rural northeast, was made into a popular movie.

Isan literature presented the Thai northeast as utterly distinct from Bangkok—writer Lao Khamhawm once said that Isan and Bangkok were like two separate countries (Platt 2002, 76). The unique content, setting, and language (Isan dialect) of this literature distinguished it as a new body of work, something distinct from the previously unmarked literature of the center. Interestingly, many Isan writers sought not to represent Isan specifically, but the Thai village or Thai countryside generally (Platt 2002; Yiwa 2005); as a result, this work came to be regarded as "rural literature." A clear dichotomy emerged between "rural" and "urban" literature, and subsequent literary production came to be categorized into one of these two genres. This method of categorization has had significant implications for the recognition of rural-urban migration literature, a genre that by definition cuts across rural and urban settings. Even though some of the earliest Isan works described the push factors driving farmers to the city, these works were categorized as "rural literature." By turning our focus to the migrant in these narratives, then, we can break away from rigid spatial categories and rural-urban dichotomies in favor of a more flexible, mobile perspective. This perspective allows for a fuller examination of the

---

5. Isan is the northeastern region of Thailand.

increasingly globalized realm in which contemporary stories are set and the marginal boundary areas where the migrant's negotiations take place. It is at these sites of border-crossing—where the migrant transcends well-established spatial or psychological boundaries—that we find writers' most compelling visions of contemporary Thai life. Here, at the "contact zones,"[6] migrant protagonists struggle to define their place in the world and, as they do so, sketch the boundaries of a rapidly shifting social paradigm.

Paiwarin's *Banana Tree Horse* was the first major work of Thai literature to call critical attention explicitly to the migrant and his journey. In doing so, the text claimed many of the tropes associated with modernization and bound these explicitly to the experience of migration. Paiwarin's status as a rural-urban migrant has lent weight to his vision; he has stated publicly that much of his writing is based on personal experience and that he is speaking on behalf of the many migrants who do not write.

> Although I've been in the city for over twenty years,[7] I still have the foundation of a country person [*khon ban nok*].[8] Even now, I feel like a country person who has come to live in the city. I bring stories of the city

---

6. Here I employ Mary Louise Pratt's concept (1992) of the "contact zone" to refer to the "border areas" where the migrant negotiates new notions of identity as he or she comes into contact with new ideas and norms.

7. This interview was conducted in October 2005. Since then, Paiwarin has married and returned to live in the countryside.

8. The term *ban nok*, which literally means "house/village outside (the city)," defines the village in terms of what it is not: the urban realm, the center. As such, it is a loaded term, and when used by Bangkokians expresses disparagement toward the countryside. The use of this term is manifold, however, and it is often appropriated by rural migrants living in the city to refer to themselves. In such cases, the word can take on a tone of defiance: it calls attention to the prejudice to which they are subjected and acts as a refusal to let such terms, spoken by others, define them. Sridaoruang commented in an interview with the author that the meaning of *ban nok* depends very much on who is using the term and in what context. "Children and country people use it in everyday speech," she said. Her son Mone Sawasdsri added, "But no matter how long people from the countryside live here, Bangkok people still see them as *ban nok*," suggesting that the term is so loaded in his opinion that to suggest it simply connotes "the village" or "the countryside" would be inaccurate (Interview with Sridaoruang and Mone Sawasdsri, September 13, 2007).

to the countryside, or stories of the countryside to the city, so that people can read about each other. I am the person who communicates between different worlds: the inside world, the outside world, the country, and the city. (Yiwa 2005, 89)

If Paiwarin is the quintessential migrant writer, a spokesperson for those who share his journey but do not write, then *Banana Tree Horse* has become the archetypal migrant's tale. In bestowing the prestigious S.E.A. Write Award on the text, critics proclaimed "migration literature" a significant part of the Thai literary canon. The award further guaranteed *Banana Tree Horse* a wide audience since high schools and universities throughout Thailand use S.E.A. Write texts in their curricula, and the S.E.A. Write seal (always prominently displayed on a book's cover) ensures a broad public readership.[9]

Despite the canonization of *Banana Tree Horse* and the focus on migration literature that it engendered, many Thai literary critics still view Paiwarin's text as a one-off: as *the* work of Thai literature about migration. *Bangkok Bound* highlights the hundreds of Thai novels, short stories, and poems about migration written before and after *Banana Tree Horse* and argues that this body of work constitutes an important contemporary genre of Thai literature. *Banana Tree Horse* should be viewed not as the definitive Thai literary text about migration, but as an exemplary text that explores many of the themes treated throughout the genre.

Thai literature about rural-urban migration emerged as a genre in the late 1960s in response to the rapid industrialization of Thailand. The production of literature about migration increased along with processes of industrialization, urbanization, and globalization, reaching its height during Thailand's economic boom years of 1986 to 1996. The Asian financial crisis of 1997 halted this period of extended economic and urban growth, and migration literature in the post-crisis years reflects a tapering off in production and a more cynical view of global processes.[10] Post-crisis

---

9. This is particularly true of poetry, which otherwise garners a small niche audience.

10. Literature of the boom period (1986–1996) celebrated the dynamism of globalization and its power to create rapid growth, but such "dynamism" is viewed much more suspiciously in the post-1997 period. Post-crisis literature expresses an anxiety about globalizing processes and their potential for destabilization.

literature presents a more uncertain view of development, one in which unequivocal statements about the migrant's place in the world or role in global processes seem like hubristic luxuries of the past.

URBANIZATION AND RURAL-URBAN MIGRATION IN THAILAND

Traditional Southeast Asian conceptions of space locate power firmly at the center, with the king, palace, and capital seen as "pivots and embodiments of the kingdom" (Geertz 1980, 13). In Thailand, this concentration of power in the capital has been present since the city's founding, and the various transformations that Bangkok has undergone since then have only increased the capital's preeminence in the Thai national hierarchy. From Bangkok's establishment as a sacred city in 1782, to its colonial-era incarnation as a commercial headlink, to its late twentieth-century roles as primate city[11] and core of the Extended Bangkok Metropolitan Region (EMBR), Bangkok continues to dominate Thailand socially, economically, and culturally. The capital's hegemony over the rest of the country has drawn migrants to Bangkok from the city's earliest days and continues to do so today.

Rama I founded Bangkok as the seat of the Chakri dynasty on a small trading settlement known as "Bangkok," or "the water hamlet of the wild plum tree" (Askew 2002, 15). The king renamed the site "Krungthep," or "city of angels," and declared it a sacred center. As a sacred city, Rama I's new capital benefited from Indic-derived notions of power, prestige, and legitimacy. This religious and royal center was also a trading entrepôt, where a local commercial elite amassed wealth while playing host to a cosmopolitan community of traders. From the city's earliest days, Bangkok concentrated the wealth, commerce, and governance of the Thai kingdom in a single site, one linked to the hinterlands as well as key points abroad.

By the reign of King Mongkut (Rama IV, r. 1851–1868), European commercial and imperial interests in Southeast Asia had grown substantially. King Mongkut understood that England's stake in Siam was primarily

---

11. Urban primacy is the ratio of the population of a country's largest city to that country's next largest city.

economic, and he reasoned that by allowing England access to Siam's markets and raw materials he might avert direct colonization. The issue came to a head when Sir John Bowring arrived in Bangkok to negotiate a trade treaty— with the backing of military forces. King Mongkut welcomed him at court, and the Anglo-Siamese Treaty of 1855 (Bowring Treaty) was signed. The Bowring Treaty opened Siam to foreign trade, reduced import and export taxes, and abolished most government trading and commercial monopolies. King Mongkut subsequently negotiated similar bilateral treaties with other countries, firmly integrating Siam into the global market, while steering it clear of the exclusive trading relationships typical of colonized countries.

Despite King Mongkut's efforts to avert direct colonization, pressure on Siam's borders continued to mount during the late colonial period. King Chulalongkorn (Rama V, r. 1868–1910) responded to this pressure by bringing outlying regions of Siam directly under the control of the capital, thus protecting the political integrity of Siam. This centralization also benefited the economy, with profits going to Bangkok's commercial elite, whose businesses grew with the center's increased control over the procurement of raw materials from the hinterlands. Bangkok boomed as the commercial center for an increasingly globalized Siam.

> With the expansion of trade came a refashioning of the waterfront and commercial quarters of Bangkok, with new wharves and warehouses, steam-powered rice- and sawmills, and rows of brick shops vending imported goods, while upon newly paved roads horse-drawn carriages bore merchants around the bustling city. (Wyatt 1984, 186)

As the city expanded, a number of royal projects were undertaken to transform Bangkok into a modern, *siwilai*[12] city that would stand proudly alongside the metropoles of Europe. Italian architects were commissioned to construct Western-style buildings in and around the palace, and the

---

12. A Thai transliteration of the English word "civilized." One of the earliest English words to be adopted in Thai, *siwilai* was used as a noun, adjective, and verb to describe the state of being "civilized" in the European sense of the word. The implication is similar to the French use of *mission civilisatrice*; if the Siamese were already *siwilai*, then there would be no need for a *mission civilisatrice* to be undertaken in Siam. See Thongchai (2000) for a full discussion of this term.

court itself became "the fulcrum of modern symbolism—from bodily adornment to the adoption of European furniture" (Askew 2002, 34). Askew argues that a new vision of Thai kingship emerged during this period as well, with the monarch figured as the "benevolent sponsor of progress" and modernity.

This period marked Bangkok's first significant experience of in-migration. The majority of migrants who poured into Bangkok during the early twentieth century were overseas Chinese who came to work as wage laborers and traders. Thais also began to trickle into the capital to take advantage of the new opportunities that Chulalongkorn's modernization policies created.

> In the modernising polity of Chulalongkorn, sources of social mobility and status in the capital shifted to education, and the opportunities offered by an expanding bureaucracy drew increasing numbers of Thai (children of lesser officials and rich peasants) from outside the capital. (Askew 2002, 37)

Population growth due to Chinese and Thai migration transformed Bangkok into an incipient primate city. By 1913, Bangkok's population had reached twelve times that of Chiang Mai, and by 1937, it was fifteen times as large. Thai rural-urban migration had not yet begun in full force, though; incoming waves of Chinese laborers kept Bangkok's wages low, acting as a disincentive to rural Thais who might consider moving to the capital (Askew 2002, 37–38). It was not until King Prajadhipok (Rama VII, r. 1925–1935) introduced immigration restrictions targeting the Chinese that Thai rural-urban migration began to increase. Thai migration streams became even more pronounced following the Great Depression, when Chinese migration to Thailand dropped precipitously (Skinner 1957, 176–77; Apichat 1995, 4).

The post–World War II period saw migrants driven from agricultural areas to the city by accelerating population growth, slow agricultural growth, and, in some cases, political instability. Although rural-urban migration streams were well established by the 1950s, there was little growth in manufacturing at that time. As a result, Thai rural-urban migrants tended to occupy informal-sector jobs and to live in squatter settlements. Robert B. Textor's 1961 study of migrant pedicab drivers describes one such informal economy. Seasonal and long-term migrants from the rural northeast found a niche in the pedicab industry, which provided one of the few reliable means of getting around Bangkok by land.[13] This niche was enhanced by a 1933 law that restricted pedicab work to ethnic Thais (thus eliminating competition from Chinese laborers).

With the first National Economic Development Plan of 1961, Thai rural-urban migration began in earnest. Under the auspices of the World Bank and the United Nations, Field Marshal Sarit Thanarat (1958–1963) launched Thailand on a program of import substitution industrialization centered on Bangkok. This modernization policy brought about the rapid industrialization of Bangkok, while stimulating the growth of the city's construction, real estate, finance, and business services sectors (Ruland 1996, 24). The deliberate concentration of production and services in the capital facilitated the growth of the Thai economy as a whole, but urban-led growth took place at the expense of the countryside and, in fact, fed rural-urban inequality. Overall incomes grew during the period of rapid industrialization, but the disparity in incomes between rural and urban regions grew much more quickly.[14] Medhi Krongkaew has noted that the increasing internationalization of the Thai economy exacerbated these inequalities.

> The benefits accruing to foreign-related economic sectors were not fully shared by the population at large, and the trickling down of benefits was quite slow. The result was that large urban centers like Bangkok enjoyed all the fruits of the increasing internationalization of the Thai economy, leaving other areas, particularly rural areas, far behind. (Medhi 1996, 309)

Such rural-urban disparities created a pool of flexible rural labor ready to migrate to Bangkok for work. A number of factors on the rural end

---

13. As the city was transitioning from a river- to land-based system of transportation, new sites were opening up faster than the formal transportation infrastructure could provide access to them.

14. As in earlier periods, Bangkok drew raw materials and labor from the countryside, and policies such as the rice premium subsidized the urban workforce at the expense of the rural farmer.

were pushing farmers to migrate to the city as well, including poverty, landlessness, and changes in the agricultural sector. The mechanization of agriculture reduced the need for human labor while forcing farmers to go into debt if they wanted to take advantage of modern inputs and machinery. Such debt generally took the form of land mortgages, and farmers whose crops failed subsequently lost their land (making them potential migrants). Land pressure also made it difficult to increase agricultural employment through the traditional means of expanding the area under cultivation. Finally, and perhaps ironically, national development projects that targeted rural youth through improved education increased aspirations for non-agricultural employment—of which there was very little outside Bangkok. If Thailand's development policies initially generated rural-urban migration through the creation of urban jobs, the inequalities brought by increasing urbanization deepened these migration streams over time. Migration to Bangkok grew over the period of rapid industrialization from a rate of 2.6 in 1965–1970, to 5.8 in 1975–1980, and to 7.4 in 1985–1990.[15]

Bangkok's greatest period of growth began in the mid 1980s with the "golden age" of the Thai economy, which lasted from 1986 to 1996. During that time, the economy grew by 10 percent per year, faster than any other economy in the world (Bello et al. 1998, 12–13). Three factors accounted for the tremendous economic growth during this period: the Thai government's transition from a policy of import substitution industrialization to one of export-oriented industrialization; the devaluation of the Thai baht in November 1984 (which generated demand for Thai exports) (Medhi 1996, 301); and the massive Japanese investment that poured into Thailand after the Plaza Accord of 1985. Bello, Cunningham, and Li argue that it was Japanese investment in particular that cemented Bangkok as *the* industrial center of Thailand.

> The massive wave of Japanese investment that swamped Thailand in the late 1980s . . . consolidated the political economy of Bangkok-dominated industrialization and foreclosed the possibility of a pattern

---

15. The net migration rate is derived from the difference of the number of the migrants into the urban area and the number out of the area, divided by the number of population (over five years of age). The migration rate is per 1,000 (Chakchai 2004, 57).

of development with a more prominent and more equitable role for agriculture. This [investment] . . . reinforced the policy of keeping down the price of rice and accelerated the outflow of able-bodied and young men and women from rural areas, particularly the northeast, to serve as workers for the proliferating factories in Bangkok. (Bello et al. 1998, 160)

Because a full 70 percent of foreign direct investment (FDI) was concentrated in the inner ring of the Bangkok Metropolitan Region (BMR) (Bello et al. 1998, 117), the tremendous growth of the 1980s and '90s deepened rural-urban migration streams to the center. Thailand's boom years, in particular, saw ever-increasing numbers of migrants converge on the capital, pushing the borders of the capital itself outward over the surrounding countryside.

The urbanized area of Bangkok in 1974 was already more than twice the size of urbanized Bangkok in the early 1960s (the inner core of old Bangkok and Thonburi), when it began to expand in earnest. By 1984 . . . urbanized Bangkok already covered the fringes of the surrounding provinces. In the early 1990s, the areas within a 40 km radius of Bangkok Metropolis filled up quickly with housing estates, commercial establishments, and such recreational places as amusement parks and golf courses, thanks to the economic boom of the late 1980s. (Medhi 1996, 316)

It was during Thailand's boom period that the government developed the Eastern Seaboard (ESB) region as a new growth pole, with the support of Japanese FDI. Although this project was meant in part to decentralize development away from Bangkok—making the core city more livable through the reduction of truck traffic, pollution, and industry—it actually had the effect of transforming the central part of Thailand from the western suburbs of Bangkok to the eastern border with Cambodia into a vast "peri-urban" area.[16] The process of peri-urbanization, whereby "rural areas located

---

16. Douglas Webster (2002, 8) describes such regions as characterized by a mixed but rapidly industrializing economy in which more than 20 percent of the labor force is employed in manufacturing (with this percentage rising) and more than 20 percent of the labor force employed in the primary sector (with this percentage diminishing).

on the outskirts of established cities become more urban in character, in physical, social, economic, and social terms, often in piecemeal fashion," is driven by FDI as well as land speculation (Webster 2002, 5). FDI tends to locate in these perimeter areas because modern manufacturing requires large plots of land for production as well as access to government decision-makers and higher-order business and personal services that are located in major cities (Webster 2002, 8–9). The pattern of peri-urban growth continues to this day, with the majority of growth now occurring in the suburban and peri-urban areas around Bangkok.[17]

Despite the incredible growth that Bangkok and its environs have undergone over the past fifty years, Thailand remains an overwhelmingly rural country. Nearly 70 percent of the Thai population still lives in rural areas, while 90 percent of the country's GDP comes from non-agricultural sectors (particularly urban-based manufacturing) (Chakchai 2004, 66). Thailand is thus considered "under-urbanized" and is expected to experience rapid and pronounced surges of urbanization in the years to come (Webster 2004, 28).

A BRIEF HISTORY OF THAI MIGRATION LITERATURE

The earliest stories in the migration genre, produced in the late 1960s and early 1970s, reflect Thai writers' first attempts to come to terms with the rapid industrialization and urbanization of their country and the impacts of this cataclysmic shift on the individual and society. Stories by writers such as Surachai Janthimathorn tended to focus on the poor, examining the ways in which modernization was affecting the country's most vulnerable citizens. This period, which came to be known as the "Era of Search," was

---

17. In 2002, the core city contained 8 million people, the suburbs 3.5 million, and the peri-urban area 6 million, resulting in a population of about 17.5 million people for the Extended Bangkok Metropolitan Region. Interestingly, in the aftermath of the 1997 financial crisis, when 120,000 manufacturing jobs were lost in the capital (resulting in out-migration from core Bangkok), the Eastern Seaboard actually gained 57,000 manufacturing jobs (engendering migration to the periphery). The devaluation of the baht at that time strengthened the economy of the ESB, which relies heavily on exports (Webster 2002, 15).

characterized by "rapid social change and dislocation [that] gave rise to new problems without easy or obvious solutions. Students and other young intellectuals questioned their society, and their own place in it, as well as the world in general. They sought ways of understanding, and then improving, what they saw around them" (Platt 2002, 81). Writers of the 1960s and '70s addressed a number of social "dislocations," including the mass migration of laborers from the countryside to Bangkok. Although few of these writers were workers themselves,[18] many were, in fact, migrants.

> Most of [these writers] came from a small-town lower-middle class that, in their generation, for the first time in Thai history gained access to higher education—thanks to the huge American-pushed and shaped schooling-boom of the period. The same social riptide that swept dispossessed peasants into the slums of Bangkok carried capable, ambitious children from local schools in Phetburi and Khorat, Chiangmai and Nakhon Sithammarat, up the steep, expanding pyramid of learning to the universities of the metropolis. (Anderson and Mendiones 1985, 41–42)

As rural-urban migrants, these young writers were in a unique position to describe the mass migration of rural Thais to the city. They could draw on personal experience in their portrayals of the effects of migration on the individual, and they possessed a sensitive eye for the impacts of migration more generally. Nitaya Masavisut has commented that these writers wrote about migration because "the subject was close to their heart. It was something they felt deeply about, something they wanted to express."[19] These writers also had a personal stake in writing about migration. The writing process functioned as a means of catharsis and social adjustment for them, helping them come to terms with their own experiences as new

18. An important exception was Sridaoruang, who came to the city as a laborer and only later took up writing. Rachel Harrison points out that most of the writers of the 1970s proposed solutions to social problems in their texts, while Sridaoruang simply described these problems (Sidaoruang 1994, 48). I would suggest that this literary stance may reflect Sridaoruang's personal background as a poor worker who knew from first-hand experience that large-scale social problems had no simple solutions.

19. Interview with Nitaya Masavisut, September 21, 2007, Bangkok.

migrants in the city. Kajohnrit Ragsa describes how he turned to writing shortly after arriving in Bangkok because it provided a constructive means of working through the stresses of city life.

> When I was in technical school [in Bangkok], twelve of us rented a house. We used to sleep all lined up in a row on the floor. A friend brought his nephew to stay with us, and he used to sit and drink all night right next to me while I was trying to sleep. How could you sleep? It was lucky I'm a writer, so I could let out my feelings that way. That whole book [*The Fisherman*] was stories I wrote during that period, things that happened to me when I first moved to Bangkok.[20]

The production of literature about migration for an urban audience also had the power to raise awareness about the writers' own plight. Armando Gnisci describes a similar phenomenon among African immigrant writers in Italy who choose to write in Italian, even when this requires entering into a co-authorship agreement with an Italian writer because their Italian skills are not strong enough.

> Italian is preferred by immigrant writers because it enables direct contact with the audience they seek: the native citizens of the place where they now reside, those same citizens who can become—through the art of the word—their hosts and neighbors. We Italians. The Italian language is used, in sum, because these writers want to be heard by us.[21]

In both the Thai and Italian cases, migrant writers occupy a position between two worlds. They are the relative elites of the periphery; they are the relatively marginalized of the center. As such, they can communicate and move between realms, both social and spatial. The educated Thai migrant

---

20. Interview with Kajohnrit Ragsa, September 13, 2007, Bangkok.

21. "L'italiano viene preferito dagli scrittori immigrati perché permette il contatto diretto con l'udienza che essa cercano, con il pubblico che a loro interessa: i cittadini indigeni della nuova residenza che possono diventare, attraverso l'arte della parola [...] ospiti e conviventi. Si tratta di noi, altri italiani. La lingua italiana viene decisa, insomma, perche questi scrittori vogliono farsi ascoltare propria da noi" (Gnisci 1998, 17).

writers of the early 1970s were in a position to convey knowledge about the rural poor with whom they grew up to the urban elite among whom they now lived. But why did these writers not simply tell their own stories? Why did they write specifically about the poor? Benedict Anderson argues that the writers of the early 1970s focused on the disadvantaged because they had "a painful consciousness that the *same* forces made possible their own success and the degradation of the people and the environment with which they had grown up" (Anderson and Mendiones 1985, 43). Migrant writers knew that they were on the privileged end of this social wave: they were moving to the city to pursue educational opportunities, while their co-villagers were migrating to survive. Indeed, the justice-seeking tone of these stories hints at a measure of "survivor's guilt" on the part of the writers. By representing the plight of the poorest migrants, relatively well-off migrant writers found a way to "atone" for their privilege. Their stories gave voice to the most vulnerable, describing extreme cases of vulnerability, poverty, and abuse. In this way, migrant writers expanded the public discourse on "development" to include its negative undersides, and their stories served as warnings to urban power-holders who professed the benefits of urban-led growth.

Migration literature of the 1970s was also deeply influenced by the leftist political movements and social realist literary trends of the day: literature was, above all, to serve a social purpose. The student revolution in which many of these writers participated ushered in a three-year period of intense political mobilization and expressive freedom. Censorship was abolished, and progressive and radical left-wing works reemerged—the most influential of which was Jit Phumisak's *Art for Life, Art for the People*. This book, first published in 1957 and reprinted in 1972 by a group of Thammasat students, was "in effect a manifesto for the Art for Life movement, expressing its characteristics, criteria, and aims" (Platt 2002, 83). The text calls for a social realist paradigm for art, denouncing "art for art's sake" in favor of a Marxist vision of "art that serves the lives of the people." Literature was viewed as a tool for depicting the experiences of the poor and revealing their oppression in order to incite social action and change. Jit calls out to his readers,

> Wake up, Thai poets, use your poetry to serve the masses who labour so hard. You must use the voice of your poetry to reveal their suffering, to arouse the spirit of fight that can change their lives. Such is the highest

duty of the poet. You must sacrifice every drop of your life blood in the quest for the freedom of mankind; the chance to join the people in fighting to change life is the highest honour that the poet can carry! (quoted in Sidaoruang 1994, 24; translated by Rachel Harrison)

The Literature for Life credo had tremendous influence on a generation of artists, intellectuals, and student organizers who came of age between 1973 and 1976. As Vieng Vachirabuason commented, "At that time, if it wasn't literature for life, it wasn't literature."[22] Writers visited factories and villages in an effort to better understand the lives of the poor. Literature for Life narratives generally portrayed a Dickensian vision of city life, revealing the exploitation and oppression migrants experienced in the urban realm. Stories such as Kon Krailat's "There Was a Day" and Wat Wanlayangkun's "Red Hot Morning Glory" depicted migrants struggling to survive (and, where possible, maintain their dignity) under conditions of extreme exploitation and abuse. In "There Was a Day," the protagonist Pen, a rural woman trafficked into urban prostitution, reaches a point where she refuses to be treated "like an animal" and stabs her oppressor (Kon 1976, 177). In Wat's "Red Hot Morning Glory," a factory's kitchen staff become mobilized when Lamduan, a cook they admire, is fired simply because he commands a salary higher than a newcomer who could take his place. After Lamduan is dismissed, the kitchen staff begins to rebel in various ways, from "accidentally" splashing water on the boss to chasing her with a knife. The story ends with the narrator describing how Lamduan's dismissal ultimately leads to the factory's first organized strikes. Both Kon Krailat's and Wat Wanlayangkun's narratives offer dramatic portrayals of rural-urban migrants who reject their oppression and pursue a Marxist path toward change.

Herbert Phillips has argued that the Literature for Life movement ended abruptly on October 6, 1976, when a right-wing mob attacked student demonstrators at Thammasat University, killing scores and wounding hundreds. A military regime was installed, and left-wing writers and activists went into hiding in the jungles of Isan, where they continued their struggle underground in association with Communist movements in Laos, Cambodia, Vietnam, and China. Martin Platt has noted that Literature for

---

22. Interview with Vieng Vachirabuason, September 29, 2007.

Life persisted in this context, particularly in the form of Songs for Life, written by groups such as Caravan.[23] I would argue that Literature for Life has made a lasting impression on Thai writers, one that can be seen in the deep social conscience that persists in Thai literature—in new and evolving forms—to this day.[24] Susan Kepner believes that "the Literature for Life movement per se may have gone. . . . Yet the idea that a good person—and a good and acceptable society—ought to care for the poor and marginalized has become entirely normalized and is part of the fabric of contemporary Thai literature."[25]

The exile of Literature for Life writers ended in 1978 when the Thai government issued an amnesty. These writers returned from the jungle and reintegrated into society. After their experiences with hardcore Marxists in the border regions, many of these writers had become just as leery of the radical left as they had been of the radical right.[26] In Nitaya Masavisut's words, "they had mellowed."[27] Their move away from political extremism was reflected in their writing, which by the 1980s had lost the bitter tone and political didacticism of the 1970s. These writers had not lost their social consciousness—they simply expressed it in a lighter and more detached way. A new generation of writers, including Prachakom Lunachai, Nirunsak Boonchan, and Jamlong Fangchonlajitr, was also emerging on the scene—and they introduced new perspectives and concerns.[28]

---

23. The leader of Caravan was Surachai Janthimathorn, a prominent writer of early migration narratives. His stories "Train" and "On the Third Class Train" are analyzed in chapter 2.

24. Recent stories by Warop Worrapa, Uthain Phromdaeng, and Siriworn Kaewkan all deal extensively with social problems—however these writers treat the subject with more lightness, humor, and detachment than did the writers of the 1970s.

25. Interview with Susan Kepner, October 27, 2007.

26. Herbert Phillips has noted that "internal ideological differences, the devastating mass murders in Cambodia, and the real hostilities between their mentors, China and Vietnam, began to eat away at the moral and political authority of the Marxists; returning defectors frequently spoke of 'our hardcore CPT [Communist Party of Thailand] members being crazier than those in Cambodia'" (Phillips 1987, 9).

27. Interview with Nitaya Masavisut, September 21, 2007.

28. It must be acknowledged that these writers were not completely free of the influence of Literature for Life. The martyrdom of Jit Phumisak and the deep respect for elder

The 1980s saw the beginning of Thailand's boom years, and the acceleration of processes of urbanization, rural-urban migration, and globalization between 1986 and 1996 provided ample material for social commentary. Writers expressed a new middle-class consciousness, and stories about migration began to focus not only on poor labor migrants, but also on students, office workers, and other middle-class Thais who were pursuing upward mobility through migration to the capital. Literature for Life visions of Bangkok as a hellish dystopia gave way to lighter—but still critical—images of the city as a realm of traffic, pollution, and overdevelopment. Writers continued to describe the alienation of city life, but they began to treat it in a new way: literature now explored not only the Marxist alienation of the worker, but also the subtle and complex personal alienation experienced by city dwellers of all walks of life. The mall became an important symbol of this alienation, as it expressed city dwellers' entrapment in a world of consumer capitalism as well as their inability to connect with one another—even when rubbing shoulders in close quarters.

The Asian financial crisis of 1997 confirmed these negative impressions of city life, and stories written about rural-urban migration in this period expressed a deepened anxiety about capitalism and globalization—processes now revealed as both inexorable and capricious. Vieng Vachirabuason has underscored the sense of bewilderment and distrust toward global processes that characterizes post-1997 literature: "The capitalist used to be viewed as the enemy [in socially conscious literature]. Now, we can't see the face of the enemy, or where they are—of if they are even in our country. But we know they're there."[29]

Writers such as Siriworn Kaewkan and Jamlong Fangchonlajitr depict globalization as a force so insidious that it can quietly transform even the most steadfast individuals. Siriworn's "About a Cell Phone" opens with a depiction of "Mr. Thrifty," a middle-aged man set in his ways, who takes the cheapest open-air bus to work and refuses to buy a cell phone. It is Mr.

---

writers who had paved the way for free expression ensured that the influence of this era would persist, if in somewhat attenuated form, for years to come. Only in the post-1997 period has a group of writers emerged that seems totally free of the Literature for Life influence.

29. Interview with Vieng Vachirabuason, September 29, 2007.

Thrifty's refusal to buy a cell phone in particular that distinguishes him as particularly "thrifty" to his colleagues, all of whom view mobile phones as a necessity. Mr. Thrifty stands firm against their teasing and even seems to delight in his "thrifty" identity, until one day he inexplicably enters a cell phone store as if in a trance.

> The truth was, he wasn't aware at all. He didn't even know what sort of force had induced him to go stand there in front of that cell phone store in a mall in the center of Bangkok. He didn't say even one word to the saleswoman, and it was as if he didn't hear anything she was saying either. He just stood there silently with his arms down at his sides and his back slightly bent. Then he slowly lifted one arm as if in a dream and silently pointed at one of the many phones in the glass case. Mr. Thrifty paid and silently walked out. (Siriworn 2003h, 50)

With this induction into the world of consumerism, Mr. Thrifty's characteristic behavior begins to give way. He becomes more and more like the other people in his office: showing off his cell phone, going out after work, and spending money liberally. By the end of the narrative, his transformation has become so complete that it permeates his home life. When Mr. Thrifty arrives home uncharacteristically late one night, his myna bird greets him with a new word. Until now, his bird had always squawked "Thrifty!"—pronouncing his name and reaffirming his identity. Tonight, the bird squeals, "It's past midnight!" Mr. Thrifty is shocked by these words, which document the extent to which Mr. Thrifty has changed and the infectiousness of this change on those around him. Even his home setting has become mutable, unpredictable. The story ends here, with the words, "After this, no one could be sure what else might happen" (54).

Jamlong Fangchonlajitr's "Those People Have Changed" offers a similar portrayal of the evasive, yet transformative power of globalization. The village-based protagonist, Grandmother Sa-ngiam, expresses bewilderment and disbelief when she hears that a migrant from their village is now rubbing shoulders with the prime minister's son in Bangkok. It seems impossible to her that a mere move from country to city could transform one's social status so profoundly. When she shares this rumor with her son who has lived in Bangkok, he is not as ready to dismiss it, however. "With globalization," he tells her, "anything is possible" (Jamlong 2005b, 31). She harrumphs in response, declaring, "globali-strange-tion." But at this very moment, the transformative force of globalization/globali-strange-tion overtakes her as well, morphing her body through a magical realist sequence. Grandmother Sa-ngiam's transformation is met with typically postmodern ambivalence on the part of her son, who comments simply, "Mother's voice and behavior seemed different today" (31).

In recent Thai literature a new lightness and humor prevail—often with a perceptible undercurrent of anxiety and the absurd. Heavy-handed visions of the impact of society on the individual have disappeared, yet social commentary persists. Post-1997 literature employs a more widespread use of experimental forms, including surreal and magical realist literary techniques, as well as postmodern self-reflexivity and references to well-known texts. Boreetat Hootangkoon's "The Witch of the Building," which exemplifies this new style, retells *The Wizard of Oz* with "Dorothy" as a young rural-urban migrant to Bangkok. The story addresses the economic inequalities that drive poor rural women into urban prostitution and the difficulties migrants face in adapting to the urban environment, but these weighty issues are treated as a backdrop to the real action of the text: the journey of a new Dorothy and the author's self-conscious act of transforming her story through parody.

The migration genre has thus been shaped not only by the social and economic development of Thailand, but also by the evolution of Thai literature itself. Once a critical mass of migration narratives was achieved with Literature for Life, this body of work began to influence subsequent production in the genre. Writers needed to find new ways to express familiar issues and themes, as migration was becoming increasingly prevalent in both literature and society. Commenting on literary production in the migration genre today, Duanwad Pimwana notes,

It is a subject that is old at this point—it's been around for forty or fifty years. Writers are trying to get past this topic because it's one that has been so thoroughly explored that it's hard to attract the reader's attention. If the writers can't find an interesting or unique angle, they won't write about it. The problem [rural-urban migration] is still there: how to express it in an artistic, interesting way—that is the issue.[30]

If the subject is now "old," the extent to which the original concerns of the genre persist can been glimpsed by examining the writing of Sunee Namso, a factory worker who has recently begun to publish short stories. Sunee's "The Exemplary Worker" describes the destructive impact of factory work on a migrant woman's health and livelihood. In Sunee's portrayal of the harsh conditions of factory life, her condemnation of the factory owner, and her indignation about the abuse of workers, this work can be aligned with the Literature for Life stories of the 1970s. Yet Sunee's story is firmly set in the contemporary period of globalization: the protagonist expresses a clear awareness of global supply chains and of her own position in this economic hierarchy. Sunee wrote this story while working as a seamstress in a factory that has close connections to a Thai labor rights NGO—she thus writes from a human rights perspective that closely resembles the activist paradigm that informed Literature for Life. If established writers now seek to transcend such narratives through innovative and experimental forms, the work of first-time migrant writers like Sunee reminds us that these stories remain current and relevant to many migrants today.

Thai literature about migration continues to explore the personal, social, political, and artistic impacts of urbanization and rural-urban migration in Thailand. The uneven pace of urbanization and globalization—and the varying impacts of these forces on particular segments of the population at particular moments in time—means that aspects of the migration experience that were new to some in the 1960s are new to others today. As processes of globalization and urbanization continue to permeate Thai society ever more deeply, the conditions and experiences of migration evolve, as do the artistic responses to them. The stories in this book offer a window onto the diversity of vision and range of expression about what it means to be Bangkok bound in a world that is becoming ever more urban.

---

30. Interview with Duanwad Pimwana, October 2, 2007.

CHAPTER 2

THE TRAIN

Thai literature about migration depicts the train as more than a means of transportation: it is an icon for the urban-industrial realm, a vessel that transports migrants to the city, and a symbol of the migrant's journey. The train is both the engine of development that urbanizes the countryside and a vehicle that transforms the individual into a migrant, "urbanizing" him. The train plays a key role in many of the processes associated with modernization—including industrialization, urbanization, and migration—so Thai writers have returned to it again and again in their portrayals of the country's transition from an agricultural society to an urban society.

The symbol of the train as a vessel of migration arose against the backdrop of rapid industrialization in Thailand. As the first industrial-urban element with which rural migrants interact, the train functions as a beacon of modernity and of the urban-industrial realm. Hurtling past villages toward Bangkok, the train evokes the power of movement and the primacy of the urban destination. If prospective migrants who watch the train pass through their villages view it as a symbol of power and possibility, seasoned migrants tend to hold a more jaded view. Those who have migrated on the train see it in more concrete terms, noting the limitations of the migration experience and the constraints that an urban lifestyle can impose. Seasoned migrants tend to link the train with the undersides of rural-urban migration, particularly the loss that migration can entail.

Writers figure the train itself as an important site of transition between the rural and urban realms. As the migrant journeys to the city on the train, he or she moves literally between country and city and figuratively between rural and urban ways of life. The train inducts the migrant into the urban-industrial world: it is on the train that the migrant begins to engage with urban logics and paradigms for the first time. In this way, the "urbanizing" journey that the migrant makes on the train becomes an allegory for the broader experiential journey of migration.

The train itself functions as a space of migration. Migrants travel to the city in such great numbers that they imprint a collective migrant identity on the train. A community of migrants is both encapsulated and constituted in this space, and it is on the train that many come to see themselves as migrants for the first time. Through observations of and conversations with others like them, the train's passengers begin to understand their experience in terms of a migrant narrative—and to evaluate their success and failure as migrants with reference to others like them. The train thus enables the migrant to take on a new perspective—one rooted not in the static realms of country or city, but in a new, mobile paradigm.

WATCHING THE TRAIN

> She had seen the train ever since she was a young girl. She watched it, filled with people and cargo, as it flew over the narrow tracks that stretched out ahead, straight as a ruler. It arrived with its whistle roaring and left this sound behind as it continued on its way. Day after day she saw it. The train seemed to her like a village animal that came growling to visit every morning, afternoon, and evening. And yet the train remained an unfamiliar animal until the day Kamsoy became a young woman and got to know and feel it for herself. (Ussiri 2002c, 160–61)

Kamsoy, the heroine of Ussiri Dhammachoti's story, "Fifth Time on the Train," watches the train pass through her village and gains a glimpse of the world beyond. The train hints at alternate spaces, new ways of life, and the possibility (and possibilities) of movement. The train seems to her an icon of the modern realm: in its mechanization, power, and momentum, it evokes a way of life radically different from the agricultural world of Kamsoy's village. And every time the train passes, it beckons her there.

Yohda Hasaemsaeng's "Return from the Battlefield" depicts another young protagonist who watches the train pass through his village:

The boy saw the train come around a curve and then move swiftly past him and his father. It flew and flew until he could only see a little of it left. "How far does the train go, Dad?"

"How far? Very far," his father said, pointing.

"To the end of the sky?"

"Hua Lampong[1]—that's the end of your sky." (Yohda 1999a, 75)

In both of these texts, the train transcends the borders of the child's known world, hinting at spaces and experiences beyond. The children know that the train is "foreign," but they cannot decipher its true nature because it passes so quickly. Part of the train's evocative power lies in its inscrutability. The train represents not only the physical realm beyond the village, but also a world of possibilities that the children have yet to explore. This limitless possibility is exciting, and these rural-born children view the train as a heavenly chariot that can take them to "the end of the sky."

The children's lofty impressions of the train are contested in these narratives by the adults' jaded visions. In "Return from the Battlefield," the young protagonist's father corrects his son's assumption that the train travels to "the end of the sky," telling him that the train's destination is not heaven, but the Hua Lampong train terminal in Bangkok (a destination that Thai readers will immediately recognize as far from heavenly). He goes on to say that his son is mistaken to assume that the passengers are excited about their journey on the train; as an experienced migrant, he can tell from their expressions that some are filled with anxiety and others have lost hope.

Through this father-son dialogue about the train, Yohda Hasaemsaeng contrasts before and after visions of migration—the prospective migrant's overwhelmingly positive view of the world beyond the village and the experienced migrant's firsthand knowledge of the undersides of migration. Yohda's young protagonist will come to understand his father's message only later in the narrative, once he too boards the train.

Ussiri Dhammachoti's protagonist Kamsoy exhibits a similar shift from initial, positive imaginings of the train to tainted visions based on direct experience. As a young child, she is curious about the train and attempts to

---

1. Hua Lampong is a train terminal in Bangkok.

understand it by comparing it to known elements in her world. Noting the train's "roar" and motion, Kamsoy likens it to a "village animal that came growling to visit."[2] Through metaphor Kamsoy incorporates this foreign body into her rural-based worldview, while simultaneously expanding this worldview to encompass something radically new. She later realizes, however, that her tentative knowledge is incomplete: Kamsoy can only truly understand the train and the broader industrial realm it inhabits when she boards it for herself and fully enters its urban-industrial world.

THE TRAIN AS TRANSITION

Village-based impressions of the train are put to the test when migrants board the train for the first time. Although Kamsoy has formulated tentative ideas about the train by likening it to a "village animal," she realizes once she actually boards the train that it in fact remains "an unfamiliar animal until the day she becomes a young woman and gets to know and feel it for herself." Ussiri Dhammachoti thus depicts the train ride as an important rite of passage for Kamsoy—it enables her to transition from a young girl with hopeful ideas about the world beyond to a woman immersed in a modern, new realm. Kamsoy's act of boarding the train marks the beginning of her journey as a migrant and as an adult.

A number of writers, including Ussiri Dhammachoti, Yohda Hasaemsaeng, Raks Mananya, and Surachai Janthimathorn depict the train as a transitional zone between country and city, past and future. The train is at once an icon for the industrial-urban realm and an integral part of that realm. The train journey thus initiates migrants into modern life, while providing them with a test run for it.

---

2. An interesting counterpart to this vision can be found in Sridaoruang's "Plaeng Phanom's Story (1)" where the migrant protagonist's Bangkok-born son, upon being taken to his mother's village and seeing buffalos, claims that he, too, has a buffalo in Bangkok and that its name is "Train." In this instance, the urban protagonist comes to understand the rural agricultural paradigm through a comparison to the urban-industrial realm with which he is familiar.

First-time migrants view the train as a space of possibility, a blank slate, where village-based images of the urban realm can be built upon and strengthened. While on the train, migrants imagine the city ahead and discuss their visions with other passengers. Such conversations—particularly conversations with seasoned migrants—enable first-time migrants to express their excitement about the journey and to gain a deeper understanding of what the city ahead will be like. Discussions on the train thus represent the migrant's first adaptations to the industrial-urban realm.

In Raks Mananya's "Along the Way," a first-time migrant shares his image of the world ahead with a seasoned migrant.

> In the industrial factory there would be new uniforms, friends his own age, and majestic chimneys shooting up to the sky. These thoughts made him confident about his decision to migrate. His quality of life would definitely be improved with migration—he would have a job, money, and a brighter future. (Raks 1993c, 52)

Although the young migrant is nervous about moving, he believes that the urban life ahead will be better than the difficult rural life he has left behind. His family's rice fields have been flooded by a government dam, and the compensation his family received for their loss was not enough to start a new farm. The young man could find no other work and so was forced to move.

With this young man's story, we see how an utter lack of opportunity in the sending area can encourage positive visions of migration. The migrant has no choice but to migrate, so he constructs a hopeful vision of the destination in order to facilitate his own adaptation to that place. Through this psychological negotiation, he gains a sense of peace with his decision to move and prepares himself for rapid integration into his new environment.

The older migrant rejects such psychological maneuvers, however, and insists on grounding the young man in the reality of the industrial-urban realm ahead. The seasoned migrant believes that there may still be time to convince the young man to turn back, so he points out the negative elements of the industrial world that are visible even on the train.

"Take a good look at the people around you." The old man spoke slowly, as if urging the young man to take a really good look. But there was nothing strange about these people who were crowded into his train car, nothing he wouldn't have expected. New clothes, expensive accessories—weren't those the things he wanted, too?

"You don't see anything strange, do you?" the old man asked when he saw the young man sitting quietly.

"No, I don't," the young man said, shaking his head, puzzled.

"You're not seeing what's strange because you're only looking at the things the passengers are wearing—you're not looking deep enough to see the things that speak to their humanity. Can't you see how little of the normal person is left in them? You're still young, naïve. I feel a little sorry for you." (52–53)

In this passage, the old man instructs the protagonist to examine the other migrants on the train, insisting that they are marked with the negative signs of industrial life. All the new migrant can see, however, are icons of urban success: money, jewelry, and expensive clothing. The signs of emotional trauma linked to migration are still invisible to him; they are so removed from his own experience that he cannot even perceive them. Over the course of the train journey, the old man tries repeatedly to convey the negative implications of urban life to the new migrant, but the young man remains steadfast. He holds firmly to his positive vision of the city—until the train itself initiates him into the reality of this new world.

The third-class train is crammed with migrants on their way to the city, and many of them climb onto the roof to escape the stifling heat and claustrophobic environment of the train car. The old man suggests that the young migrant climb up as well, but the young man refuses, saying he is scared. The old man responds, "Of course you are. That's because you're still a normal person. You still have the instinct of fear, like normal people do. Those [people on the roof] are hardly people anymore. They only have enough consciousness to take orders, like radio receivers" (54). He explains that if the young migrant continues on his journey to the city, his own dehumanization will be inevitable.

Shortly after this conversation, the train takes over the old man's lesson, making the undersides of the modern world known to the new migrant and inducting him into the industrial way of life. A loud crash sounds, and there is a flash of light. The older migrant who has heard this sound before calmly explains that some of the passengers have fallen from the roof and been run over by the train. The young migrant is horrified.

> "Why doesn't anyone signal to stop the train?" he asked. His voice was shaking, and his face began to get pale.
> "Why stop?"
> "Stop to help the people who have fallen."
> "None of them could have survived, son." (55)

The inexorable motion of the train, unyielding even for death, shocks the young migrant. The train's speed, which had earlier impressed him as a sign of power and possibility, now strikes him as evidence of a monstrous indifference to human life. It is at this moment that the new migrant begins to understand that the industrial realm operates on a radically different logic from anything he has known before. The train's mechanized motion scares him, but he is even more frightened by the indifference of the other migrants on the train. They seem to have lost their humanity, just as the old man claimed. None of them reacts to the deaths of their fellow migrants—like the train, they simply move on. Worse, they unconsciously, mechanically, take their place.

> The train kept rushing through the darkness, leaving behind the bodies of those who had fallen as if they were worthless. And still, there were others who climbed up through the darkness onto the roof each time the screams died down. (56)

In this passage, Raks Mananya depicts the train journey as a clear allegory for the rural-urban migration experience. The passengers who climb onto the roof replacing those who have fallen represent the unending waves of migrants who move to the city, replacing those who have come before. Each of these migrants, the author implies, risks his life by migrating. Moreover, they are entrenched in a system of flexible labor whereby the risk or opportunity of migration is intimately connected to the loss of those who have come before.

Raks' protagonist ultimately understands his experience on the train as his induction into the urban-industrial world. The deaths of his fellow passengers and the train's mechanized indifference to these deaths constitute an unwelcome lesson for him—a lesson that he chose to ignore when it came as kindly advice from an old man. The act of migration jettisons this young man into a new paradigm whose rules he could not have understood from his pre-migration standpoint and which he now must struggle to learn. He comes to view his industrial surroundings and the city ahead with a sense of dread. It now seems that migration may not provide this young man with an escape from the difficulties of the sending area, and he expresses this realization with a metaphor that recalls his original reason for leaving home: "He had never considered that this trip would be like drowning in a nightmare" (56). The "drowning" of his family's fields was the push factor that forced this migrant to move in the first place. His vision of an unsuccessful migration experience, then, is one that brings him back to the place where he began—or to a new place steeped in the same problems.

The protagonist's fear that the train may not transport him to a better realm is linked to his growing sense that migration will entail loss at a number of levels. The old man has already warned him that the industrial realm will steal his humanity, and the protagonist now acknowledges this transformation in other migrants on the train. The migrant's very ability to make this observation by the end of his journey speaks to his own loss of innocence: he can now see negative aspects of the industrial world that were invisible to him when he boarded the train.

This linking of the train ride—and, allegorically, the journey of migration—with loss is evident in a number of Thai migration narratives. The protagonist of Ussiri's "Angel-Slave" equates her move to the city with a loss of youth, innocence, and virginity (Ussiri 1992c, 93). Kamsoy, the protagonist of Ussiri's "Fifth Time on the Train" links her train ride with the loss of her home: "The first train ride to the city threw her from her home—and left her floating between dream and reality" (Ussiri 2002c, 161). And the father of Yohda Hasaemsaeng's "Return from the Battlefield" links the train so closely with the physical and emotional losses he experiences as a migrant that it continues to recall and embody this loss for him even years later, long after his migration experience is complete.

"The last two times I took the train, it wasn't a good experience. I left our village to be a soldier on the battlefield." He stopped for a moment, and a vacant look came over his eyes. "When I came back from the battlefield, one of my legs was gone." He started to breathe unevenly. . . . "The train took me from here to the battlefield," Father said loudly. "That train cut off my leg!" Now he was almost yelling. "When I came back, you and your mother didn't see my leg anymore." (Yohda 1999a, 76)

Yohda's protagonist has ridden the train on many occasions, but it is the journey he makes as a migrant that defines "the train" for him. As the vessel of migration, the train enables—and, in his mind, executes—all of the events that occur while he is a migrant. He conflates the train in particular with the defining moment of his migration experience: the loss of his leg. "That train cut off my leg!" he exclaims, ascribing a monstrous power to the train and projecting his anger over this loss onto the train itself. With each passing of the train, these feelings of anger and loss are renewed.

The protagonist's metaphorical amputation, moreover, presages the literal amputation of his son's arm by a factory saw when the son, too, becomes a migrant. The train and the factory machine thus become two manifestations of the same industrial force that unfeelingly transforms the migrant's hopes and struggles into loss.

Surachai Janthimathorn offers a similar vision of the train as a monstrous machine.

I wonder why this machine doesn't organize a place for everyone. It should cut off their legs and store them in one place, cut off their heads and store them in another, and cut off their arms and store them in yet another. It would all be so neatly organized—not messily crowded as it is now. (Surachai 1982b, 150)

The dystopian vision takes the train to its ultimate level of mechanized efficiency. In cutting off the limbs of passengers and storing them in a designated place, the train finds space for everyone, providing a "comfortable" and efficient ride. This tongue-in-cheek vision recalls John Ruskin's famous critique of the train: that it "transmutes a man from a traveller into a living parcel" (Ruskin 1903, 159). Surachai underscores the pernicious power of this mechanization, which operates without regard to the effects of "efficiency" on the human being. Such industrial logic can have profound consequences on those who must endure it. Surachai's protagonist tells a young migrant: "We work with machines. This turns our hearts into steel and stone, too" (Surachai 1982b, 149).

In all of these narratives, migrant protagonists become permanently changed through their relations with the train and the mechanized world. The father and son in "Return from the Battlefield" are physically transformed, as the train/migration journey takes their limbs. In Raks Mananya's "Along the Way," the train produces a psychological transition in the protagonist, changing him into an "industrial person." By the end of Raks' narrative, the young protagonist who had exhibited "the instinct of fear" towards other migrants' "mechanical" behavior now walks numbly to the factory, choosing to embed himself in the industrial realm.

> He decided to follow the crowd, even as he heard the old man's words in his head, words that now rolled over and over through him: "As soon as you become part of it, you'll be no different from these people. Your brain will be like a radio receiver. The electric signals will urge you toward the factory, like a lifeless robot. And all you'll do is receive orders." (Raks 1993c, 59)

In this final scene, Raks' protagonist joins the mass of migrants who walk mechanically toward the factory. His experience on the train has convinced him that entering the industrial realm will lead to further loss and, most likely, irrevocable change. The train has led him to this vision. However, it has already begun his induction into this realm. The protagonist represses the words of warning in his head and enters the factory.

As we watch the young migrant bury his fears, we gain insight into the unseen psychological processes of the other migrants in this narrative. The migrants who traveled on the roof now move toward the factory—"with expressionless faces, as if they hadn't seen what happened to their friends on the journey." The words "as if" (*muean*) are important here: they suggest that the migrants have, in fact, been affected by the tragedy, but that they suppress their emotional response to it. These migrants know that they must continue onward or risk being replaced by those who come after them.

The migrants' "blindness" to the train tragedy serves a further purpose: denial. All of the migrants travel on the same train; all share a single journey. The link between the journey and death is all too clear. Any of these migrants could have been killed in the train accident. Moreover, the train deaths stand emblematically for the broader dangers of migration. By refusing to acknowledge the deaths of their fellow migrants, the survivors suppress the truth of the risk they continue to take as migrants. Severing their connection to those who have died enables them to dissociate themselves from a tragedy that could have happened to them and *still might*. Numbness becomes a defense mechanism, one that allows them to continue on their journey.

A VESSEL OF MIGRATION

Migrants travel to the city in such great numbers that they imprint a migrant identity on the train—particularly on the third-class car, which Surachai Janthimathorn refers to as "a vessel of migration" (Surachai 1982a, 113). Those who travel third class are poor, and the most common reason a poor villager would travel to the city is for work; those aboard the third-class train car are thus de facto identifiable as migrants. Commenting on the symbolism of the train in the Thai imaginary, Ussiri Dhammachoti has noted, "The train was the way that poor people came to the city; it was a symbol of people in the countryside."[3] This remark is compelling given the usual associations of the train with modernity—particularly for the rural-born migrants who gain their first taste of the industrial realm through the train. Ussiri, speaking from a thoroughly urban perspective, reminds us that for those based in Bangkok, the train is associated with the waves of migrants it brings to the city.

The close identification between the train and migrancy is clear not only to those who watch the train, but also to those who ride it. In Surachai Janthimathorn's "Train," two young migrants chat over the course of their journey. One mentions that his destination is Bangkok and asks where the other is heading. The other does not answer, but simply leans against the

---

3. Interview with Ussiri Dhammachoti, October 19, 2007.

train door and smokes, allowing the train to answer on his behalf: "The train's wheels rumbled against the tracks, as if answering for the many people on the train—"Bangkok, Bangkok, Bangkok, Bangkok, Bangkok. . ." (Surachai 1982b, 152). To respond to the question would be redundant: the individual's very presence on the train announces his migrant identity and rural-urban trajectory.[4]

In "On the Third Class Train," Surachai Janthimathorn offers a striking image of the way that the train, by providing a collective space for the community of migrants, frames the migrant identity and makes it apparent to the group: "When the train went around a curve, those at the front and the back of the train would wave at each other and smile. No one could say why they did this. They would smile at each other, even though they had never met" (Surachai 1982a, 114–15). As the train's passengers look through their windows, they see people just like themselves, framed by the train that is taking them to the city. The train plays an active role in the construction of this visible identity, encapsulating the migrant group in its windows and displaying the community in the act of migration. If the young protagonists of Ussiri's and Yohda's narratives saw a similar vision as they watched trains of migrants pass by their fields, in this case, association between train and migrant is personal. Now, the observers are also passengers: they know that the train they watch is the train that carries them as well. And this knowledge enables them to feel that they are looking at themselves. As these migrants wave to other passengers along the curvature of the train, they acknowledge themselves as migrants and acknowledge those with whom they connect as members of a shared journey.

The train functions as a key space where a collective migrant identity is forged. As passengers observe others on the train, they begin to "see themselves" in those around them—recognizing their own migrant identities and understanding themselves as part of a broader community

---

4. Surachai Janthimathorn recently commented on this story, noting that Bangkok was *the* destination for villagers migrating during the period of rapid industrialization. "Where I come from [in Isan], everyone came to Bangkok once they finished school. It didn't matter if you came to study, to work, or whatever—Bangkok was your destination. It was the place you went to seek success, to make money, so you could help back home." Interview with Surachai Janthimathorn, October 19, 2007.

of migrants. The protagonist of Ussiri Dhammachoti's "Angel-Slave" notes that everyone on the train is of her "breed."

> This train car was like a microcosm of the village. All of us were the same breed. We were all sticky rice farmers. Here, though, we all had different jobs. Some were factory workers, others waiters, construction workers, tuk-tuk or taxi drivers, and from the conversations she had heard since dusk, some were housekeepers just like her. (Ussiri 1992c, 94)

The migrant initially describes the passengers' shared origins, but goes on to reveal a more complex shared identity. All of the passengers on the train are identifiable not only by their rural origins, but also by their urban positions. In this space, the dual rural-urban identity is simultaneously apparent. The train encapsulates a group—and, in doing so, constructs a community—that is defined by migrancy and by a dual identity (rice farmer and an urban occupation). Although the group will disperse upon the train's arrival in Bangkok, the collective migrant identity does not disappear, as it has already been forged in the passengers' minds. Moreover, this group will be reconstituted (and its collective identity refreshed) each Songkran (Thai new year), as the migrants return by train en masse to the village.

Because the train fosters a heightened awareness of the migration experience, the train journey lends itself to meditations on what it means to be a migrant and the success of one's migration experience. When the protagonist of Ussiri Dhammachoti's "Angel-Slave" rides home after two years of working as a housekeeper in the city, she reflects on the many changes that she has experienced, including the loss of her childhood, innocence, and virginity: "It's been exactly two years since she went to live in Bangkok, along with her girlhood which was now gone" (93). The migrant's self-evaluation begins in earnest, however, when she sees a group of childhood friends—also migrants—emerge from the more expensive second-class sleeper car. The protagonist knows that these women have been working as prostitutes in Bangkok, but she is struck by their fashionable clothing and beautiful appearances—they look like "angels" to her. Compared with these "angels," the protagonist feels backward, as if she were still the poor village girl she had been two years earlier (97). The protagonist notes the angels' thick gold necklaces and compares them with her own gold bracelet, so thin it looks like "dried shrimp's whiskers" (98). The bracelet was a gift from the man she loves, her employer's son, who will never marry her due to her class status and rural upbringing. Evaluating her urban experience from the space of the train, the protagonist now realizes that her own life in the city is a lot like the angels' (and the angels have at least been well paid for their labor).

Over the course of the narrative, the protagonist evaluates her urban life with respect to those she has seen on the train. She listens to the women's stories and imagines their lives in Bangkok as if she were a rural dweller who had never been to the city. The story ends as the protagonist prepares to return to the city on the train, wondering whether she should go back to her previous job as a maid or follow the angels to Patpong. It seems likely that she will begin a new trajectory of migration, one that may lead to greater material success and to the status and urban manners she now associates with the angels. The train ride has brought her full circle: she writes off two years of her migration experience and prepares to begin again. As she does so, the train becomes imbued, once again, with possibility for her—this time in the form of the second-class car.

THE TRAIN AS ENDURING SYMBOL

The train represents possibility and alternate realms not only for the new migrant, but also (in slightly altered form) for those who have already moved to the city. The train and its tracks form an enduring link between the rural and urban realms. As such, they act as physical reminders that the migrant can leave the urban environment at any time.

In Samrung Kampa-oo's "Oriole" (2005), Lut and Pigun, two migrants from the countryside, are stuck at a Bangkok bus stop in the rain. The story's title, "Oriole" refers to a popular song about a bird that leads an itinerant life, never knowing where it will sleep at night. Lut and Pigun have ended up in a similar position—despite their original hope that migration would lead them to upward mobility, it has led them to itinerancy and homelessness. Lut has lost his job, and the couple stands in the rain, not knowing where to go next. Pigun suggests that the couple return to the countryside. She argues that Bangkok's higher salaries barely cover their cost of living, and that in the countryside they can at least be sure that their hard work will yield the food they need to survive. Lut agrees, and the couple decides to return to their village on the first morning train. As they wait at the bus stop, they begin to fantasize about the new life they will build once they return to the village. Soon after, however, they are robbed. Pigun is devastated, but Lut assures her that they do not have to abandon their dream of return. As soon as they have enough money, he will bring her home on the next available train. The story ends on a hopeful note, as Pigun gazes at Lut with trust in his promise.

In "Oriole," the train becomes a symbol of hope for migrants already living in the city. The train thus emerges once again as a beacon to alternate realms and a new life. This symbolic function is important not only for urban-based migrants like Lut and Pigun who decide to return to the village, but also for those who decide to stay. The mere possibility of return suggested by the train enables the migrant to choose to stay in the city, thus reconfirming the original migration decision. This choice provides the migrant with a measure of agency and hope. And in this way, the train brings the migrant to the city over and over again.

A RELIC OF MODERNITY

If the train served as the quintessential vessel of migration during Thailand's period of rapid industrialization, in recent years, migrants have begun to take the bus. The expansive road-building projects of the past decades have brought buses to many previously remote regions, making bus travel a more convenient means of moving from country to city. Buses now penetrate more deeply into the countryside than do trains (making the journey more direct) and travel much faster than trains, given Thailand's excellent road infrastructure. The train, once a symbol of speed, industrialization, and development, has now become a "relic of modernity" (Ward 2003, 1191).

Thailand's road, port, and air infrastructure have been routinely updated, but the train system has not. As a result, the train now seems out-of-date, forever connected to the era of industrialization in which it represented something modern and new. Stories about migration on the train—even stories written only fifteen years ago—now feel dated, as if they depict an experience rooted in another time. In 2007, I interviewed Eur Unchalee about her 1996 story "There's No Water Under the Bridge,"[5] and she expressed surprise at the anachronistic feeling of the train setting, particularly because the story was based on a real event and written only a decade earlier. She wondered aloud whether her story would make sense to contemporary readers, given the extent to which uses and perceptions of the train have changed.

> The train used to be romantic. Now it seems dilapidated and out-of-date. The train never changes. Looking back ten years [to when I wrote the story] the train seems antique. Transport wasn't as easy then as it is now. The train's time has passed. Now we take the bus.
>
> Yesterday, as I took the Skytrain,[6] I thought to myself, "If someone reads this story today, they might not be able to imagine what the train is really like. They'd probably picture something like the Skytrain. Reading about the train is like reading ancient literature."[7]

Sridaoruang, who has spent her life around trains and who has written several stories about trains, agrees.[8] "Most people use the bus. Farang[9] use the train. It is slow." She goes on to say, "You can relax on the train, look at the view, walk around, drink."[10] With these comments, Sridaoruang suggests that the train has moved from the realm of functionality into the realm of recreation. If the train was once the fastest means of getting to the city—and therefore the quintessential vehicle for modern life—it no longer satisfies

---

5. This story details a young rural-urban migrant's return to the countryside (on the train) to visit her ailing mother.

6. The modern elevated rail system in downtown Bangkok.

7. Interview with Eur Unchalee, September 13, 2007.

8. Sridaoruang's father worked at the railway station while she was a child—a subject she depicted in her short story, "Father." Sridaoruang still lives near the train, now on the northern periphery of Bangkok, and uses the train as her main means of transport to and from the city.

9. Farang is a blanket Thai term referring to "white foreigners"—here it implies foreign tourists.

10. Interview with Sridaoruang, September 13, 2007.

the country's need for rapid and efficient transportation. Instead, the train offers a way to get away from the demands of the contemporary world, enabling the passenger to "slow down," "relax," and "look at the view." The train has become a space of tourism and recreation, one that harks back to a pre-modern era when life was not tied to the clock.

Sridaoruang's son, Mone Sawasdsri, an upcoming writer and lifelong train aficionado, touches on many of these issues in his 1997 short story, "Traveling in Sweden (2): The Train and My Favorite Hat." In this travel narrative, Mone depicts his excitement in riding Sweden's trains for the first time. The Swedish trains impress him not only in their speed (which far exceeds Thai trains'), but also in their relevance to everyday Swedish life. They seem to him, like the Japanese bullet train, perfectly in step with the contemporary world. The author contrasts the Swedish train, which facilitates an engagement in contemporary life, with Thailand's train, whose time has passed.

The [Swedish] train sped ahead at over a hundred miles per hour. I couldn't believe my eyes when I looked out the window. We passed car after car, leaving them easily behind. Comparing this train to the Thai train would be like comparing black to white. Our train still swings and rocks about with a thundering sound, while emitting jet black smoke from its engine . . ., and there are many other ways that our [train] does not live up to theirs.

But if anyone asks me which train I prefer, my answer is I like ours the best. Because the shaking of our train makes it fun to ride, the loud rhythm of the train is like music that lulls one to sleep (some people might not be able to sleep, but I can). . . . Our train is the symbol of the first communication between the city and the countryside, and in this way it stands in full contrast to Sweden's train today. It's clear to see. The electric cables resting on poles that drive the foreign train are signs that development has thoroughly permeated that country. In Thailand, we still use gas—this is because some lines of our train pass through areas where there is still no electricity (or, to put it another way, we might say that our country may not want to make such improvements yet). (Mone 2001, 132–33)

Mone envisions Sweden's train in much the way that Thai writers viewed Thailand's own train thirty years earlier: as an icon of the modern world. The tones of these assessments vary dramatically, however. Writers of the earlier generation viewed the train as a symbol of industrialization and as such a potentially destructive force for the landscape and humanity. They understood the development gap between rural and urban regions in Thailand and viewed the train as a symbol of Bangkok's industrial/urban hegemony over an overwhelmingly agricultural country. Mone, looking at the Swedish train in 1997, views this train in a positive light because the train seems to him perfectly integrated into contemporary Swedish life. He argues that modernity has permeated all regions of Sweden, and the sleek and efficient Swedish train functions as an icon of this development. The Thai train, on the other hand, seems to hark back to a past project of modernity—one that Mone acknowledges may have remained incomplete, but one that he can now view with cheerful nostalgia.

CHAPTER 3

NATURE AND THE CITY

The urbanization of the countryside continues inexorably in Thailand (Webster 2004), with pronounced effects on the natural environment, village society, and rural-born individuals (who either experience the urbanization of their rural homes or are forced to migrate as a result of local urbanization). This chapter explores the ways in which Thais of all walks of life are grappling with the increasingly urban nature of their surroundings. The personal negotiations involved in adapting to urbanization are particularly pronounced in the case of rural-urban migrants, who experience the shift from a rural paradigm to an urban one almost instantaneously with their move to the city.

Rural-urban migrants hold a privileged perspective on Thailand's transition to an urban society. Their roots in the agricultural realm enable them to identify aspects of village society that are absent in the urban realm, and their rapid shift to an urban way of life makes it possible for them to see changes that are so subtle they are invisible to long-term residents. The speed with which migrants must adapt to the urban environment forces them to confront disjunctures in their sense of self, home, and social norms. For some migrants, a recognition of the changes required to become urban leads to a refutation of the urban identity and a return to the village. For others, the modern urban lifestyle comes to seem "natural," as they adopt urban ways of life in an effort to keep in step with the times.

If the train brings the industrial realm to the village, giving migrants a first taste of urban life, it is the migrants' own evolving relationship with nature once they arrive in the city that drives this lesson home. Migrants seek nature in the city, noting its absence or the disparity between what they understand to be "natural" and what city people do. Some migrants

43

recreate nature in the city in an attempt to bring life to a "lifeless" urban existence. Others seek to understand the city through natural metaphors. A number of migrants view their own rural-to-urban trajectory as an allegory for humankind's broader evolutionary journey from a life rooted in nature to a modern urban existence. These protagonists view their own loss of a natural environment through migration to the city as symptomatic of a deeper loss. Their sense of personal alienation in the urban environment thus comes to represent something much more profound: a society-wide crisis over the loss of human beings' natural way of life.

URBANIZATION OF THE COUNTRYSIDE

> All big cities were country once, and what used to be the property of all has become the property of city power holders and gradually been pushed back by urban growth. (Seinee 1996, 147; translated by Marcel Barang)

The expansion of urban areas over the countryside forms the backdrop for countless Thai stories about rural-urban migration. Many writers allude to land pressure as the push factor driving migrants to the city, and a few take a sustained look at this process and its effect on rural-born individuals. Kosol Anusim's "The Marvelous Leaf-Blown Song" and Ussiri Dhammachoti's "The Bountiful Fields" portray the urbanization of the countryside over many years, describing the multiple decisions that rural-born individuals must make in response to the ever-changing nature of their surroundings. As urban areas encroach on rural land, rural-born protagonists must decide whether to adopt a more urban way of life or retain their agricultural traditions. Those willing to become more urban can do so by selling their land and moving to the city or by remaining on their land and adopting modern lifestyles and professions. Those who choose to maintain a rural way of life must do so in the face of increasing land pressure and social change or by migrating to a new rural area beyond the borders of the city. The decision to maintain a rural way of life is not made just once; continuous urban growth means that rural-born individuals must confront this decision again and again.

Kosol Anusim's "The Marvelous Leaf-Blown Song" portrays one family's efforts to respond to the increasing urbanization of their home by migrating in search of new agricultural land. When "the city expanded and grew until the forest that surrounded it ran away into the mountains and the trees scrambled for space there," the family moves hundreds of kilometers away to claim land deep within a forest (Kosol 1994, 73). This new site is an intensely natural environment, wholly isolated from modern ways of life. Here, the family's youngest son befriends an elderly man who has lived in the forest for many years. This man, steeped in traditional culture, works hard to pass his local knowledge on to the boy, sharing folktales and teaching him skills such as basket weaving. The only skill the old man is unable to impart is the one he most wishes to convey: the "marvelous leaf-blown song" made by holding a leaf to one's lips and blowing.

Time passes, and urban growth overtakes the forest area where the protagonist's family lives. They decide to remain on their land, upholding rural traditions to the extent that they can. At the same time, the proximity of the city makes it possible for the boy to attend school while his parents work in the fields. In school, the boy learns scientific theories and comes to adopt a modern, urban-based frame of reference.[1] As a result, he rejects the elderly man's spiritual worldview and insists that science represents the only truth. And when he becomes old enough to leave the village, he does so, migrating to Bangkok to pursue higher education in the city.

Upon arrival in Bangkok, the protagonist immerses himself in urban life, throwing himself completely into this new identity—until one day, years later, he realizes that he has become completely estranged from the place and people of his youth. On that day, he stands in his scientific laboratory and "the old memories returned to him one by one. He thought about the old man and his marvelous leaf-blown song. Now I understand! . . . All I ask is to hear the leaf-blown song and be close to the old man once again" (73). At that moment, after years in the city, the protagonist suddenly understands that he needs a connection to home in order to feel truly fulfilled.

He returns to his village shortly after only to find that the home he left behind has been thoroughly transformed. The area has urbanized so

---

1. The standardized national school curriculum is set in Bangkok.

quickly that it is barely recognizable: "He had never thought that his city could change this much. For the last ten years, whenever he thought about this place, he thought about a small town nestled in the mountains. Not a city of bricks and concrete with people running around chaotically like this" (73). It is not only the physical landscape that has changed, but the personal linkages that made it home for him as well. The protagonist learns upon his return that the elderly man has died. He feels a chill upon hearing this news—the person with whom he longed to connect and the traditional music he longed to hear once again were now gone forever. The protagonist's own failure to learn the leaf-blown song as a boy—despite the old man's efforts to pass it on—meant that this tradition was now dead. It becomes clear at this point in the narrative that the protagonist's sadness over the loss of the leaf-blown song is symptomatic of a much broader loss: that of Thailand's traditional way of life.

Kosol Anusim has stated that he wrote "The Marvelous Leaf-Blown Song" to convey how tradition can be lost with urbanization and migration, while the emotional connection between loved ones, as well as religion and spirituality, persist.[2] The story is in large part autobiographical, and Kosol Anusim wrote it with young rural-urban migrants like himself in mind. In pointing to the ongoing connections that migrants hold to their families in the countryside, he hoped to make his migrant readers more aware of the broader (urban and rural) context in which they live. In particular, he hoped to "plant the idea of return" in them so that they would remain aware of their roots and engage in a fruitful relationship with the home they have left behind—even as this home continues to urbanize and change.

And, in fact, the protagonist learns at the end of the narrative that some elements of his earlier life do persist. The old man has willed his land to the protagonist, and this gift facilitates his ongoing connection to the man and his home. The protagonist's father has planted new trees there, regenerating the land and paving the way for ongoing development and growth in this space.

Ussiri Dhammachoti's "The Bountiful Fields" offers a sustained look at the impacts of rural urbanization on one family. When the story begins,

---

2. Interview with Kosol Anusim, September 13, 2007.

the family is just starting out: the father and mother claim land "at the edge of the fields where there is only desolate brush," planting fruits and vegetables (Ussiri 1992e, 150). Their land is so far from town that when they go to the district office to register it, the clerk does not even want to bother processing the deed. "Don't worry," he tells them. "No one's going to contest your rights to a haunted plot of land at the edge of the cremation grounds" (150). The family insists on the deed, however, and they are right to do so: in the years to come, the city expands rapidly, and their land becomes much more valuable.

The family's three children are born and raised on the farm. The first two children, sons, grow up before the city reaches the edge of the farm, and they follow the rural traditions of their parents. The experience of the third child—a daughter—is different. She comes of age as the city expands, and she attends school near the farm. By the time she graduates, the city has grown so much that it completely surrounds their rural land.

> The farm was no longer far from town. A gleaming new highway was laid, and cars sped by night and day. The cremation area where father and so many others were cremated had long since been moved, and in its place stood a municipal water processing plant, complete with a system of dikes and sewers. Mother's ten-*rai*[3] plot of land now looked small squeezed in among row houses, a wood-processing factory, a new market, a school, government offices, and a cluster of private homes buried under a web of television antennas and cables (153).

The urbanization of this area changes the meaning of the land. The farm remains intact, but the city permeates its barbed wire fence in myriad ways. Car horns and television babble drown out the sounds of cows and chickens, and gasoline fumes overpower the scents of night flowers. Economic forces permeate the fence as well: the value of the family's land, now in the center of town, increases exponentially. Mother loves this land and cannot bear to part from it, but she also recognizes that the farm is no

---

3. A ten-*rai* plot of land is equivalent to approximately four acres; 2.53 *rai* = one acre; one *rai* = 1,600 square meters.

longer the natural place or family home it once had been. Her sons have left for the city, and although they struggle as day laborers there, they have no plans to return to the countryside. She decides to sell the land and join them in Bangkok, using the money from the land to improve her children's lives as much as possible.

Ussiri's "The Bountiful Fields" and Kosol's "The Marvelous Leaf-Blown Song" reveal the disjuncture between the older generation's attachment to the land and the agricultural way of life and the younger generation's willingness to leave these behind. The elderly characters are so connected to the land that they function in the narratives as symbols of nature itself. Kosol's elderly protagonist lives and dies on his land, maintaining a traditional lifestyle to the end. Ussiri's elderly protagonist is just as connected to the land, but she must grapple with estrangement from it—first through the area's increasing urbanization and later through her physical departure from the farm. When she arrives in Bangkok, she experiences a sense of displacement and alienation so profound that even reunification with her family cannot cure her.

The sons in Ussiri's narrative, on the other hand, are much more adaptable to Bangkok life—particularly after their mother's financial infusion enables them to improve their standard of living. The sons came of age when the area around the farm was already beginning to urbanize, and urban ways seem relatively "natural" to them. Their sister, who grew up along with the city, easily adopts an urban way of life, becoming a teacher and settling in the now urbanized area where she was born. Both Kosol's and Ussiri's narratives suggest that early exposure to urban lifestyles facilitates the ultimate adoption of and adaptation to an urban way of life. These stories show further how this process of urbanization can proceed quietly over long periods of time, revealing an effect on rural-born individuals only years later when they unquestioningly adopt urban homes as adults.

If this process of urbanization is inexorable (and potentially insidious), there are a number of protagonists who rail against this force and refuse to succumb to it. Authors Tadsanawadee and Duanwad Pimwana depict protagonists who go to great lengths to preserve a rural way of life—both for themselves and as a political gesture—even when they recognize that the rural life they are attempting to "preserve" may have already slipped away.

Tadsanawadee's "Wall" portrays a young man who refuses to take on an urban way of life—even when this means breaking up with the woman he loves. The story takes place on a single day, when the protagonist journeys to Bangkok to discuss whether he and his fiancée will live in Bangkok or the countryside once they are married. This has been a long-standing point of contention for them (and, in fact, the only issue on which they disagree), and they are eager to come to a decision. The couple has now been together for five years; they met and fell in love in the countryside, and shortly after, the female protagonist moved to Bangkok to pursue a business career in the city. She is now a successful businesswoman, fully immersed in urban life, and she wants her fiancé to join her there. The male protagonist, on the other hand, has lived in the village throughout their relationship, working as a writer and teacher. He believes firmly in the rural way of life and has no desire to move. Moreover, he views his fiancée's wholehearted acceptance of Bangkok life as an affront to their love, which blossomed in the countryside, and to their family and community traditions.

The story unfolds through each of their arguments. The female protagonist maintains that the couple should live in the city where they can pursue a modern way of life. The country is urbanizing quickly, she reasons, so they should embrace an urban lifestyle and seek success within that framework: "Soon, the [rural] lifestyle will cease to exist," she tells him. "The countryside will turn into the city, and your dreamland will disappear" (Tadsanawadee 1995, 49). She offers signs of the village's imminent demise by pointing to fundamental changes in the rural lifestyle that have already taken place: "Do people back home still use ox carts to till the fields? No. They place them in front of restaurants, bars, and discos as decorations" (49). These essential farming tools, she notes, have become fetishes of a lost agricultural way of life. It is not only Bangkokians who feel nostalgia for the rural way of life—villagers do, too.

"The world has changed," she tells him. "We have to run after it. We can't just sit still immersed in the way things used to be" (49). She chooses a metaphor of migration to describe contemporary life: "Life must travel" (*chiwit tong doen thang*) (47). To keep pace with the world today, she asserts, one must keep moving. Her double entendre is significant: she hopes that her fiancé will *move* to Bangkok to engage in modern life with her.

He does not want to move to the city, however, and he rejects her arguments that modern life must be lived quickly and in constant motion. The male protagonist views urban life as a "culture of business," imbued with unnecessary stress and motivated by ill-conceived goals. He rejects the notion that money should dictate lifestyle, and he feels that ambition is a negative trait. His perspective holds strong Buddhist overtones, and he figures the city as a site of worldly pursuits that lead only to suffering. He tries to convince his fiancée that there is a simple way out of the urban rat race: return to the village and eschew an urban way of life altogether.

Ultimately neither protagonist will compromise and the story ends with the dissolution of their relationship. The male protagonist's decision to end their engagement—despite his love for his fiancée and her undeniable arguments that the country is urbanizing[4]—represents a definitive stance against modernization and the changes that are encroaching on his world. He would rather hold on to whatever traditions he can than give in to a social shift that he believes is wrong.

Duanwad's "City of Flowers" depicts an even more proactive effort on the part of the protagonist to maintain a rural way of life. This protagonist not only aborts his act of migration en route, but decides to create an alternative "city" in the countryside: a rural utopia that functions as a counterpoint to Bangkok.

Duanwad's story opens as the protagonist prepares to leave his nearly deserted village. All but three villagers have migrated to Bangkok to take on factory work, and Uncle Choom has invited the protagonist and his mother to go as well. The protagonist proposes this to his mother, but she refuses to go. She has lived in Bangkok before, she explains, and she will never return. Bangkok turns people into "lifeless machines," she says, and she would rather remain alone in the village than become an urban machine (Duanwad 1993, 251).

When Uncle Choom learns that the protagonist's mother has decided to remain behind, he is overcome with respect for her and sadness at his own departure. He begins to think about the negative aspects of urban life,

---

4. The protagonist's occupation—teacher, not farmer—belies his assertion that the rural area has remained unchanged.

admitting to himself that he would rather stay in the village (but no longer has this choice, as he has already sold his land). As Uncle Choom and the young protagonist begin their journey to the city, Uncle Choom describes the negative undersides of urban life, comparing the city's bricks and cement to the village's natural environment. Development, Uncle Choom asserts, is not the positive force people believe, since it comes at the expense of the rural areas.

> I don't know how much dirt they have to dig up, how many mountains they have to explode, how many trees they have to cut down until it will be enough. Taken all together, there's no development. No matter how much they build, nature is destroyed that much, along with the souls of the people that are pulled down with it. (254)

Upon hearing Uncle Choom's description of urban life, the protagonist thinks twice about his decision to migrate, asks the truck driver to pull over, and begins to walk home. The protagonist's transition from motorized transport to foot on his return is important: he not only reverses direction, but rejects the truck's mechanized movement. When the protagonist arrives home later that day, he finds his mother standing in the sun, surrounded by the flowers that have bloomed after the rain. "This," he tells himself, "is true development" (254).

With these words, the protagonist takes a stand against urban development, going so far as to appropriate the term "development" and inscribe it with new meaning. Development, he suggests, is not the creation of a built environment and an economy that feeds off the countryside, but natural growth—the emergence of flowers after the rain. He goes on to propose a new vision of "urbanization" as well: "I've decided to start my own city right here," he tells his mother, a "city of flowers" (255). The story thus ends with a new urban experiment. We are not given details about this incipient "city," but we can assume that it will evolve organically and that it will be a radical departure from the urbanity of Bangkok.

Both Tadsanawadee and Duanwad Pimwana take staunchly anti-urban stances in their stories. Tadsanawadee leads his reader to identify not with the successful urban businesswoman, but with the poor rural writer. Tadsanawadee endows this rural protagonist with a strong moral authority by aligning him with Buddhist values. Through a Buddhist lens, the protagonist's poverty becomes a sign of non-attachment to worldly things, while the female protagonist's urban success becomes a sign of materialism. In this way, Tadsanawadee reverses the usual identification readers are led to make with the wealthy, urban protagonist and leads the reader to reexamine his values.

"Wall" and "City of Flowers" were written at the height of Thailand's economic boom, and these stories can be read as responses—and backlashes—to new values associated with rapid economic growth. Tadsanawadee's "Wall" turns contemporary visions of success inside out by exposing their incompatibility with long-standing Buddhist values. Duanwad's "City of Flowers" challenges the very notion that "development" is a positive force—particularly when it involves the destruction of nature. These narratives thus raise important questions about the nature of development, leading readers to think critically about the benefits and drawbacks of migration and economic growth.

SEEKING NATURE IN THE CITY

The protagonists of Uthain Phromdaeng's "Desert," Supachai Singyamoot's "Butterfly," Paiwarin Khao-Ngam's "Morning Song," and Ussiri Dhammachoti's "The Bountiful Fields" recognize only once they arrive in Bangkok what they have lost by leaving the countryside: their natural homes. As these rural-urban migrants engage with their new surroundings, they come to understand that many of the natural elements they took for granted in the countryside are missing in the city. Uthain Phromdaeng and Supachai Singyamoot describe this absence of urban nature not as a *lack*, but as a *loss*. In the tradition of Seinee Saowaphong (who viewed the countryside as a predecessor to the city[5]), these authors figure the urban environment as the culmination of an evolutionary process away from nature. The protagonist of Uthain Phromdaeng's "Desert" states,

---

5. "The countryside has always preceded the city" (Seinee 1996, 147).

Humans used to be surrounded by nature—by plants, forest animals, mountains, and streams. But now the things that surround us are crude concrete structures devoid of life. How is it possible that this rough concrete existence will not have an effect on our souls? (Uthain 2004d, 142)

In this passage, Uthain's migrant protagonist describes his personal experience of moving from a rural to an urban environment as an allegory for human evolution. He locates the green, life-filled environment of the countryside in his (and human beings') past and the concrete "lifeless" environment of the city in their present. The modern environment is the urban environment—and this scares the protagonist. His experience of Bangkok has convinced him that the city lacks many of the necessary elements for life, and he fears for a society that is moving inexorably toward an existence at odds with man's very nature.

Songkram, the protagonist of "Butterfly," views urbanization in similar terms. He aligns the past with man's natural surroundings and the present with the unnatural, "lifeless" environment of the city.

Before I came to Bangkok to become a teacher, my home was in Nakorn Sawan. I lived with water, with forest animals, with nature. But I didn't realize the incredible value these things had for my mental health. When I came to Bangkok and began to live amidst skyscrapers immersed in smog . . . that's when I began to see their value.

If all of these buildings were trees, Bangkok would be a dense forest. And all of the cars that jostle chaotically on the streets—they would be all kinds of forest animals. But no. The difference is like black and white, earth and sky—the difference between my country home and Bangkok. Here, everything is dry and vapid. Life seems so lifeless that I have to ask myself if I am still a person. In what ways do I differ from the many cars that move over the streets of this concrete jungle? (Supachai 1994, 140)

Songkram's original point of reference is the countryside, and he attempts to understand his new urban environment through comparisons with the rural realm. Skyscrapers remind him of trees, cars of animals.[6] But there is a key difference for Songkram between these rural and urban elements: the urban landscape lacks vitality. The city reveals itself to him as a dry forest, a concrete jungle—a mere simulacrum of the natural environment man needs to survive. Within this context, Songkram himself becomes no more than a lifeless machine, a "car . . . mov[ing] over the streets of this concrete jungle" (140).

The protagonist of Paiwarin Khao-Ngam's "Morning Song" notes a similar loss of nature when he moves to the city. The story takes place over the course of a morning as the protagonist lies in bed meditating on the differences between his original country home and the Bangkok apartment where he now lives. The protagonist's alarm rings at six o'clock in the morning, but he finds himself unable to get out of bed. In the countryside, he had a real reason to get up: he was responsible for feeding the buffalo and tilling the fields. Here in Bangkok, where he is a writer, the natural cycles of day and night have become meaningless to him. He lies in bed, thinking back on the "beautiful land and beautiful days" of his youth (Paiwarin 1993, 34).

> Going out to the fields very early in the morning became a habit that I enjoyed. I didn't have to fight with the intense laziness I feel in the mornings these days. Wherever I went with Father, a warm mist encircled us. Even though the work was tiring and I had to help Father with many different chores, going out to the fields was more interesting to me than staying at home. (31)

As the protagonist compares the countryside where he was raised to the high-rise apartment building where he now lives, he notes the lack of nature in his current space. He feels sympathy for the children who grow up in the urban environment without the chance to play in fields or swim in rivers as he once did. "They are born children of the tall building—not children of the open fields like I was when I was young" (34). Despite the

---

6. This perspective recalls the young Kamsoy's efforts to understand the train from her village perspective—it seems to her like a village animal.

protagonist's sympathy for the "children of the tall building," these kids exude pure pleasure as they play in their urban space. The protagonist watches in amazement as one small child fills an enamel jug and splashes around in it "as if he were in a big open river" (37). Although the protagonist views the jug as an inferior substitute for the rivers he swam in as a child, the child sees it as a refreshing pool. For these children, the city is a "natural" home, the only environment they have never known. If the protagonist finds it oppressive, it is only because he compares it with his earlier experience in the countryside. And although he pities the children for their "loss" of a rural home, the children feel no such loss.

The protagonist's refusal to abandon his rural-based perspective, despite his decision to live in Bangkok, turns his urban life into a purgatory (34): he is caught between nostalgia for his rural past and his inability to adapt to a present he declares "unnatural." Fittingly, he remains stuck in bed through the end of the narrative, unable to physically or psychologically integrate into his surroundings.

The protagonist of Ussiri Dhammachoti's "The Bountiful Fields," like Paiwarin's protagonist, remains deeply tied to the rural realm. Although she recognizes that selling her rural land will mean losing her natural surroundings, when she arrives in Bangkok she comes to understand that her loss will be much more profound. In the city, she finds it impossible to relate to nature in the familiar way she always has and, as a result, experiences a deep sense of alienation.

> On the days when Mother went up to the roof of the two-story townhouse to gaze at the sky, a sky almost totally obstructed by tall buildings, she felt bereft and totally alone in the world. The Bangkok sky looked sullen to her, covered by a veil of smog and noise. This was not the clear sky she knew, the sky that sent warm showers falling down on the fields. This Bangkok sky looked as if it had no mercy to show strangers like her who had lost their way. (Ussiri 1992e, 155)

Mother's inability to connect with nature in the city leaves her feeling lost and alone. Communing with nature has always given her a sense of comfort and connection to the world; now tall buildings, pollution, and noise block the connection she seeks. Attempts to interact with nature in the city thus deepen her feelings of exile—both from her immediate surroundings and from her original, natural home. And the new types of nature the city offers—parks and manicured gardens—seem to her as pathetic simulacra of the true nature she has always known. The "flowerpots filled with creeping vines that grew along the eaves, balcony, and entryway" of her Bangkok townhouse rub salt into the wound, reminding her of the nature that she has lost (155).

> Mother often felt that she had lost her way and lost her home. She felt like an old woman wandering around searching for the road back home, but unable to find it. And she felt like the home she was searching for, her real home, had been destroyed by her own hands. (155)

Mother experiences a severe sense of guilt for destroying the natural environment she loved and the connection to nature on which her happiness and her identity had been based. Although mother understands that the urbanization of her land was underway before she sold it, she continues to blame herself for contributing to nature's—and her own—demise.

In an effort to bring some nature back to her life, Mother decides to move from her sons' home in Bangkok to her daughter's home in the suburbs, which is near the original site of her farm. Here, Mother hopes to revive some of the connection to nature she has lost. In the final scene of the story, she walks out onto her daughter's suburban yard to commune with nature once again.

> Outside the suburban house, there was a small yard with a few trees where Mother could be with nature. Mother gazed at this yard and cried. Then, she walked out onto the yard, lowered herself slowly to the ground, and buried her face in the bountiful fields. (156)

Mother has now come as close to her natural home as she will ever get. She is back in the province where she was born, and she stands on a plot of green grass. Yet even this is not the nature (or home) for which she longs. As the old woman lowers her head to the earth, she cries, knowing that she has lost both the land she loves and the connection to nature that gave her life meaning. This moment marks the woman's ultimate tragedy and irresolvable exile: she can no longer return to nature, and she can no longer return home. Her geographical proximity to the original fields by the end of the narrative underscores her estrangement from them. Even if she were to stand on the exact site of the farm—a site that has now been thoroughly industrialized—she could not return home. That nature is gone forever, lost with migration and urbanization, relegated to a permanent place in the past.

The final words of the narrative drive home the woman's exile, as Ussiri Dhammachoti ironically refers to the suburban yard with the honorific title he used earlier in the story to describe the woman's original land: "the bountiful fields" (*phuen phaendin trinnachat*). This elevated, Sanskrit-derived term conveys the idyllic nature of the woman's land at the start of the story and now ironically alludes to a small suburban plot of grass, underscoring the extent to which the protagonist's Paradise has been lost. This yard has now become her "bountiful fields"—even if it can never substitute for them.

CREATING NATURE IN THE CITY

Songkram, the rural-migrant protagonist of Supachai Singyamoot's "Butterfly," views his new urban surroundings as "lifeless" (Supachai 1994, 140). To combat the harmful effects of this urban environment, Songkram decides to plant a garden, filling the empty concrete space in front of his Bangkok townhouse with flowers and trees. By recreating nature in the city, Songkram attempts to "bring more life to his life" and make Bangkok feel more like home—his childhood home in the countryside and mankind's ancestral home in nature (141).

As Songkram's garden takes hold, however, he begins to exhibits a capricious relationship toward this urban nature. He is excited when his garden attracts butterflies, but becomes irate when caterpillars eat through the leaves of his favorite tree. Songkram wants to bring "life" to the urban environment, but not life that ruins his manicured space. Songkram seems to feel that the nature he cultivates in the city should be subject to the same urban parameters that constrain him.

The extent to which Songkram has truly lost touch with nature becomes clear on the day that butterflies are born in his garden. When the first butterfly emerges from its chrysalis, Songkram brings it into the house so it will be safe. He sets the small butterfly on a curtain to rest. A few minutes later, he finds the butterfly mangled on the floor—his indoor cat has attacked it. Songkram then returns to the garden to find a second butterfly fluttering around; it has emerged on its own and grown strong amidst the flowers and trees. It is at this point that Songkram understands his mistake: animals thrive in the wild, not in captivity. Moreover, the author has drawn a clear parallel between the butterflies and Songkram himself with Songkram's pronouncement that he and the butterflies are "both animals" (147). The reader is left to wonder, then, whether Songkram is blind to the negative impacts of the urban realm on *him*. Has the process of rural to urban adaptation that led Songkram to view the house as a "safe" environment for butterflies also skewed his ability to evaluate his own needs?

The protagonist of Siriworn Kaewkan's "About the Person Who Turns Off the Lights" remains in tune with nature and human beings' basic needs—despite his intensely urban environment. He views Bangkok as a palimpsest,[7] looking through the built environment of the city to see the natural site underneath. In order to reveal this natural environment, he obsessively turns off and destroys lights, taking particular aim at the illuminated advertisements behind bus stops—in his view, these signs not only obscure the city's natural state of darkness, but they divert Bangkokians from their essential needs toward the pursuit of consumer products. The protagonist's contemporaries view him as mad, but the author tells us that doctors have examined him and that he is "saner than we are" (Siriworn 2003c, 75).

The citizens of Bangkok do not appreciate the protagonist's "lights out" policy, and they band together to protect their lights, going so far as to assault the protagonist to keep him from destroying them. Feeling unsafe on the street, the protagonist retreats to the safety of his apartment where he remains alone in the dark. In the evenings, he looks out his window at the millions of lights of the city and whispers, "I'm sorry. I'm sorry" (79). With

---

7. Similar visions are found in other texts: "The country-side has always preceded the city. All big cities were country once" (Seinee 1996, 147); "He looked up at the sky and the stars that were flashing in it and thought, this place is no different than the countryside, except that it's the site where they built a large city" (Chatchawan 1994, 63).

these words, he offers an apology to the environment, the sky, and the gods for what human beings have done. He apologizes for the city he sees before him, whose lights mask nature and destroy it through the consumption of resources. And he apologizes for having failed in his efforts to turn the city back to a natural state by destroying "development."

Defeated in his broader social and environmental agenda, the only thing the protagonist can do is modify his own behavior. He paints the walls of his apartment black and starts to conduct his activities in the dark. In doing so, he succeeds in revealing a bit of Bangkok's pre-modern identity—if only for his own eyes.

> When he stood in his window frame looking out over the city in the dark, he saw all the lights of the city as stars and the skyscrapers as trees in a primitive forest. And from here, he went to draw some things on the black walls of his dark apartment. . . . The pictures that began to appear in faint outline on those walls were of strange animals, stick figures of nude people, pictures of hunters hunting animals, pictures of tools made from stones and animal bones, and pictures of many other things that people of our day and age probably wouldn't understand. (80)

With the final phrase of the story, "that people of our day and age probably wouldn't understand," Siriworn identifies the protagonist as a visionary. We are reminded that although society has called this protagonist "mad," the doctors who have examined him (and the writer who gives these doctors the last word) insist that "he is saner than we are." The protagonist's anger at the inexorable "development" of the city is thus the *sane* reaction—even if society does not acknowledge it as such. The protagonist's return to a primitive era within the confines of his room must therefore be viewed as a success, even though it is a success only a hermit can enjoy.

DESERT

Literary depictions of the northeastern Thai countryside invariably include images of the dry, cracked earth. Such portrayals are based in reality: Isan has always been prone to drought, and the dryness and poverty of the region continue to push migrants to Bangkok. Given the close association of dryness with Isan, however, it may seem surprising that a number of Thai narratives about migration to Bangkok depict the city as a "desert." Such portrayals respond to the trope of Isan aridity and build upon it, declaring Bangkok a place so inhospitable that it makes Isan seem like greener pastures.

Uthain Phromdaeng's "Desert" and Taratip's "On the Road" execute this metaphor through a play on words. In both texts, migrant protagonists observe that Bangkokians (and even rural-urban migrants who now live in Bangkok) lack the "watery heart"[8] (*nam chai*) that is a hallmark of Thai social interaction. The urban environment is therefore a dry and lifeless place, where human connections cannot take root.

Uthain's protagonist, a rural-urban migrant who has lived in Bangkok for ten years, says that trying to find *nam chai* in the city is like searching for a drop of water in the desert (Uthain 2004d, 142). The story is set on a Bangkok bus, and the protagonist notes the lack of *nam chai* all around him. The man next to him spreads his legs out "as if to show he's the owner of this seat," and the protagonist imagines that this man would probably ignore an elderly woman in need (144). The protagonist then thinks back on the selfish behavior he has seen over the course of ten years of bus riding: the worst is when children, the handicapped, pregnant women, or the elderly get on

---

8. *Nam chai* (also written "*naam jai*"), literally "watery heart," is generally translated as spirit, generosity, or good will. Christopher G. Moore offers an extended definition:

When you make an effort to remember someone, or take into account his or her feelings, for example, by bestowing a small gift after returning from a trip abroad or when invited to dinner. Traditional recipients of such gifts are friends, family, an employee, staff, or servant. If you make this gesture you are said to possess *naam jai*. The phrase translates literally as water of the heart. Everyone likes to feel they are important, that they matter, and that others take them into consideration. In Thailand, one way of expressing your *naam jai* is through a simple gesture of appreciation. Often *naam jai* translates as acts of common courtesy. Giving up your seat on the bus for an elderly person or a pregnant woman, allowing the person with one or two items to go ahead of you at the check-out at the supermarket, or permitting another car to enter the traffic in front of you. *Naam jai* doesn't take much effort. Inside such a heart is the understanding that these small gestures are part of the glue that holds society together, and make us all a little more human and decent. It reminds us that there is something to admire in people who take into account the fact that other people have feelings. The way a person with *naam jai* treats another touches all of us. (Moore 2006, 67–68)

and passengers pretend they are sleeping or simply look away in order to retain their seat. This lack of compassion, the protagonist concludes, is what makes Bangkok seem dry as a desert. "The sad thing is that [such people] are becoming more numerous everyday. Bangkok is becoming just like a desert of *nam chai*—completely dry" (145). The protagonist offers a potential solution for the "drying out" of urban life: the city could be turned from a "desert" into "a plentiful lake" if Bangkokians would become more generous in their daily interactions (147). Shortly after he makes this suggestion, however, his own actions belie his dedication to this effort. He sees an old woman get onto the bus as he is falling asleep. Through half-closed eyes, he watches the man next to him get up from his seat. It is unclear from the narrative why the man has gotten up, and Uthain deliberately leaves this final scene open to interpretation.[9] It is possible that the man has offered his seat to the woman, thus refuting the protagonist's assertion that there is no *nam chai* in the city. Or, it is possible that the man has simply reached his stop. Either way, it is the protagonist's own reaction to the arrival of the elderly woman that is important. Despite his critique of the lack of *nam chai* in the city and his call for a collective effort toward greater selflessness, he fails to give up his own seat. We are thus left wondering whether the protagonist is a self-righteous individual with no awareness of his hypocrisy or the latest victim of the dehumanizing power of the city.

The protagonist of Taratip's "On the Road" (1993) also laments the loss of *nam chai* in Bangkok—and the impact of his own loss of *nam chai* on others. This protagonist notes that when he first moved to Bangkok, he regularly offered his seat to others, but now that he has lived in the city for a few years, he is much more selective. Watching an old woman stand on the other end of the bus, he feels a bit of sympathy for her, but when confronted with the possibility of losing his own seat, he simply stares out the window, ignoring the person in need. The protagonist's awareness that his lack of *nam chai* may cause difficulties for others is not enough to change his behavior. He, like Uthain's protagonist, perpetuates the "drying out" of urban life.

Paiwarin Khao-Ngam's "Morning Song" offers yet another vision of the "drying out" of human interaction in the urban realm. As this protagonist

---

9. Conversation with the author.

meditates on the lives of the children who have grown up in the city, he asks: "Are these children simply dewdrops that must yield to the strong sun?" (Paiwarin 1993, 39). With this question, the protagonist, who has lamented the children's estrangement from nature over the course of the story, uses a water image—dewdrops—to express their fragility with respect to the city environment. His vision of their future is inauspicious, reflecting the loss of humanity he believes growing up in the city will entail. The children's natural, delicate, and watery essences, he predicts, will likely be overcome by the harsh, urban sun.

RAIN

Rain, welcomed for its regenerative power in the countryside, is met with annoyance in the city. Rain is not essential for urban life; on the contrary, it slows down the efficient functioning of the city, causing traffic and delay. Bangkok rain enacts a force of nature on a modern system that "should not" be subject to nature. As a result, Bangkokians view rain as a nuisance, something to be avoided at all costs. Yohda Hasaemsaeng's protagonist notes that although rain "washes away the dryness and filth of this big city," Bangkok people do not like it (Yohda 1993, 125). In Samrung Kampaoo's "Oriole," the protagonists spend the entire narrative hovering under a bus shelter to avoid rain and the splashing water created by passing cars. In these stories, the cleansing attributes of rain are overshadowed by dirty floodwater that grinds the city to a halt.

Migrant protagonists who arrive in the city after having waited, season after season, for rain to fall on their fields are shocked and dismayed when they observe Bangkokians' response to the abundant rainfall in the capital. It seems to these new migrants that urban dwellers do not appreciate the gift of water they are receiving. Once these migrants have lived in Bangkok for a while, however, they tend to take on Bangkokians' views. As these migrants integrate into the urban realm, the meaning of rain changes for them, and they start to focus on the ways in which rain wreaks havoc on time, efficiency, and convenience in the city. They begin to notice the extent to which rain washes away the positive elements of urban modernity, leaving behind a city mired in floodwater.

In Tadsanawadee's "Wall," the protagonist's visit to Bangkok begins and ends with a rainstorm. He leaves behind the dry countryside in need of rain and observes that rain finally falls just as he reaches the city.

The damn sky threw down a torrent of rain to greet the passengers who had just traveled from the dry countryside. I had to waste almost two hours. The rain drove everyone to huddle together under the stuffy roof, where they waited like insects that go in search of food after the rain. Water rose, flooding the streets, and garbage floated in the floodwater. Many people stared at the rain as if they hated it. (Tadsanawadee 1995, 44)

"Rain," the protagonist notes, "falls often here, but no one here wants it" (52). This thought is confirmed by a conversation he overhears at the bus terminal between a father and son who have just arrived from the countryside. The boy, gazing at the sky, says, "Dad, it's going to rain. Let's go home" (52). His father swallows hard and responds, "I've sold our land, son. We don't need rain anymore" (52). With this comment, the man socializes his son to transition from a rural-based to an urban-based view of rain. The family no longer has agricultural land, so they do not need rain or benefit from it. A lack of rain has pushed them from their land, and rain's arrival in the urban realm cannot save them or bring back their home. The father suggests they simply forget about rain and adjust their relationship to their new environment accordingly.

On the rare occasions when migrant protagonists *do* abandon themselves to rain in the city, however, they reconnect with nature through it. In embracing rain, they assume rhythms based on nature and eschew urban schedules. Water becomes a rejuvenating force that can cure the "dryness" of the urban realm, bringing *nam chai* and natural human connections back to the city.

The protagonist of Paiwarin Khao-Ngam's "Morning Song," states that the day he celebrates the Songkran water festival is his best day in Bangkok: "On that Songkran, I was totally drenched with water. And maybe I was drenched to my very soul. . . . That was truly one of my happiest days in Bangkok" (Paiwarin 1993, 36). Songkran's water both revitalizes the protagonist and forges a connection between him and the urban children in his apartment block. Significantly, Songkran is a tradition associated with the village. By recreating the rural ritual of cleansing and rebirth in the city, the protagonist connects with his roots *and* with the urban children around him. Through Songkran's flowing water, the rural enters the urban and brings life back to the city.

Manot Promsingh's "Kao Pradapdin Night"[10] depicts a similar trajectory, whereby a rural-urban migrant ultimately transcends his feelings of isolation in the dry, inhospitable city by embracing water—and with it, natural, fluid interactions. Maen, the protagonist of "Kao Pradapdin Night" works as a guard in a Bangkok mall. When he first takes on this position, he believes that his polite behavior will gain him the attention and respect of customers; he soon realizes, however, that he is virtually invisible to the thousands of people who pass him every day. He feels invisible not only at work, but also in the evenings when he takes off his guard uniform and "turns back into one of the many strangers in the city" (Manot 2005a, 124). These feelings of isolation lead Maen to conclude that Bangkok "is no different from a broad, empty desert" (124). This vision is intensified when Maen's girlfriend leaves him, severing all human connections he has in the city; the night of their breakup, he dreams of a desert.

Maen's search for love and human connection in the city can be traced through his relationship with water. Maen becomes obsessed with waterfalls, examining plastic waterfalls at the market every afternoon and eventually settling on a large poster of a waterfall to hang on his bedroom wall. Whenever he looks at the poster, Maen imagines a world of fluidity and human connections. He dreams of bringing women to play there with him. The waterfall thus becomes a site of fluid interpersonal relations as well as fertility—a welcome oasis from the urban desert in which he lives.

When Maen finally achieves a real human connection in the city, "the hot desert disappeared in a flash" (133). And when the woman he loves visits him in his home soon after, the scene overflows with images of water. On that day, Maen walks home from work through the rain to find his waterfall

---

10. Kao Pradapdin is a day on which northeastern Thais make offerings of food, betelnut, and tobacco to ancestors. They place these offerings in small bundles under trees in the temple. The festival falls thirteen days after the full moon in the ninth month of the lunar calendar.

poster rippling on the wall, so that it looks like the water in the image is flowing. This vision of flowing water makes him "dream on and on, and made his heart feel happy" (133). The waterfall seems to "come to life," just as his relationship is coming to life—not in the two-dimensional world of the poster, but in the three-dimensional world of the city in which he lives.

In the final scene, Maen's prospective girlfriend appears across the street from his apartment, as a river of Bangkok floodwater flows between them. This seamstress has told Maen that she would rather die than cross a street of Bangkok floodwater, but she now wades through the knee-deep water toward him. At this moment, Maen's "whole world turned into a wide and crystal-clear waterfall" (135). The human connection is so powerful that it not only revitalizes his dry urban existence, but literally transforms the hated Bangkok floodwater into a clear stream (as far as the couple is concerned). Maen and the seamstress revel in the revitalizing power of this water, as nearby Bangkokians whose cars are stuck in floodwater shout out that the couple is crazy. Maen and his partner are oblivious to these taunts, however—they simply enjoy the water that christens their emerging relationship.

In all of these stories, the happiness that rural-urban migrant protagonists experience as they give themselves up to nature in the city can be read as a celebration of their own rural identities. When they stop struggling to live by the city's rules—rules that they often find isolating—these migrants experience a deep sense of joy and freedom. As they embrace their "natural" selves through water fights or rainstorms, they reinvigorate their identities and begin forging connections with others in the city, a city that previously seemed to them dry as a desert.

CHAPTER 4

ANIMALS AND THE CITY

Animal imagery pervades stories about rural-urban migrants now living in Bangkok, evoking the undersides of migration and urbanization. Given the low status of animals in the Buddhist worldview and Thai cultural consciousness, authors use this animal imagery to explore the city's dehumanization of migrants and the vulnerable positions that rural-urban migrants occupy in their new urban homes.

In some stories, migrants are shown sharing space with animals, despite the migrant's persistent efforts to eliminate these dogs, mice, and insects from the urban space. As animals "invade" the migrant's urban surroundings, they hint at a "ruralness" that the migrant cannot shake off (despite aspirations for a modern lifestyle). In stories where a migrant's inability to reclaim his urban space drives him to sadistic behavior toward these encroaching animals, we watch as the migrant himself is turned into an "animal" by his urban environment.

In a number of stories, authors explicitly compare migrants to animals in order to express the ways in which the city dehumanizes the individual. This dehumanization can be subtle, as migrants become "mice" forced to run through the maze of a capitalist "rat race."[1] Other comparisons are more severe, as the physical and psychological violence that city dwellers inflict on one another make their victims seem like "abused dogs." And as migrant city dwellers perpetrate this violence, they too become "animals" engaged in a Darwinian struggle for survival of the fittest.

---

1. The animal imagery of this phrase reads the same way in English and Thai.

The authors of these texts repeatedly call into question the notion that the urban environment is "civilized," portraying it instead as a jungle. Migrant protagonists, in fact, express nostalgia for the "civilized village" where social structures are clear and respected. The city is, for them, a concrete jungle where Social Darwinism prevails.

ANIMAL INVASIONS

Nirunsak Boonchan's "Middle Class People, Second-Hand Car, and Mangy Dogs" (1992) details a young couple's efforts to forge a middle-class life for themselves once they move to Bangkok—and the foiling of these effort by a group of mangy dogs. The story offers a glimpse of the complex orchestration of purchases and upgrades involved in becoming middle class in Thailand today—as well as the tenuousness of this middle-class status for those who have recently attained it. Nirunsak's protagonists raise their social position by purchasing a private home, car, and other middle-class accoutrements, but in doing so, stretch their finances, incurring both anxiety and debt.

After years of working in the city, Prueang and Sophit finally save up enough money to buy their own home. They are proud of this small townhouse on the periphery of Bangkok because they have earned it with their own hard work. At the same time, they are worried about their ability to handle a mortgage. The townhouse, they soon learn, requires a number of unanticipated expenditures, and its location on the outskirts of the city forces them to make a second expenditure: a car. They purchase a second-hand car on installment, and their standard of living improves significantly—that is, until the car begins to break down. Prueang and Sophit pay to have the car fixed again and again, until they no longer have the funds to repair it; at this point, they simply leave the defunct car in front of their house and resign themselves to taking the bus.

Not long after, a group of mangy dogs comes to live under the car. The first time Prueang spots these dogs, he chases them away, shouting, "This is a home for people, dammit! Not for mangy dogs!" (Nirunsak 1992, 51). The dogs see no reason to leave, however. Prueang and Sophit repeatedly attempt to rid their home of these dogs, but the dogs continue to treat the space as their own.

Although Prueang and Sophit have handled the challenges of upward mobility with relative aplomb up to this point, the dogs push them over the edge. The dogs seem to call the couple's very achievement of higher social status into question. By claiming space under their car—a symbol of their middle-class status—the dogs become visible signs that something is lurking beneath the migrants' middle-class image. The mangy dogs hint at a "ruralness" that these rural-urban migrants cannot shake off, contesting the notion that the migrants have ever really transcended their village origins.

There is a clear parallel, moreover, between the dogs and the migrants themselves. Both claim space in the city, and both exhibit a measure of insecurity about their ownership over this space. The couple's anxiety about the dogs' invasion of their home underscores their own fear that they too may be encroachers on this urban space. To banish this fear from their minds, they attempt to force the dogs out, but in doing so, they underscore their own precarious position in the city.

Kajohnrit Ragsa's short story "Cockroaches" portrays another rural-urban migrant whose urban space is invaded by unwanted animals. The cockroaches that infest the protagonist's apartment make it impossible for him to feel at home in the city; in fact, they make him feel that he has no control over his environment at all. Each time it rains, the protagonist's apartment (and his ground-floor bedroom in particular) is flooded with water and infested by cockroaches. The protagonist is disgusted by these insects, which smell bad, eat through his clothes, and chew his skin at night. He attempts to rid his space of these insects, but the cockroaches always get the best of him.

> As soon as he sprayed the insecticide, the cockroaches would run for cover into the drain. They would stay away for a night or two before returning with a vengeance once they were really hungry. He'd sprayed so many times that the poison didn't even make the cockroaches dizzy anymore. It was as if his spraying angered them and brought them back even stronger than before. (Kajohnrit 1998, 82)

Fighting with these cockroaches brings the protagonist to the verge of a nervous breakdown. To save his sanity, he abandons this space and moves to a new apartment. But the cockroaches seem to follow him there, albeit in a new incarnation. In this second space, his roommate's nephew, who moves in shortly after the protagonist, is a "cockroach" in the protagonist's eyes. He dirties the apartment, steals, and holds frequent parties, generally encroaching on the protagonist's space—just as the cockroaches had done.

The protagonist's fights with this roommate (and with the occasional real cockroach) drive him to insanity. He begins to dream about cockroaches at night and to hallucinate their presence during the day. The protagonist continually hears the sounds of cockroaches, only to spin around and find that his "ears deceived him" (88). Cockroaches not only invade his space— they invade his mind. This is made clearest in the final scene, when his roommate's friends appear at the protagonist's door ready for a party. In a Kafkaesque sequence, these partygoers turn into cockroaches before his eyes.

> I stood silently looking at them [the group of partiers] in alarm. I saw the shiny dark brown wings slowly emerge from their bodies. And all of a sudden, thin antennae popped out of their heads. They began to move their wings and crawl with their six legs towards me. (90)

The protagonist screams as these "cockroaches" approach him, and the story ends here. Whether we read this final sequence as a dream, a hallucination, or magical realism, the message is the same: the protagonist cannot find peace in the urban realm because animals continue to invade his space. As in "Middle Class People, Second-Hand Car, and Mangy Dogs," encroaching animals make it impossible for the protagonist to forge a new life for himself in the city. It becomes impossible for him to experience the city as a modern, efficient, and "civilized" place because an element of animal disorder keeps creeping in. If the protagonists of Paiwarin Khao-Ngam's "Morning Song" and Manot Promsingh's "Kao Pradapdin Night" solved this problem by ultimately embracing the nature in their urban environment and in themselves, the protagonists of Kajohnrit Ragsa's "Cockroaches" and Siriworn Kaewkan's "About Animals of All Kinds, Especially Dogs" do not have it in themselves to take this step. As a result, animal invasions in these texts drive the protagonists increasingly mad.

In Siriworn Kaewkan's "About Animals of All Kinds, Especially Dogs," the protagonist Chatcharin struggles endlessly against the many animals that invade his Bangkok space. Chatcharin believes that "the world is not fit for any animals except humans" (Siriworn 2003f, 122). He hates animals of all kinds, but particularly detests "*sat na khon*,"[2] which he says "look way too human" (125–26). Chatcharin is angered by Darwin's suggestion that human beings evolved from *sat na khon*; as far as he is concerned, humans are thoroughly distinct from animals. Chatcharin wants more than anything to live in a truly "civilized" environment, one that is free from all non-human life.

To accomplish this goal, Chatcharin goes to war with the many insects and animals that invade his personal space. It is not enough for him to rid his home of these animals, however—he wants to eliminate them from the world. We learn shortly into the story that Chatcharin has selected his Bangkok housing development as part of a wider genocidal plan: this housing development has more stray dogs than any other he has seen, and he reckons that if he kills one stray dog per day, he will have a measurable effect on the animal population.

The animals Chatcharin tries to kill, however, repeatedly outsmart him. When he offers an orangutan in the zoo a poison-laced banana chip, the animal sniffs the chip and angrily throws it back at him. And although Chatcharin's feigned "love for animals" impresses the owner of Lion, a dog across the street, the dog himself sees right through Chatcharin's act. Whenever Chatcharin approaches, Lion growls ferociously, as if he senses Chatcharin's evil intentions.

The futility of Chatcharin's efforts to turn Bangkok into an animal-free space is rendered in the unyielding onslaught of insects, rodents, and dogs that flood his urban home. The more animals Chatcharin kills, the more he falls victim to this animal onslaught. And while he does ultimately succeed in killing Lion, the dog's death *increases* the number of dogs that encroach on Chatcharin's space. In a scene reminiscent of Kajohnrit Ragsa's "Cockroaches," where the protagonist's use of insecticide makes the

---

2. The term *sat na khon* refers to animals with hair on their faces. This word has a negative connotation and is usually used to distinguish "animals" from human beings.

cockroaches come back "even stronger than before," Chatcharin's murder of Lion opens the floodgates for a pack of dogs to enter the neighborhood.

> When he was sure that no one was looking, Chatcharin threw the food he had prepared into Lion's cage. The dog swallowed the food as if it were the most delicious thing he had ever eaten. After that, Chatcharin returned home satisfied, opened his fridge, and took out a beer. He poured the beer into a glass slowly—so that there wouldn't be too much foam—and then took it up to the balcony. He lit a cigarette, sipped his beer, and watched as Lion writhed around inside his neighbor's fence. . . . That first night after Lion died, all of the stray dogs in the development got together to celebrate, howling at the tops of their lungs as if to announce that now there was no part of the *soi* where they could not wander freely. (134–35)

Chatcharin realizes only after he kills Lion that he has unintentionally unleashed all of the dogs in the neighborhood—dogs who apparently disliked Lion as much as he did and who had avoided this street because of him. With the death of Lion, these dogs are now free to howl and roam through Chatcharin's environment, penetrating it even more deeply than before. By the end of the story, it becomes clear that Chatcharin's efforts to rid his "civilized" urban environment of animals is doomed—not only because his exterminations bring these animals back in greater force, but because Chatcharin's killings turn *him* into an animal as well.

SURVIVAL OF THE FITTEST

"There Was a Day" and "In the Mirror" by Kon Krailat, and "Lost Dog" by Sila Khomchai depict Bangkok as a site where migrants are dehumanized by the city's unnatural environment and the psychological and physical violence that city dwellers inflict upon one another. This violence is not depicted as random, but rather as an integral part of urban life—a strategic way to get ahead in the city. In all of these texts, city dwellers are engaged in a struggle for survival of the fittest, where dehumanization is used as a tool to prove the perpetrator's power over his victim.

Pen, the protagonist of Kon Krailat's "There Was a Day," describes her life in the city as "more and more like an animal's every day" (Kon 1976, 177). A human trafficking victim duped into urban prostitution, she is the subject of constant physical and sexual violence. In the brothel where Pen is forced to live and work, women live "like animals in a cage, piled up ten to a room" (182). Pen attempts to discuss this abuse with other women in the brothel, but she finds that they are already so dehumanized that they simply accept their reality. Eventually Pen tries to escape, but she is quickly dragged back by the traffickers, as a passerby watches in silence. Pen is troubled by the lack of empathy among Bangkok residents, noting that "back home, if even a buffalo went missing, everyone in the village would drop what they were doing to help search for it" (178). In the city, Pen is treated worse than an animal would be treated in her village.

One day, a group of men enters Pen's room in the brothel. The man who returned her to the brothel is among them, and he commands her to have sex with him. When Pen realizes that she has no choice, she agrees and tells him to send his friends away. "There's no need to send them away," he says. "I'm going to do it in front of them."

Pen refuses. "I'm not an animal," she tells him, "I won't do it!" (186). In response, he rapes her. Pen struggles against him, cursing him and calling him an animal: "Animal! Lizard!"[3] (187). Recognizing that her own dehumanization is almost complete, Pen thinks to herself, "I can't take this anymore. I can't let him treat me worse than an animal" (187).

> Pen had never realized before that there is a point at which human beings can no longer endure being taken advantage of. On the day when their endurance has reached its ultimate limit, they have to fight back. And on that day all of the pain that they have endured and held inside will be paid back. (187)

She grabs a knife and stabs him. Pen's struggle with the forces of urban dehumanization is played out in this scene. As she murders the man who

---

3. The word used for lizard here, "*hia*," is a strong curse word in Thai. With this word, Pen both curses him virulently and responds to his dehumanization of her by calling *him* an animal.

treats her "worse than an animal," she fights her own dehumanization in the most dramatic way possible—by killing another. Kon Krailat thus poses a moral quandary: is it possible to save one's humanity by descending into the animal-like role of murderer? If Siriworn leads us to view the protagonist of "About Animals of All Kinds, Especially Dogs" as culpable and "animal-like" (as his murders of various neighborhood animals are unjustified and sadistic), Kon Krailat leads us to empathize with Pen and her struggle. Throughout Kon Krailat's text, we have watched Pen endure extreme dehumanization through no fault of her own (she was trafficked into prostitution and forced to endure slavery and rape). We have also watched her fight consistently against this fate—for herself and for the other women with whom she works. By the time we witness Pen's murder of her oppressor, then, there is no doubt in our minds that she has been utterly abused. Pen herself does not believe her actions to be morally wrong. When she arrives at the police station, she explains the situation to the officer and is truly shocked to learn that she is guilty of murder.

Once Pen gave her statement at the police station, she no longer feared anything. This was the first time in months that she had been outside her small room at the "hotel." She straightened her hair. The drops of blood were now drying on her skin. "That's okay," she thought to herself. "When this is all over, I can wash it off." But who could wash away the stain on Pen's life?

The policeman stared at her for a long time. "There's a small problem, dear," he said. "The punishment for killing someone like this is several years in jail."

"I have to go to jail?" she asked.

"Huh? You killed someone."

"But he hurt me first. I was defending myself."

"It's not that simple. You went too far."

Pen started to hurt all over. She stood up and held onto the edge of the table to steady herself. "And what about what they've done to me? They've turned me into a living corpse. And done the same thing to I don't know how many other hundreds of women." She stuttered in disbelief. "Why don't the police arrest those people and put them in jail? Instead, police protect them, take money from them."

"Be quiet. If you talk like that you'll be brought up on slander charges too." (187–88)

Pen repeats her accusation. And although she refuses to silence herself, the policeman covers her mouth and drags her to a jail cell. As Pen is condemned and silenced for her actions, the reader is left with a deep sense of injustice. All of the protagonist's attempts to maintain her humanity have been in vain. When Pen is ultimately silenced for speaking the truth about the abuse she has endured (abuse that we now realize will continue through this complex and deeply ingrained system), we come to understand that she has no way out of this black hole. Her very migration to the city has launched Pen on a downward spiral that she has no power to end.

In Kon Krailat's 1977 story, "In the Mirror," the author once again portrays Bangkok as a fiercely dehumanizing environment, but offers a glimmer of hope that the rural-urban migrant who struggles against dehumanization may prevail. Chiwin, the protagonist of "In the Mirror," moves to Bangkok with the goal of becoming a teacher. After months of searching unsuccessfully for a teaching job, however, he is forced by hunger and desperation to take on work in a go-go bar.

When he'd set off for Bangkok, carrying his teacher's certificate with him, who could have known that for months he'd be clutching at straws, trying to compete with tens of thousands. . . . At first his hopes had still been bright. . . . But, as time passed, they'd faded, like a candle that melts itself completely away, dimming down to his last baht. Then a friend of his, who worked as a bartender in a go-go club, had invited him along to try this line of work. (Anderson and Mendiones 1985, 216; translated by B. Anderson and Ruchira Mendiones)

The bar where Chiwin works is a space "so dark . . . that people can't see each other's faces" (208). The bar is a place of non-connection and obscurity; although a community of patrons congregates here, they never communicate face-to-face. Chiwin has been working in this environment for a long time and has become desensitized to it. A letter he receives from his mother in the countryside shakes him from this numbness, however: "Win, my dear son, your father isn't very well. The rice planting season's already here, but there's no one at home. How are things going for you in Bangkok? Have you found a job yet or not? We haven't heard from you at all" (207). The words of this letter resound in Chiwin's mind and keep him from falling mechanically into his work routine that day. With his rural home in mind, Chiwin approaches the urban environment with a new critical eye. He notes the club's false lighting, conditioned air, and "endless, indolent" music (211). He becomes aware of the artificiality of this environment and of the deleterious effects it has on him (and on everyone else who enters the bar). That day, as Chiwin performs, he looks out at the audience for someone with whom he can share a human connection. In response to his gaze, "he sees nothing but faces burning more hotly than ever with satisfaction and excitement" (214). The audience sees only the performance—not the humanity of the performers. Chiwin concludes, "We're all animals of the city, who live lives of pain and suffering in the midst of a demented society" (214).

> All of them [the audience members] feel the pressure of the society outside. So they come here for emotional compensation, to build up a superiority complex. . . . This allows them to feel contempt for people they can then regard as lower than themselves. Man has a deep abiding instinct to shove his way up over his fellow men. (214)

The audience's dehumanization of the performers is part of their pleasure. As Chiwin begins to understand the system of dehumanization in which he is enmeshed, he realizes that he is not only a victim, but also a perpetrator. When the audience goads him on in his performance, he feels a sense of rage toward them, but "doesn't dare do anything" (215). Instead, he transfers his rage onto Wanphen, his partner onstage. He does this instinctively, without even realizing his role in Wanphen's dehumanization until she points it out: "Take it easy, Elder Brother Win," she tells him. "I'm not a cow or a water-buffalo" (215). Hearing these words, Chiwin is humbled. He now realizes that he has responded to his own dehumanization by treating another person like an animal.

> So that's it! He's turned Wanphen herself into a victim of his own oppression. He comes to himself at the nip of her nails and the sound

of her voice. Suddenly the tears well up in his eyes, mixed with drops of sweat. He pushes his body up, leaning on his outstretched arms, and stares Wanphen full in the eyes. When he bends over and gives her a kiss, she's surprised by a touch she's never felt from him before. Just then the song ends and the stage-lights dim to darkness. (215)

With this moment of understanding and human connection, Chiwin experiences a flood of emotion. His tears mark the end of his numbness and denial about the harmful effects of the urban environment on him. As Chiwin gazes at Wanphen, he truly connects with her for the first time. This affirmation of their shared humanity is so powerful that it brings the "endless, indolent" music and performance onstage to a close (211).

From here, the story moves immediately to its climax—Chiwin's confrontation with his own image. "Indeed man encounters his real self when he stands before a mirror" (215). Scrutinizing himself in the bathroom mirror, Chiwin thinks about his mother's letter: "How are things going for you in Bangkok? Have you found a job yet?" (215). For the first time, he admits to himself that he has been afraid to tell his mother the truth about his life in the city. "How [could] he possibly tell his mother about the kind of work that he has found? She would faint dead away" (215). As he continues to gaze at himself in the mirror, Chiwin asks, "Is this the true image of a man who's studied to become a teacher?" (216). His answer is purely emotional. He vomits uncontrollably, purging himself of the past and clearing the way for a new beginning.

"In the Mirror" depicts the dehumanizing force of the city, yet opens a space to transcend this dehumanization. As Chiwin awakens from his numb acceptance of the urban environment to identify and reject many of its dehumanizing elements, he leads the reader on a journey upward from hell through purgatory (literalized in his purgation at the end of the text). Whether Chiwin will continue on a Dantean ascent to Paradise—perhaps through a return to the rural realm, or by forging a new life in the city—remains to be seen. But by the end of the text, this possibility has clearly emerged.

Sila Khomchai's "Lost Dog" (1993e) portrays another protagonist who comes to understand her own role in the dehumanization of another over the course of the story. Thongmuan, a housekeeper, has been abused by so many people that the author compares her to one of the maltreated dogs that wander Bangkok's streets. And while Chattaphon, Thongmuan's employer, is not the first to hurt her, she reproduces this dehumanization by refusing to empathize with her and ultimately forcing her back onto the streets. Chattaphon tries to dismiss her own role in this abuse, but she is left at the end of the story grappling with guilt about the animal-like nature of her own actions.

Chattaphon's mother invites Thongmuan to come work for their family after she learns of Thongmuan's history of abuse; she feels sympathy for the old woman and wants to help her out. Chattaphon and her siblings are not happy that their mother has hired Thongmuan, however. They are in need of a housekeeper who can lessen their burden and are worried that an older, crippled woman will simply add to it. They also find Thongmuan's demeanor strange—she seems fearful and suspicious, and the family worries that she will pose a threat to their safety. Chattaphon's mother is saddened by her children's lack of compassion but ultimately agrees to send Thongmuan away.

Chattaphon feels a slight sense of guilt about turning Thongmuan away, but her siblings make light of the situation, going so far as to mimic Thongmuan's crippled movements. This mockery pushes their mother over the edge, "cutting her like a sharp knife and slicing a hole through which everything she held inside came tumbling forth" (Sila 1993e, 131). Although she has tried to be discreet about Thongmuan's past, she can no longer keep Thongmuan's sad story to herself.

"Do you know why Thongmuan is [crippled] like that?" The serious tone of her voice silenced them all immediately. "She was beaten. Beaten until her nerves were destroyed." Mother emphasized the word "beaten" with an expression of pain on her own face.

"Her older brother was a drunk. When Thongmuan was a young woman, no matter how much money she made working, he would take it to fill his bottle. If she didn't have any money, he would beat her instead. Then, when she got married, her husband beat her, too. If she ran away, he'd bring her back and beat her some more. She endured beatings from the time she was a young girl until she was thirty or forty years old. Her arms were broken, her ribs cracked, her body became swollen. There were times when she became unconscious for two days . . . until all she had left was the shell of a body, filled with fear. Her soul has already left her.

"What do you think it's like to feel the sting of a raging man striking your skin with a bamboo stick? Snap! Snap! Your arm breaks. Crack! Or he strikes your nerves over and over again until they snap like a taut string. Your leg becomes so dead that you have to drag it behind you . . . ." Mother was panting now, exhausted after this flood of words and emotions.

"Like a lost dog [*muean ma thi sia ma*]." (131–32)

The final line of Mother's impassioned speech, from which the story takes its name, is an important play on words. The phrase "*sia ma*" literally means a dog that is lost or wasted. "*Muean ma thi sia ma*" could thus mean "like a lost dog." Dogs are one of the less esteemed animals in Thai culture, and stray dogs are particularly disliked. Here, Mother employs the metaphor to express the extreme nature of Thongmuan's dehumanization and abuse.

Another interpretation of this line is rooted in the common phrases "*sia khon*" (lost or wasted person) and "*sia phuyai*" (lost or wasted elder). A person described as *sia khon* is seen to have lost the essence of "personhood," to have lost his integrity as a human being by not living up to the expectations of what a human being is. With the author's substitution of *ma* (dog) for *khon* (person), then, the phrase comes to mean "a dog that does not behave as dogs are supposed to behave, a dog that can no longer even be called a dog." Mother thus points to the incredible dehumanization that Thongmuan has endured. She is not only reduced to the status of "dog," but her degradation extends further—she is a dog who has lost even the usual attributes of this (negatively viewed) animal.

Usually dogs are happy and playful, faithful to their owners. Or they're aggressive, growling at strangers. But there are also those dogs that have been beaten so much that they become nervous. Wherever they go, they hang their tails in fear. They run unsteadily, as if they can't balance themselves. They shift their eyes from left to right, constantly watching their surroundings with fear and jumping in fright at even a falling leaf.

> They can't be loyal—whenever anyone gets close to them, they run away, or if they aren't fast enough, they shiver there on the ground groaning and trembling in fear. The streets are filled with these pitiful creatures. (132)

Hearing these words, Chattaphon and her siblings begin to feel guilty about their actions—until one of them counters that Thongmuan must have done some bad things in her past life to incur such abuse now.[4] All of them latch onto this idea, allowing it to assuage their sense of guilt—except for Chattaphon. The story ends with her gazing gloomily into the kitchen where the fearful Thongmuan seems to lurk. Although she does not want to admit it, Chattaphon now acknowledges that her earlier twinges of guilt were founded. She, too, has committed violence against Thongmuan; she, too, has contributed to the woman's dehumanization by robbing her of a home. The final pun on the title "*sia ma*" becomes clear at this point: with Thongmuan's departure, Chattaphon has "lost a dog," or, rather, a human being that she has treated like one.

THE UNCIVILIZED CITY

A number of Thai migration narratives question the notion that the city is civilized. It is the incoming rural migrants in these texts who identify the "uncivilized city," noting that the village they left behind was more civilized than the city in which they now live. These rural-urban migrant protagonists not only proclaim the city's lack of civilization, but also critique it. In "Desert," Uthain's protagonist notes that citizens completely ignore the plight of poor beggars in "this developed, civilized city" (Uthain 2004d, 142). Kon Krailat's protagonist Pen notes that buffalos are treated better in her village than people are in the city. In Bangkok, she explains, everyone

---

4. Chattaphon's siblings try to justify their failure to demonstrate the Buddhist value of compassion by suggesting that Thongmuan has bad karma and very little merit. This is clearly a flimsy excuse, however, and the author implies that it is not Thongmuan who is the "animal," but these siblings who fail to exhibit the basic elements of human kindness and mercy.

struggles to survive without concern for others. "In this [urban] society, everyone struggles for his own survival. The smart people snatch what they want from the stupid people. The strong ones take from the weak. Don't bother hoping that the big fish is going to help the small fish" (Kon 1976, 181–82).

The urban environment reproduces the base struggle of the jungle through the logic of capitalism. The patron-client system that operated in the village, a system in which "the big fish" helps "the small fish," disintegrates in the urban realm. Pen must learn to fend for herself, and as she does, she finds herself thinking back on the village with nostalgia—a village where clear social laws pertain. Kon Krailat thus reverses the traditional alignment of the city with order and nature with untamed jungle: here, Bangkok becomes the jungle.

Boreetat Hootangkoon and Yohda Hasaemsaeng offer similar depictions of the "uncivilized city." In Boreetat's "The Witch of the Building," a postmodern parody of The Wizard of Oz set in Bangkok, the lines between people and animals are blurred. Animals are anthropomorphized, and Boreetat Hootangkoon uses these part-human, part-animal protagonists to offer his vision of the "civilizing" process of the city.

When Muansaikham (the Dorothy character) meets the cowardly lion for the first time, the lion has just been beaten up by a gang of Bangkok teenagers. Hearing him cry, Muansaikham calls out,

"Excuse me, Mr. Large Dog! When you cry, you sound just like a person."

"Humph! I'm not a dog. I'm a lion!"

"Oh! You speak the same northern dialect as I do. You're a lion—are you going to eat me?"

The young lion sat up on his hind legs. He rubbed his eyes and smoothed down his hair. The light that shone from the lamppost above illuminated his dirty fur, which was covered with scratches. Although he no longer held the grandeur of the king of the jungle, an awesome power still lurked in his large paws and sharp claws.

The lion tried to stop crying when he noticed that Muansaikham was staring at him. She mustered her courage to go up to him and hand him a penguin-patterned handkerchief. Then she asked why he was crying.

"I just killed someone! I tore apart his flesh," the lion responded, hiccoughing.

"Oh!"

"I was hired to kill him. It was horrible. I've never killed or eaten anyone before. But this time, I had to do it. Boo hoo!"

"You're a murderer!" Muansaikham exclaimed.

"I know. But I'm not really the one to blame. We should really blame all those dogs and cats, those ignorant people who laughed at me in my previous job. They all thought it was so funny that the king of the jungle was working at a gas station washing windows and waving in customers. To tell you the truth, the job never bothered me. But after hearing their insults again and again, I couldn't take it anymore. So I quit, becoming a poor, homeless lion who wandered the city streets. After a while I got hungry, and I began to miss those days of the past when I used to play with porcupines, elephants, and bulls. I needed money to get back to my jungle home. And someone suggested this work."

"Your boss made you kill someone," Muansaikham broke in.

"That's right, Sister. He hired me for 30,000 baht to eat the person who loaned him money." (Boreetat 2002, 96–97)

This passage offers a remarkable vision of the "civilizing" process of the city. Boreetat presents us with a lion who lives a peaceful vegetarian life in the countryside, becoming a meat eater only once he migrates to the city and is forced out of humiliation to become a "murderer." Urban society thus pushes him toward a way of life he considers barbaric. In Boreetat's world, the city dehumanizes even animals.

The lion begs Muansaikham to let him join her journey. He wants to visit the witch who can seal off the cowardly chambers of his heart. With these sealed, the lion will be able get on with his work of murder without suffering the tormenting guilt he currently feels. In doing so, he can earn enough money to move back to the jungle, where he will live once again in peace.

Boreetat's text, like Siriworn Kaewkan's "About the Person Who Turns off the Lights," uses an iconoclastic protagonist to portray the uncivilized nature of city life. In both texts, the protagonists define "civilization" in a manner that is counter to society's definition (and the reader's expectation), and the authors stand firmly on the sides of these iconoclasts. In Boreetat's text, we are not surprised to learn that the lion eats people, as we expect this to be part of his nature; rather, we are surprised that he would rather work as a gas-station attendant than do so. The urban environment forces the lion into a role that the reader views as "natural" but the lion himself identifies as degrading. The reader's attention is thus drawn to the question of what it means to be "civilized." And we watch as the lion chooses forest over city.

Similarly, in Siriworn Kaewkan's text, the doctors who examine "the person who turns off the lights" conclude that "he is saner than we are" (2003c, 75). The author thus suggests that an iconoclast who wants to return the city to its pre-urban state is right to feel this way. It is the rest of society, which tries to jail him and get on with "development," whose sanity should be questioned.

In all of these texts, Bangkok is portrayed as a place that masks itself as "civilized" but is truly a jungle. Humans are depicted as animals, either literally or figuratively, and the underlying logic, motivations, and processes of the city are those normally associated with the jungle. A wide range of stories point to this conclusion, from the raw depictions of jungle-like violence in Kon Krailat's "There Was a Day" to more benign narratives that seek to reveal the animal-like logic embedded within acceptable—and even esteemed—urban frameworks. In this latter group of stories, the struggle for "survival of the fittest" in the city is depicted as one version of the socially acceptable "rat race."

In Yohda Hasaemsaeng's "Trap," urban life turns the protagonist into a "mouse" and traps him within its capitalist cage. The ironic twist of Yohda's story (and its central message) is that the urban capitalist system not only sets traps for human beings, but that the system is itself a trap—a trap that even the "winner" of the rat race cannot escape. The only way to avoid the trap, the protagonist ultimately concludes, is to remove oneself from the urban realm altogether. Yet it is not at all clear by the end of "Trap" that the protagonist can extricate himself from this system: when he gains enough distance to recognize the trap as such, he ultimately "chooses" not to extricate himself. It is unclear how much agency the protagonist actually has in this decision—or whether his foray into the urban realm has embedded him in the trap for good.

The story begins with the protagonist struggling to get to work on time. The night before, he has set a mousetrap, and he now sees that the trap has caught its first victim. The protagonist drowns the mouse in a bucket of water and hurries off to work. He walks quickly to the bus stop, but loses time waiting for the bus. Then, he loses time as the bus inches through traffic. The protagonist complains about the insufferable nature of Bangkok time, which alternates between rushing and unpredictable delays.

> I should be able to make it to work on time, if only I didn't have to wait so long each time I changed buses—I end up wasting at least half an hour each day waiting for the bus. Or if the traffic weren't quite so bad, or if I didn't have to mess with mice in the mornings, or if I could pull myself out of bed a little earlier. . . . But there's no use thinking about it—no matter what I do I'm always late. The strange thing, though, is that once I get to work, there really isn't anything urgent for me to do here anyway. What kind of important work could there possibly be for a suburban house salesman like me anyway? (Yohda 1993, 123)

The protagonist describes himself as a setter of traps—traps for mice and traps for people.[5] In his work as a home salesman, he traps unsuspecting buyers by selling them poorly constructed houses. Mousetraps, he explains, do not hunt actively; they simply wait with an "enticing" bit of rotten meat for their next victim. The victim, a "stupid mouse," sees the bait and goes after it without any understanding of the larger system in which it is entrenched or the life-and-death implications of the trap (132). City people, he concludes, are just like these mice. Mice sacrifice their lives for rotten bait; urbanites run themselves weary for money, titles, and status, never considering that these goals may be embedded in traps—or may be traps in and of themselves. "And I," he concludes, "am probably one of those stupid mice, too" (132).

When the protagonist accidentally steps on the mousetrap he has himself set, he interprets this event symbolically. It causes him to worry that he may be more ignorant victim than purposeful predator. He also begins to consider the possibility that he may have unknowingly set other traps for

---

5. The defective house he sold to a picky customer is given as a perfect example of the human traps he sets.

himself that he may fall into at any time. "If I can fall into my own trap," he says, "how can I count on escaping the big trap that is waiting to snap on me one day, or that may already have?" (132). He begins to worry that the financial and career goals he has set for himself may be no more than rotten bait embedded in a larger capitalist system from which there is no escape.

Concluding that the urban realm is filled with traps, the protagonist makes a bold move: he decides to return to the countryside and save himself from the fate of "stupid mice" who drown, one by one, in the city. In doing so, he plans to extricate himself from the urban capitalist system once and for all. In the ten years he has lived in Bangkok, he has considered returning home many times—but he has always rejected this idea because he was afraid that villagers would view him as a failure. This fear is no longer powerful enough to hold him within the urban trap, however.

> Even if others call me crazy, I should still go back. Even if they make fun of me for graduating in the big city and then returning to be a rice farmer, I don't care. At least I've realized that [in the city] I was reaching for rotten bait and running around in circles in a trap—a trap that was about to snap on me, taking my life, just as it did to that stupid mouse this morning. (132)

The protagonist's decision to return to the village represents a decisive stance against the dehumanizing nature of the city—he refuses to be a mouse in a cage any longer. On the protagonist's final day in Bangkok, he abandons the urban schedules that always oppressed him, waking without an alarm and waiting for the rain to cease before leaving his house. "There's no more competing with the clock. There's no more rushing" (133). As he leaves his apartment, the protagonist throws away his alarm clock and his mousetrap, ridding himself of the schedules and traps of the city.

As he travels to the bus terminal on the outskirts of Bangkok, the protagonist passes "armies of mice" heading toward the "big trap" in the center. When he arrives, he finds the terminal empty, since it is a working day. He thinks to himself that the others around must be "outsider mice like me" (133). The bus to his village is waiting at the platform, but there is some time before it is scheduled to leave, so he goes to buy a snack. As the protagonist walks through the terminal, it morphs before his eyes, becoming a "world of mice"[6] (133). He sees a "group of mice at a store crowding around a trap called the lottery" and "a taxi making itself into a trap for a mouse fresh off the bus from the countryside"—"it seemed like there were traps everywhere" (133–34). As the protagonist looks around at these "mice" and "traps," he feels as if he is seeing the urban realm as it really is for the first time. Finally understanding the truth of the city, he makes a firm decision not to fall into such traps any longer.

Soon after, he runs into a colleague from work. "There's good news from the office," she announces. "If you didn't go in this morning, you may not have heard yet" (134). She informs him that they have both gotten raises and that she has been promoted. The protagonist listens, feeling pity for the poor "little mouse who is falling for rotten bait into a trap she will not be able to get out of" (134). He remains unfazed by the news of his own raise and seems to have truly extricated himself from the system of bait and reward.

She continues, "And as for you. You've had the highest sales of anyone in the last six months, and you sold that house that no one could get rid of. So, you'll be promoted to Director of Sales" (134–35). The protagonist is stunned. He stands on the bus platform unable to decide what to do next. He looks at the road out of town and then at the city buses that head toward his Bangkok apartment and office. One bus departs for his village, then another, as he stands there undecided on the platform.

The story ends here, with the protagonist vacillating between return to the village and reintegration in the urban system. It is unclear whether his promotion will be enough to draw him once again into the "rat race" or whether his awareness of the trap is enough to save him. The promotion has clearly enticed him, and it may well prove too much to pass up.

---

6. This scene employs magical realism, so that the people around him literally become mice.

CHAPTER 5

URBAN MOBILITY

A key motivation for rural-urban migration is the expectation that spatial mobility will lead to social and economic mobility. By moving to the larger and more diversified urban realm, the migrant hopes to gain access to a wider range of opportunities and, in doing so, achieve a measure of upward social and economic movement. Urban success is thus deeply linked in the migrant imaginary with notions of dynamism: the move to the city enables success, and upward mobility in the urban realm defines it. It seems ironic to many new arrivals, then, that the overwhelming landscape of Bangkok is one of traffic.

Bangkok reveals itself to new rural-urban migrants not as the fast-moving city they envisioned from the village, but as an overcrowded bog, thick with millions of migrants just like them trying to navigate a single clogged space. Traffic functions in these narratives as the setting for the migrant's struggle. As a literal obstacle to movement, traffic represents the challenges that migrants face in negotiating the city and attaining a level of "mobility" there. The connection between spatial and social mobility is more than metaphorical: because Bangkokians generally take the most comfortable means of transportation they can afford, different modes of transportation become segregated along class lines. Each mode of transportation is associated with a particular class of urban resident: the bus with the poor; the Skytrain, private car, or taxi with the middle class; and the chauffeured car with the elite. For the poor who have no choice but to take the bus, the interminable wait at a bus stop evokes the social "immobility" in which they are immersed. The ability to "escape the bus stop" through a taxi or private car speaks not only to the migrant's greater physical mobility in the urban sphere, but also to the higher level of socio-economic status he has attained. The Skytrain[1] engenders similar notions of middle-class mobility and access through its unimpeded vistas and efficient service to the heart of the city. Once in the center, middle-class migrants express their social mobility further through the consumption of middle-class status symbols.

There is some room for slippage in these categories, however. Middle-class mobility can stall through overconsumption, and maximizing the relationship between "mobility" and debt becomes a preoccupation of the middle class. Similarly, even the poorest beggar can find spaces of free movement by subverting "fixed" social categories or breaking them down altogether. Those who are forced outside society ultimately have nothing to lose by trampling on it, and they may gain a measure of power and mobility by doing so.

CLASS MOBILITY

The traffic was always jammed, no matter if it was morning or evening. (Yohda 1993, 123)

Traffic forms the backdrop for modern Bangkok life. It is an integral part of the urban space, and its unpredictability forces Bangkokians to adapt their rhythms, schedules, and plans to it. Although traffic affects everyone who lives in Bangkok, individual responses to it vary. For those who adopt a Zen-like attitude toward traffic, delays can be more readily endured. The protagonist of Sila Khomchai's "The Family in the Street" ceases to feel frustrated in Bangkok traffic jams once he succeeds in modifying his rhythms to the unnatural environment of the city. He eats, sleeps, and works in the car, and although this lifestyle originally seemed awkward to him, he has come to embrace it. Now, rather than be frustrated during the many hours of gridlock he endures each day, he gets out of the car to network

---

1. The Bangkok Transit System (BTS) "Skytrain" is an elevated train inaugurated in late 1999. The subway, also known as the metro, or MRT, opened in 2004.

with other businessmen on the street or relaxes with his wife in the intimate comfort of their car.

> It was when I learned to like the conditions of my life in the car that our family began to grow closer. Luncheon on the expressway became a time for warm communion, sharing funny stories and whispered confidences. Often when we've been stuck in the same place for over an hour, we think up amusing games. (quoted in Yamada 2002, 212)

For those who are more easily frustrated by traffic's ills, psychological refuge is usually found by taking the most comfortable means of transportation one can afford. Short stories about transit in Bangkok thus reveal an intimate connection between transportation and class. The connection between spatial and social mobility goes even deeper, however. The interminable wait that the urban poor must endure at the bus stop comes to represent the broader social immobility in which this group is immersed. The middle class's ability to escape the bus stop—literally and figuratively—declares their social and spatial mobility. And the stillness of the elite as they sit in the backs of their chauffeured cars (as legions of others move for them) expresses their transcendence of the everyday categories to which most Bangkokians remain subject.

Bangkok's poorest citizens have no choice but to take the bus, enduring traffic's pollution, heat, and delays. The bus itself feels like an extension of the trafficked road, crowded and slow. The lower-class experience of "urban mobility" is thus characterized by waiting. Stories about poor Bangkokians waiting at bus stops (or stuck in traffic on crowded buses) convey the lack of agency these individuals can feel in the city. The only power they have with regard to this environment is the emotional means to endure it. Such agency is most often played out in the protagonist's mind: through an interior dialogue in which the migrant comes to terms with his environment or in which he psychologically escapes to a more pleasant place.

For urban dwellers with more money to spend, the heat and pollution of Bangkok's traffic can be avoided through the use of more expensive modes of transportation. Prior to the Skytrain's opening in 1999, the only way to avoid the ills associated with bus travel was to take a taxi or private car. As a result, the automobile became the symbol par excellence of middle-class mobility: it was the vehicle through which one could escape the congestion of bus travel as well as the long wait the lower class had to endure. With a car one could travel through the city in privacy and comfort along a self-determined route. Most middle-class Bangkokians ply the streets in private cars.[2] Sandra Cate has noted that "cars symbolize the wealth, and, *ironically*, the social mobility of an increasing middle class participating in international systems of status and display" (1999, 25; italics added). Cate argues that with increasing car ownership, middle-class Bangkokians cause additional traffic and, in doing so, ironically thwart their own "mobility." I would suggest, however, that the "systems of status and display" to which Cate alludes enable middle-class Bangkokians to turn the negative experience of traffic inside out: a middle-class Bangkokian can more readily be seen in his middle-class status symbol if he is sitting in traffic.

In recent years, the Skytrain and subway have provided additional means of transport for those who can afford slightly higher fares than for buses. These light rail systems trump other means of transportation by providing cool, clean spaces that flow quickly through the city center. The Skytrain, with its sleek international look, embodies notions of movement, access, and cosmopolitanism. It provides direct access to the heart of Bangkok and unobstructed vistas of the city below. The sense of access one feels when riding the Skytrain is conveyed further by the Skytrain's primary destinations, the major downtown malls. Sky bridges facilitate passengers' movement from train to mall, where passengers/consumers continue "middle-class mobility" through pedestrian and capital circulations in the shopping center.[3]

---

2. The vast majority of Bangkok's car owners are members of the middle class. The wealthy also drive cars, but they represent a miniscule portion of the population. The significant numbers of urban poor ride the bus. The Thai government has consistently supported car use through the subsidization of fuel prices (until 2005, when global hikes in oil prices made this too costly), the subsidization and reduction of toll-way prices, and acquiescence to powerful real estate interests that continue to build suburban housing developments in the urban periphery. Recently, Natural Gas Vehicles (NGV) have enabled middle-class Bangkokians to continue using private cars by making fuel even more affordable. (Fuller 2007; Wanpen et al. 2006)

3. Sky bridges enable passengers to move directly into the mall without ever touching the street below. The transit/mall system thus lifts the middle class up from the life of the

Bangkok's light rail system thus provides many of the advantages of a private car—including the expression of middle-class status and mobility—while avoiding traffic altogether. However, these light rail systems remain limited in scope, serving Bangkok with only three lines. The majority of Bangkok's middle-class residents live on the outskirts of the city, where it is financially feasible for them to buy private homes. To access the Skytrain, then, they would need to drive to the Skytrain terminus and park there—it is much simpler to drive directly to one's destination. For those who live in the city center, Bangkok's superblock pattern of development represents a further obstacle to Skytrain use. Most Bangkokians live on *sois* embedded in vast superblocks, so they are too far from the main road to walk to the Skytrain. The low concentration of residents in these superblocks means that shuttle bus service to the main road is not economically feasible either. As a result, even people living in the city center use cars to commute.

Beyond these logistical reasons, the enduring symbolism of the car as middle-class status symbol cannot be overemphasized. In a study of middle-class commuters in Bangkok, Wanpen Charoentrakulpeeti et al. (2006, 703) note that middle-class Bangkokians view car ownership and the use of private cars as "both a necessity and desirable for the following reasons: ease of accessibility, enhancement of social status, safety and a reduction of one's exposure to pollution." The study's middle-class respondents viewed public transportation as "inadequate to meet their demands," noting its "poor quality of service, a lack of safety, and an absence of reliable and regular schedules." The authors of this study themselves aligned car ownership so closely with middle-class status that they made "private car ownership" one of four criteria for defining "middle-class respondents" in their survey.

The car is the vehicle of choice for Bangkok's most elite residents as well. For this group, issues of defensible space and status pronouncement easily win out over the enticements of speed. The richest Bangkokians sit still in

---

street (which is associated with heat, dirt, and pollution), providing unimpeded mobility through clean, cool spaces of consumption. A recent Skytrain advertising campaign invited passengers to "lift up your life" by using the Skytrain. The message was delivered in English (not Thai), adding a further note of cosmopolitan cachet to the campaign and to the Skytrain in general.

the backs of their cars while drivers inch through Bangkok traffic on their behalf. Given the associations of stillness and power in the Southeast Asian paradigm, it makes sense that these individuals would prefer a method of transportation that deemphasizes speed in favor of status proclamations. For those at the top of Thai society, moving through traffic becomes irrelevant— appointments and people will wait for them.

THE BUS STOP

The bus stop appears in Thai literature as a site where the rural-urban migrant's level of agency in the city is understood at the nexus of financial power and mobility. The key to escaping the wait or immobility of the bus stop is money. Again and again, migrants comment that if only they had more money, they would use an alternate means of transportation—usually a taxi—to escape this realm. The ability to circulate capital is thus the ability to circulate physically through the city. The bus stop setting facilitates a meditation on class and mobility because it exposes the difference between those who are forced to remain immobile and those who have access to economic and spatial movement. At the most immobile or financially-deprived end of the spectrum, we find beggars who are permanently installed at the bus stop (with no plans to move even once a bus arrives); at the other end, we have the more privileged riders who can choose to take a taxi if they become tired of waiting. In the middle, we have the majority of lower- to middle-class Bangkokians for whom the bus is the only option— no matter how uncomfortable the bus stop may become, members of this group must remain there if they are to become mobile at all.

The protagonist of Prachakom Lunachai's "Rain and Night" is forced to spend the night at a bus stop after he fails to push his way onto the last overcrowded bus home. He explains, "If I were to take a taxi home tonight, I would have to go without food for several days before my next paycheck. And in any case, the money I have in my pocket right now wouldn't be enough for the ride" (Prachakom 1996d, 96–97).

The bus stop functions as a sort of ground zero for those with limited economic power. Lut and Pigun, the protagonists of Samrung Kampa-oo's "Oriole" end up at a bus stop when they have nowhere else to go. They have searched unsuccessfully in Bangkok for work, and they now stand at a bus stop in the rain wondering what to do next. Having come to this end-of-the-line position in the urban realm, they decide that their best bet is to leave the city altogether. They go to sleep under the bus shelter with the intention of departing for their village the next morning.

The link between money and mobility is underscored when Lut and Pigun awaken to find that they have been robbed. These protagonists now lack the means to make it even to the train station, let alone back to their village. With this moment of bus stop bankruptcy, the couple reaches its ultimate low: a complete lack of agency and mobility in the city. Lut looks at Pigun and tells her,

> "Don't worry Pigun. We're not all that much poorer now than we were before [the robbery]. I promise that as soon as I save up enough money for the ticket, I'll bring you home."
>
> Pigun looked into her husband's eyes with trust in his promise.
> (Samrung 2005, 120)

With no clear option in the physical world, Lut attempts to regain agency for himself and his partner through a psychological negotiation. He promises to earn a bit of money so that he can reclaim physical and economic mobility. Once he does so, he promises, he will take Pigun far away from the bus stop where they are currently stranded.

Just as Lut and Pigun view power and mobility in terms of their ability to escape the bus stop, migrant protagonists who have attained a measure of social and economic mobility describe their success in Bangkok in terms of their ability to escape the bus. In Uthain Phromdaeng's "A Man," Tarin's "Fake Beggar," and Siriworn Kaewkan's "About a One Baht Coin," we find protagonists who have pulled themselves from the "bus realm" to attain a level of social and economic status that affords them greater choice. The memory of the bus remains with them, however, and all of these protagonists retain a connection to the bus realm and an awareness of the privilege they have attained with respect to other migrants who are still stuck.

Uthain Phromdaeng's Pracha, a rural-urban migrant who has achieved success as a businessman in the city, states,

I feel bad for the people at the bus stop. They wait to fight their way on the bus, struggling against the crowds that are traveling on the same route. The bus is the only option for people with low incomes. It's impossible to guess how much longer those people will have to wait there. But as for me, in only a few moments a taxi should arrive to take me home in comfort. (Uthain 2005, 152)

Pracha contrasts the unpredictable and seemingly interminable wait of those with low incomes to his own certainty of escape in a matter of minutes. In noting that "it's impossible to guess how much longer those people will have to wait," Pracha refers not only to the physical bus stop, but also to the broader context of social and spatial immobility in which poorer Bangkokians are immersed. Pracha knows that it *is* possible to escape the "bus realm"—he has done so himself—and yet, he also knows that it is "impossible to guess" when such an escape might occur. A large measure of luck is involved in achieving success in the city, and Pracha grapples with a nagging feeling that his own upward mobility has been, in part, a fluke—that he deserves it no more than the many others who are still "waiting for the bus." As a result, he feels a sense of "survivor's guilt" toward these newer migrants. Although he has ostensibly transcended the bus realm, he finds himself glancing uncomfortably back at the migrants who still stand there, as he justifies his own ability to move on. Pracha can now afford to travel exclusively by car, but he still feels a need to explain this "extravagance" by stating that his crippled leg makes it difficult for him to use the bus.

Pracha's sense of "survivor's guilt" is revealed further when he spots Chamrat, a childhood friend, at the bus stop.[4] Pracha and Chamrat have not seen each other in decades; the two drifted apart once Pracha left the village to further his studies in the city, and Chamrat remained behind to tend his family's farm. Pracha had heard that Chamrat eventually made it to Bangkok and had considered looking him up—he had even thought about lending Chamrat a hand if he needed it—but in the end, Pracha did not bother to reach out. It is only here, at the bus stop, that they are reunited.

---

4. Pracha is standing under the bus awning as he waits to hail a cab.

As soon as Pracha sees Chamrat, he knows that his old friend's situation is dire. Pracha is not simply one of the masses relegated to the bus realm: he is a thief who waits at the bus stop to steal from these masses. Pracha watches as Chamrat grabs a woman's purse and attempts to flee the scene. This vision of Chamrat—a man who started off in the same position Pracha did—signals to Pracha what he might well have become. Pracha is overcome with guilt and fear, and rather than step in to aid his friend (who is now being carted off by the police), Pracha decides instead to deny that this person was actually Chamrat. Pracha finds safety in distance and quickly hails a cab to leave the scene. As Pracha rides away, he distances himself from his past, from the stymied realm of the bus stop, and from any suggestion that he may still be tied to this realm.

Pimala, the protagonist of Tarin's "Fake Beggar" exhibits a similar relationship to the "bus realm." As she waits for the bus that will take her home after work, she compares the people she sees at the bus stop to professionals like her who lead relatively luxurious lifestyles.

> There's a small group of people who can survive on small change—an amount of money so negligible that it cannot even be compared with the amounts spent by cert\ain groups in their pursuit of comfort. Pimala didn't want to include herself in this latter group—but to tell the truth, she was pretty much already part of it. (Tarin 1993, 244)

Pimala, a rural-urban migrant cum urban professional, has achieved middle-class status in the city. She takes the bus to work, but has enough money to take a taxi when the bus becomes too uncomfortable. Pimala lives on the cusp of two socio-economic worlds, retaining an allegiance to the city's newest migrants, while identifying with the wealthier middle-class group of which she has recently become a part. Thus, when co-workers from Pimala's office laugh at the upcountry accents of street vendors, Pimala thinks to herself that their amusement is "beyond what is called for" (237). At the same time, she fails to defend the street vendors. And when Pimala overhears a group of well-dressed women discuss "fake beggars" in the neighborhood, she believes them and adopts a suspicious attitude toward the beggars at the bus stop. An elderly beggar subsequently asks her for small change to "buy a ticket home," and Pimala refuses to give her money

(242). This refusal functions as an articulation of identity: Pimala locates herself firmly in the group of middle-class professionals who are suspicious of street beggars. This refusal also reproduces the constraints within which each of the classes operate: Pimala's own (financial) ability to return home by various means stands in contrast to and reinforces the elderly beggar's inability to return home at all. Pimala's middle-class privilege is thus revealed not only in her ability to perpetuate her own mobility, but also in her capacity to restrict the mobility of others.

Once the beggar walks away, however, Pimala wonders if she has done the right thing. She admits to herself that the amount of money the elderly woman requested was so negligible that it "would have made no difference to her anyway" (243). Pimala begins to feel guilty about withholding small change from a woman in need. She thinks to herself, "Maybe she wasn't lying after all. Maybe she was trying to save money to go back to her provincial home—to the place where she once lived. The place she loved. . . . When Pimala thought about this, she began to feel a little bit guilty" (243). Pimala's subtle identification with the beggar emerges in this passage. As she turns the conversation with the beggar over in her head, Pimala imagines the woman as a rural-urban migrant who needs money to get "back to her provincial home, . . . [to] the place she loved." Here, Pimala projects what is perhaps her own desire onto the old woman, expressing a sense of nostalgia for the countryside through imaginings about the beggar. The empathy Pimala feels at this moment leads her to change her mind about the donation. She decides that if she sees the old woman again, she will give her some money and help her return home.

Despite this resolution, "Pimala stopped thinking [about the old woman] when a taxi pulled up in front of her" (243). The prospect of Pimala's own mobility pushes the elderly woman from her mind, and Pimala enters a cab, "leaving the heat and crowds behind" (244). Once in the taxi, Pimala "moves to the center of the seat in order to fully absorb the cool air from the front of the taxi" (244). In moving to the "center," Pimala eschews the marginality of the bus realm, placing herself in the core position she has earned through her class status. As she relaxes in the exclusivity of the cab, Pimala thinks to herself how different this cool, private space is from the stifling world of the bus—even though they share the same road. She looks back at the bus stop, feeling relieved that she has left it behind. But shortly after, a feeling of guilt creeps in as she thinks about the elderly beggar and the transparent lie Pimala had told: "I don't have any money, Grandmother" (244). These words play over and over in Pimala's mind, haunting her ride. The final time she hears her own words in her head, Pimala "looks away, as if to evade the thought she had a moment ago. But the cool air kept hitting her" (244). Despite her attempts to push these words (and the image they evoke) from her mind, their meaning continues to be conveyed by the unrelenting conditioned air that forces Pimala to confront her privilege.

Pimala looks out the window, hoping to find an escape from this "oppressive" taxi, but when she sees the dense traffic, she knows that she will not be able to escape any time soon. Her taxi creeps slowly past the bus stop, and as she gazes at it, she sees an image that upsets her: the elderly woman is leaning against the bus stop, crying. Pimala's fear is confirmed; the woman is not a "fake beggar" after all, and Pimala has, through middle-class affect, held this woman in a state of immobility.

As a rural-urban migrant and recent inductee into the urban middle class, Pimala is an inside-outsider. She knows what it feels like to be in both positions, but does not fully inhabit either role. The taxi that saves Pimala from the uncomfortable realm of the bus stop also traps her in guilt over its privilege. As someone who has endured the bus stop, Pimala cannot ignore the larger context around her newly claimed class status. Her own words to the old woman haunt her taxi ride and ultimately pull her back to the hot, uncomfortable space she hoped to flee. Pimala's inability to escape the immobile "bus realm" is symbolized by the impenetrable traffic, which slows her down and forces her to experience immobility and come to terms with her surroundings.

The beggar, perhaps the most marginalized member of Thai society, occupies a unique position. On the one hand, the beggar remains utterly vulnerable, subject to the good will of passersby for survival. On the other, the beggar represents a powerful wild card, someone who has nothing to lose by exposing holes in the system (or by destroying it altogether). To the extent that he can mobilize his own subversive power, the beggar can break down the class categories that hold him at the bottom and, in doing so, reclaim his mobility. In Tarin's "Fake Beggar," the elderly beggar turns the tables on Pimala almost passively, by embodying a vision of helplessness that haunts the protagonist until she is stripped of her middle-class power and mobility. In Siriworn Kaewkan's "About a One Baht Coin," the beggar enacts a similar subversion by repeatedly crossing the borders of accepted social, economic, and class categories. In doing so, he shows these categories to be less fixed than society purports them to be and creates space for his own mobility.

When Siriworn's story opens, the beggar is sitting silently on the ground near a bus stop. Passersby ignore him. "No one knew who he was, where he came from, or when he came here. Or, if we were going to say it in another way, we would have to say that no one cared who he was, where he came from, or when he came to live next to the garbage can at this bus stop" (Siriworn 2003e, 139–40). This beggar occupies a position so marginal that others hardly acknowledge him. Yet his clothing and demeanor suggest that he once held a much more powerful position in society.

> He would sit there silently [at the bus stop], looking like a businessman who was sick of the rat race. He sat there like this all-day long, rain or shine, hiding himself in an old, worn-out suit. His buttons were done incorrectly, his belt hung limply around his neck like a tie, and three or four old newspapers were rolled up and thrust into his breast pocket. In his right hand, he held an old cell phone loosely.[5] (140)

Repeated references to the Thai year 2540 (AD 1997) suggest that he may have been a businessman who lost his fortune in the 1997 Asian financial crisis. The beggar's hybrid appearance, which simultaneously suggests former wealth and current poverty, makes it difficult to place him in a clear class category. His actions, moreover, make it impossible to place him in the immobile realm of the bus stop. Although passersby may ignore him, this beggar watches *them*. He is a witness, "the man who watches the happenings on this street" (139). The agency that his gaze affords is revealed when the beggar observes an event that no one else sees: a woman drops a one-baht

---

5. The mobile phone has also become an important icon of middle-class "mobility." The 1992 street demonstrators (who were overwhelmingly middle class) were known as the "mobile mob" due to their ubiquitous mobile phones.

coin on the ground.[6] Although this event may seem minor, the beggar's witnessing of it opens a space for the rearticulation of his presence and an explosion of the class categories that hold him in place.

The story's middle-class protagonist, Lamyai, or Laura,[7] drops a one-baht coin on the ground as she rummages through her purse for bus fare. "Although she did not mean to drop the coin, she knew she dropped the coin. And while she did not mean to drop it, she meant not to pick it up" (139). This event, occurring in a blink of an eye, may have passed unnoticed if not for the beggar who witnesses it. After watching the coin roll onto the sidewalk, the beggar slowly rouses himself, goes over to the coin, and picks it up. If this seems a logical response—a beggar, in need of money, picks up a coin—the beggar's next move is surprising: he walks over to Lamyai/Laura and hands her the coin.

Lamyai/Laura turns toward him slightly, regards him with anger and disgust, and steps to the side. The beggar follows her and holds out the coin again. People at the bus stop begin noticing this interaction. No one can figure out why a beggar is handing a one-baht coin to a fashionably dressed woman (since only the beggar and Lamyai/Laura know that she has dropped it), but they find the sight amusing. Lamyai/Laura becomes increasingly embarrassed as people begin watching her, and she moves further away. The beggar follows her, all the while holding out the coin. Unable to avoid him, Lamyai/Laura considers screaming, but decides that this would call even more attention to herself—an outcome she does not want. On the other hand, she cannot bring this public interaction to an end by accepting the coin, because this would instantly reduce her to the status of someone who accepts change from beggars (making the onlookers laugh even harder). She is trapped.

Lamyai/Laura ultimately escapes the scene by ducking into a taxicab

---

6. At the time the story was written, one baht was equivalent to approximately 3 cents.

7. Siriworn Kaewkan refers to this protagonist alternately as Lamyai (a Thai name meaning "Longan," the tropical fruit) and Laura, a Western name that he aligns with her dyed blond hair and expressions of *thansamai* (modern, up-to-date) behavior and dress. The dual nature of her appearance also suggests the variability and multiplicity of identity, and the difficulty of pinning a person down with a single word.

and rushing off into the distance. At this point, the beggar begins slowly and methodically to follow the cab.[8] His determination to return the coin renders him visible by forcing Lamyai/Laura—and everyone else at the bus stop—to acknowledge him. This act also reclaims his power and mobility, as he becomes the pursuer and Lamyai/Laura is forced to respond to him.

By actively attempting to return Lamyai/Laura's coin, then, the beggar reveals the inherent flux and malleability of social status categories. In moving from the role of beggar to donor in an instant, he exposes the deeply fluid nature of status and wealth. The fact that the coin he manipulates was minted in the year 2540 (AD 1997) speaks further to these fluctuations: this very coin was reduced in value by nearly 100 percent shortly after it was minted and has fluctuated continuously since. Just as one such fluctuation brought the beggar to the streets in 2540/1997, so now does an arbitrary event—the dropping and retrieval of a coin—jettison him from stillness to movement, engendering a change in perspective for all around.

CONSUMING MOBILITY

If agency is located for the lower classes at the nexus of economic power and mobility, for the middle classes, it resides at the intersection of *consumption* and mobility, with status expressed through conspicuous consumption. Jim Ockey has noted the inchoate nature of middle-class status in Thailand and resultant "insecurity of the new rich" (Ockey 1999, 238–40). Because "middle class" is a relatively new category in Thailand (when compared with "rich" and "poor"), the parameters of middle-class status have yet to be clearly defined. As a result, those seeking to join the middle class fight an uphill battle in proving (to themselves and others) that they have actually made it. Perhaps the easiest way to achieve this goal is through the consumption of recognized middle-class status symbols, such as a car, home, and particular types of clothing, accessories, and food. The problem is that consumption is

---

8. The stories in Siriworn Kaewkan's text combine contemporary settings with fable and allegory in a humorous manner that recalls the work of Italo Calvino.

a fleeting act, one that must be continually repeated, and repeating this act too often can risk middle class status itself by transforming wealth into debt.

The promise that consumption will lead to a modern, middle-class lifestyle is one promulgated both by corporations seeking to sell products and by governments seeking to expand the economy.[9] As Thais buy into consumption's promises of modernity, however, they risk jeopardizing the very middle-class status they are trying to achieve. Pasuk and Baker have pointed out that as the economy expanded under Thaksin, so did household debt, making it increasingly difficult for the average Thai to tell "what level (of debt) is critical."[10] And when the invisible line between consumption and overconsumption is crossed, the "mobility" of middle-class status—which must be constantly reproduced—stalls. This is exactly what happens to Prueang and Sophit, the protagonists of Nirunsak Boonchan's "Middle-Class People, Second-Hand Car, and Mangy Dogs." The couple's decision to buy a home—a purchase that propels them into the middle class—leads to a spiral of unanticipated expenses. The more the couple spends to maintain their middle-class status, the more precarious their financial situation becomes. The status symbols they consume to declare upward mobility ironically drag them deeper and deeper into debt. The immobility that results from their overconsumption is figured literally in their broken-down car and symbolically in the fact that they must once again take the bus to work.

In Suthipong Thamawut's "The City That is Punished for Consumption,"[11] the middle-class protagonist falls, over the course of one morning, into a similar state of immobility as a result of his unyielding consumption. He is a consumer *par excellence*, so immersed in a world of consumption that he views the city itself as a sort of mall filled with modern products waiting

---

9. "The Thaksin government has encouraged people not to save but to consume, and to go into debt to consume" (Pasuk and Baker 2004, 130).

10. According to Pasuk and Baker, household debt in Thailand quadrupled under Thaksin (ibid).

11. The title, "*Nakhon Boripokatan*" is an invented term. The author has constructed the word "*boripokatan*" through a combination of Sanskrit roots. We might also translate the title as "The City That Punishes for Consumption"—both meanings are implied in the text.

to be possessed. "I'm still young. . . . I'm just starting out. . . . There's still a lot of modernity out there waiting for me. . . . I already know about it, I'm just waiting for the chance to possess it. . . ." (Suthipong 2004, 222–23).

This protagonist is well on his way to appropriating the urban modernity around him. His Bangkok townhouse is filled with appliances that proclaim his modern lifestyle and produce surplus "time"—a commodity that he can spend in pursuit of further "modernity." Noting the value of time, the protagonist states, "My time is not there to be *spent* wastefully" (227; italics added). With these words, we see the extent to which this protagonist aligns time and money. His use of the verb "to spend" (*jai*) time is unusual in Thai (normally one speaks of "using" [*chai*] time), and the economic nature of his words stands out. In the city, he says, time is money, and the more time/money one accrues, the more "modernity" one can access. This truth, he adds, is lost on those who "live in the countryside [*ban nok*] and don't understand the value of time" (225). "Doing things slowly like my mother does," he says, "would cost I don't know how many opportunities in this city" (225).

Suthipong's protagonist thus endeavors to use time to his utmost advantage, employing various time-saving devices in his daily activities.

In this city, I have the same amount of time as I did in the countryside where I was born, but here I have all sorts of modern appliances and conveniences to make things much easier and faster.

As fast as the thought came to me, I ran to plug in the hot water heater on the plastic shelf. I put two pieces of bread into the toaster next to it, pushed down the lever, and plugged it in. I opened the refrigerator, took out two sausages and two pieces of ham, unwrapped the plastic around them, and put them in the toaster oven. I closed the door of the toaster oven and plugged it in. I grabbed a piece of cheese and placed it next to the plate and spoon. I turned over a coffee cup that was resting upside-down and set it on a saucer. Then, I scooped three spoonfuls of instant coffee and two squares of sugar into it and left it waiting for the water that had not yet started to boil.[12]

---

12. The "modernity" of this scene is expressed not only in the protagonist's reliance

This [amount of caffeine] would be enough to wake me up and get me ready to enter the field of competition.

I spent less than three minutes preparing breakfast. After this, I had time to do whatever I wished. The switches on the machines would watch the time and temperature so that I could finish everything else. (220–21)

The protagonist's appliances go beyond saving time; they keep time. The protagonist adapts himself as closely as possible to the machines' mechanized schedules, adjusting his activities and behaviors to their clocks. When the toaster goes off, he immediately throws away his half-smoked cigarette and realigns himself with the mechanized schedule he "should" be on. Even his bodily functions adapt to this tempo: his stomach acids begin churning when the toaster's bell rings so that he is able to finish in the bathroom just as his breakfast is ready.

On this particular morning, however, his body refuses to cooperate with his appliances' schedule. The night before, the protagonist failed to consume as usual, forgetting to take the laxative capsules that keep his body running mechanically, and this lapse has thrown his entire system out of whack.

Since I've been living here [in Bangkok], there's only one thing that really bothers me: constipation. Actually, it's not that big a deal. I've learned on TV about the various medications I can take for this problem. There are several brands, and I've tried almost all of them. I can say with certainty that my favorite is the blue and pink capsules. (224)

Suthipong's protagonist is plagued by bloating—the inability of his body to excrete waste—but this unyielding consumer deals with his problem by consuming more. He has streamlined his consumption, taking one capsule per night before bed. By keeping his consumption constant and controlled, he remains in pace with the city and avoids unwanted delays in the morning.

On the night before the story takes place, however, he gets so drunk (overconsuming alcohol) that he passes out before he takes his capsule. This

on machines and his strict adherence to mechanized time, but also by the very food he eats—a Western breakfast—which implies cosmopolitanism and international tastes.

single breach of consumption has consequences the following morning, forcing him to confront the effects of overconsumption: a hangover, bloating, and delay. It is not only the protagonist's body, but the entire modern environment that seems to revolt against him on this morning. After leaving the house, he becomes plagued by the fear that he has left his appliances plugged in. When he returns to check on his appliances, he is delayed further by the state-of-the-art lock he uses to protect his belongings. Then, when he attempts to leave for work a second time, his car will not start. The protagonist finally gives up on his modern "time-saving devices" and decides to take a taxi instead. When he reaches the corner of his *soi*, however, he finds an overwhelming image of delay: traffic as far as the eye can see. At this point, the protagonist is confounded by the overconsumption (and resultant immobility) of the city at large—traffic created by millions of middle-class car owners just like him vying for modernity and mobility in Bangkok.

This moment represents the protagonist's ultimate "punishment" as suggested by the title. His lifestyle of consumption has brought him to a state of bloated immobility inside and out. Just as his body is clogged by his overconsumption of food, so is his lifestyle bogged down by the cumulative overconsumption of urban residents like him (and the overdevelopment of the city as a whole). The story ends here, with a vision of traffic as far as the eye can see and the sounds of unrelenting construction. And, although he expressed praise for development earlier in the story, he now admits that the sound of this hammer is beginning to grate on him.

MOVING BEYOND

The paradox of middle-class "mobility" is that it remains constrained along established lines. This is perhaps clearest in the case of the Skytrain, where speedy access to the city center leads the rider invariably into a mall. Once in the mall, the passenger/shopper continues his or her "mobility" by circulating capital in the consumption of pre-approved middle-class status symbols. As Yohda Hasaemsaeng puts it, such "mobility" is no more than movement through the tunnels of one's own cage.

How then can one truly attain mobility in the city? The beggar in "About a One Baht Coin" offers an interesting suggestion: pursue movement that does not strive upward along well-established routes, but that breaks these structures down to allow free flow in any direction. If Pimala's "upward" movement from bus stop to taxi leaves her feeling trapped, Glangjai's wild and directionless movement in "The Motorcycle Gangstress" enables her to reclaim agency, freedom, and the road.

Chamaiporn's middle-class protagonist Glangjai disentangles urban movement from its usual class categories by using a mode of transportation decidedly below her class, the motorcycle taxi. While Glangjai initially expresses disdain for motorcycle taxis, calling them loud, dirty, and dangerous, she ultimately turns to them when the traffic on her *soi* becomes impenetrable. On her first ride, Glangjai feels awkward and scared; she does not know quite how to sit with her long skirt, and she fears the speed and recklessness with which the driver plunges forward. This first motorcycle ride "carries her away," and by the end of it she is so scared that she cannot even ease her way down off the motorcycle (Chamaiporn 1992, 124). Once Glangjai gets over her shock, however, she realizes that she has arrived at work *early*. This pleases her.

The next time Glangjai hires a motorcycle taxi, she decides to take it all the way to her appointment (rather than to the end of her own *soi*). She is now used to the speed of the ride, but this time is frightened by the shoddy condition of the motorcycle, which looks as if it might fall apart at any moment. When she arrives at her destination quickly, however, she is pleased once again—until her colleagues see her descend from the motorcycle and laugh. "The people she worked with cracked up when they saw her step off the motorcycle taxi" (125). For them, a middle-class woman on a motorcycle is an incongruous sight, and they cannot help remarking on her transgression of class norms. Glangjai's husband, too, expresses surprise and concern at her use of this "low" form of transportation. "Don't take them anymore," he tells her. "They're dangerous!" (125). Motorcycle taxis, he insists, should be used only by those without better options. His vision of "better" implies safer and more expensive—not faster.

Glangjai's husband thus aligns himself with the upper-class paradigm for movement: the ability to "choose" to move slowly (that is, to sit in traffic in a comfortable car). If "middle class" is an unstable and amorphous category in Thailand, it makes sense that middle-class individuals would align themselves as closely as possible with the upper-class paradigm (rather than the lower-class one). And although Glangjai does not share her husband's perspective, she assents in order to appease him. But shortly after, she boards a motorcycle taxi once again.

On this occasion, Glangjai has a business meeting in an area she does not know well. She takes a number of wrong buses before running out of time. She switches to a taxi, but finds herself frustrated and immobile in traffic. She has splurged for a cab and still attained no mobility. She curses herself for not having taken a taxi from the outset (in an effort to save money) and for not having used a motorcycle from the start (in an effort to avoid embarrassment in front of her colleagues). She now realizes that she has "stuck" herself in the "middle class" by not spending freely as an upper-class person would, while avoiding the symbolic "downward mobility" that a motorcycle taxi implies to others. When the possibility of mobility emerges, then, she immediately takes it.

A motorcycle taxi weaves through the traffic and pauses in front of her taxi. The motorcycle driver is about to squeeze through the space between two cars when Glangjai grabs a twenty-baht bill, thrusts it at her driver, and dashes out. She pulls herself up onto the motorcycle taxi in the middle of the street and yells, "To Sanam Luang, on the Thammasat side!" (126).

This motorcycle is the scariest one yet. The driver weaves in and out of lanes and slips between cars—even through spaces so narrow that he must inch by with his feet. Glangjai closes her eyes and curses him, "but at the same time, she also felt happy that she was moving more quickly" (127). Here we see Glangjai's vacillation between a fear of breaking down boundaries (by moving inappropriately fast or by taking a motorcycle taxi at all) and her pleasure in speed and mobility. And when she recounts these scary but hilarious experiences to her friends, "no one could tell for sure whether Glangjai liked the motorcycle taxis or not" (128).

This inscrutability is at the heart of Glangjai's pleasure: it allows her to transcend the terrifying stasis that underlies middle-class life—that of being pinned down, fixed into categories, and ruled by social conventions. While earning status symbols ostensibly fosters upward mobility, Glangjai understands that this pattern quickly locks one into predictability. Rather than be fixed, she insists on finding mobility in her own way.

This determination is reiterated in the final scene of the story, when Glangjai boards a motorcycle taxi for the final time. Her clothing places her firmly in the middle class (she has styled her hair, wears a long skirt, and holds a carefully chosen umbrella), and yet she insists on traveling by motorcycle. When the driver eyes her with incredulity, she simply tells him to drive (while continuing to hold her umbrella). The motorcycle taxi soon loses balance, and they have an accident. Worried that Glangjai has been hurt, the motorcycle driver slowly escorts her home. She brushes off his concern, however, and even insists on giving him a tip. Two hours later, she emerges from her home limping and asks the motorcycle taxi driver to take her to the hospital. She has changed out of her long skirt (adapting to a clothing style more suitable to the motorcycle taxi), but still wears a skirt (insisting, at least in part, on retaining her own style).

"The Motorcycle Gangstress" reads as a humorous story about a woman addicted to an activity below her class, but it is not a warning tale of addiction. Glangjai seems, in fact, to come out ahead as a result of her obsession, expanding the borders of her own experience and the spaces in which she moves—without ever giving up the traits that are characteristically hers. With her accident (and her refusal to abandon motorcycle taxis after it), she gains "street cred," taming even the driver who had earlier expressed annoyance at her middle-class pretensions. By the end of the narrative, Glangjai reclaims these "pretensions" as elements of her own personality (rather than representative symbols of a class), while taking back the streets and her ability to move freely through them.

CHAPTER 6

RETURN

The migrant's moment of return to the village throws the experience of migration dramatically into light, revealing the migrant's changed perspectives, values, and needs. In this way, return to the village sets the stage for self-evaluation on the part of the migrant. This can include the ways in which the migrant has changed since leaving the village, the impact of the migrant's departure on his or her rural family and community, the migrant's altered position in that home community as a result of migration, and whether or not the act of migration has brought success. In grappling with these questions, the migrant must come to terms with the differing systems of value in the rural and urban realms, as well as a global system of value that the migrant may intuit but be unable to pin down.

Two reasons for return appear repeatedly in Thai migration literature: return for the Songkran holiday and return for a family tragedy, usually the death of a relative. While these two tropes of return share many characteristics, an important difference is the planned nature of return in the first case. Before migrants return for Songkran, they have time to prepare themselves psychologically for the shift from the urban to the rural realm. With the unanticipated return for a family emergency, no such preparation is possible. As a result, the issues migrants face upon return are intensified in the second scenario, particularly because tragedies are themselves moments of heightened emotion.

While these two tropes of return differ in specific ways, they share one important characteristic: obligation. It is expected by the migrant's family and village community that the migrant will return at these times, and the inability (or refusal) to fulfill this obligation appears as a major breach of village and family norms. As such, failure to return becomes a cause for the examination of the severe impacts that migration can have on the family and individual.

In addition to these experiences of short-term return, a number of stories deal with migrants who return to the village permanently, often after a traumatic migration experience. The work of evaluating one's experience of migration is particularly poignant for those who return to the village after being incapacitated by urban work. When migration has claimed a limb, the health, or the sanity of the migrant, how should success be evaluated? This question becomes further problematized in instances where the migrant is compensated for loss with money; in such cases, the goal of migration—financial stability—is achieved, but with dire and unanticipated consequences. These stories explore issues of sacrifice and exchange, as migrants consider what they have traded through their act of migration and attempt to determine whether the trade has been worth it.

Stories about migrant return—both temporary and permanent—detail the ongoing process of identity-making through which migrants seek to solidify their sense of self, their place in the world, and their role as "migrants." In returning to their homes, these individuals must confront any disjuncture between nostalgic visions of the village and the contemporary reality of that place. This process can be difficult work, and many migrants find themselves with an ultimate sense of living "in between," unable to settle fully into a clear identity, as the categories "rural" and "urban" become increasingly blurred.

EXCHANGE

The city sent them many good, new things. But what it wanted in exchange was all too valuable. (Plinda 1993, 59)

Grandfather Han, the protagonist of Plinda Siripong's "Exchange," mutters these words as he watches his thirteen-year-old granddaughter prepare to migrate to the city. She is moving to help their family financially, but when Grandfather Han considers the personal cost of her migration, he concludes that the trade is not worth it.

A number of Thai stories about migration explore the question of exchange—what the migrant gains and loses through the act of migration and whether the trade-off is worth it. With the decision to move to the city, the migrant expects to trade his or her labor and immediate connection to home for financial gain. Sometimes the objective in migration is even more specific: a sum large enough to save the migrant's family home, which would otherwise be lost to debt. In this case, the migrant expects to exchange a short-term connection with home for the long-term salvation of that home. And while migrants may accept these terms of exchange willingly, they may learn upon arrival in the city that they are expected to sacrifice more than they bargained for. When the terms of exchange shift quickly and additional demands are made of—and sometimes taken from—the migrant, he may find himself grappling with questions of fairness and loss. Moreover, it may become impossible for the migrant to determine whether his or her journey has been a "success" given this shifting paradigm and the migrant's own lack of agency within it.

This section examines three stories in which migrants are faced with this question: Yohda Hasaemsaeng's "Return from the Battlefield," Ussiri Dhammachoti's "What's Gone Is Gone," and Sunee Namso's "The Exemplary Worker." In these stories, the migrant protagonists willingly move to the city, but ultimately are forced to sacrifice more than they expected there. The protagonists of "Return from the Battlefield" and "What's Gone Is Gone" lose limbs to urban factory machines; the protagonist of "The Exemplary Worker," loses her health and, later, her life. Despite these dramatic losses, all of the protagonists also gain something in the city. The migrants who suffer physical losses return home with compensation money—in "Return from the Battlefield," this sum is enough to save the protagonist's farm (thus enabling him to accomplish his original goal of migration). Sunee's protagonist returns home with a deep sense of pride in having contributed to a global product that gives her work meaning beyond the borders of her known world.

These narratives deal with extreme examples of migrant sacrifice; as such, they offer a window onto the migrant's process of evaluating the migration experience. These stories reveal that the migration experience is never complete; traces of this experience remain and continue to affect the migrant even once he or she returns home. The migrants in these narratives ultimately come to understand that once they have become migrants, they will, in essence, always be migrants. Their sense of home must therefore shift to encompass their changed perspectives and experiences. Upon return, the migrants find that "home" is no longer the same—either because they cannot integrate into their families or communities in the way they once did or because their families and friends now treat them differently—despite their own attempts to return to their "old selves."

In Yohda Hasaemsaeng's "Return from the Battlefield," two migrant protagonists—a father and son—attempt to come to terms with the elusive and uneven terms of exchange that characterize their migration experiences. Father left home as a soldier, putting his "body and blood" on the line for the security of his countrymen. As he entered the battlefield for the first time, a senior solider laid out the terms of exchange: "Esteemed men entering the battlefield. You will put your body, blood, and organs on the line in order to secure the well-being of those who come after you. No matter what happens, you will return from the battlefield with pride" (Yohda 1999a, 78). Although the terms of exchange are clearly stated from the outset, the protagonist's situation does not unfold as described. He loses a limb, but does not achieve the pride or sense of security that he was promised. Upon return to the village, he is not thanked for his efforts, but is rather treated as an outcast. Moreover, the psychological and physical disability that he incurs makes it impossible for him to resume the life he once lived or to achieve a sense of peace. He is plagued by nightmares of the battlefield, which make the war seem to continue to rage. These nightmares keep him from appreciating even a positive outcome of his migration—the secure environment at home.

As a result of the father's inability to move past his traumatic migration experience, the family's debt increases and they risk losing their farm. To save the farm, his son decides to migrate as well—this time to the city for work. The son has a clear objective in his migration—to make enough money to save the family's fields—and he is willing to "exchange fatigue . . . and physical exhaustion" to accomplish this task (79). Upon arrival in the city, he finds a job in a furniture factory. The work is difficult, and the factory's loud machines damage his hearing, but he is willing to accept this impairment as a trade-off for his family's land. He draws the line, however, at taking drugs to enhance his performance. Many of his co-workers use *ya ma* (amphetamines) to work longer hours and earn more money, but he has seen the dangers of this drug use firsthand.[1] The protagonist is clear about his terms of exchange: he will work to his body's capacity (regardless of fatigue), but not beyond it. The soundness of his body remains paramount, more important to him than money or his family's land.

The protagonist reaffirms this decision after he witnesses a co-worker on *ya ma* lose his hand to an industrial saw. He comments, "Ten years of overtime couldn't buy that man's fingers back," and a number of his co-workers agree (81). These workers stop taking amphetamines, and the factory's production drops so steeply that the owner is fined for the factory's inability to fill orders. It becomes clear at this point in the story that the factory's production is predicated on the assumption that the workers will use drugs. When they refuse to do so, the factory owner takes matters into his own hands and puts drugs in their water supply.

In the weeks that follow, the protagonist works quickly and tirelessly. He feels proud of his increased productivity, attributing it to his growing familiarity with the machines (and not to the amphetamines he is unknowingly ingesting). He sends additional money home to help his family and starts to save for his future. He has fallen in love with a woman in the factory and plans to begin a life with her soon. He is happiest at this moment in the narrative; he has laid out his own terms of exchange and found success within them (or so he believes).

"The most painful day of his life" arrives when this bubble bursts (82). The protagonist, like his co-worker, ultimately falls victim to a factory accident, and worse, to the realization that he has been deceived. His "success," he ultimately realizes, is attributable to a force beyond his control—a force he explicitly rejected—rather than to his own work. Questions of value, success, and exchange become even more complex for the protagonist as he considers and weighs the various losses—and one substantial gain—his migration has brought. His greatest loss is his arm, taken by the factory saw; with this loss, he loses his ability to do work. He feels that "there is no longer any value left in his body," and this loss resonates through all spheres

---

1. Earlier in the story, the protagonist is almost killed as a result of a co-worker's drug use. The protagonist is riding in the back of a truck driven by a worker using drugs. The driver loses control of the car, and all of the men in the back barely escape with their lives.

of his life (82). His value as a potential husband, for example, diminishes: "The woman he yearned for turned down his marriage proposal [when she learned he was crippled]. There probably isn't anyone who would want to be with a cripple from the start, so he might as well give up any thought of marriage" (82). This traumatic experience moreover leads to the loss of his mental stability, as he begins to have visions of whirling industrial saws and armless workers.

All of these negative outcomes are weighed against a single benefit, the large sum of compensation money he receives as a result of his accident.

> While he was convalescing in the hospital, the factory owner came to him with a sum of money—a "compensation gift." At first, he wanted to throw it out. But when he thought back to the cornfield, he changed his mind. In the end, he succeeded in saving his father's fields. . . . They would now be returned to the family, their rightful owners. (83)

It is the protagonist's accident that ultimately enables him to fulfill his goal in migration—the restitution of his family's fields. His migration must therefore be considered a "success." However, the protagonist does not feel that he has *achieved* this success. Despite his efforts to define terms of exchange with which he was comfortable, it is only once things spiral out of control that he "achieves" his goal. He never has the chance to work toward his goal on his own terms; a sacrifice is forced upon him. Moreover, the pride he initially felt in his work was predicated on a lie. For these reasons, his return home is bittersweet.

> This time he was returning home permanently. The important thing was that his traveling bag was filled with money. Other people might not think it was very much, but it was the largest sum he had ever had in his life. It was enough to get the cornfields back for his father and his family. He felt bitter, but really, he should be proud that he had succeeded, shouldn't he? (79)

Here, the migrant's notion of success is linked with pride. Although he states twice that he has succeeded in his migration, he also notes that he does not feel proud of his achievement. The protagonist feels that he has been robbed of what is rightfully his, the chance to seek success on his own terms. If his father suffers from the feeling that his battle will never end, the son believes that his own battle ended before he could even wage it. Perhaps the only real success the two achieve through migration is the increased closeness and empathy they feel as a result of their shared loss.

Ussiri Dhammachoti's "What's Gone Is Gone" (1992f) portrays a similar story of migration and loss. In "What's Gone Is Gone," a young woman moves to the city with the intention of helping her rural family through urban factory work. Her efforts are cut short, however, when a factory machine slices off her forearm. After the accident, she is sent home with ten thousand baht in compensation—a sum greater than anyone in her family has ever seen.

If Yohda Hasaemsaeng's protagonist has mixed feelings about the monetary compensation he receives—acknowledging the value of the money for his family's fields, but rejecting the notion that money can ever replace a hand—Ussiri's heroine views her compensation in decidedly negative terms. For her, the money is a painful reminder of the accident she unwillingly endured and the loss with which she must continue to live. In particular, the red ink of the hundred-baht bills functions as a reminder of the blood she spilled in exchange for money. When the protagonist brings this "blood money"[2] home, it affects all who come into contact with it, extending the scope of her loss to the village and beyond: "The large sum of money she received as compensation for her lost hand took away everything she had ever valued in life. It was the shadow of the evil ghost that followed her home and continued to destroy her" (Ussiri 1992f, 111). The "blood money" brings an air of violence into the house, provoking conflict among family members who bicker over how to spend it. On the protagonist's first night home, thieves who have heard about her compensation come to take it by force. They fight their way into the house and ransack it looking for the red bills. Although they never get their hands on the money—the family has left it with the village headman for safekeeping—the bandits kill the protagonist's beloved grandfather and her dog. By the end of the

---

2. Significantly, her compensation is paid in red 100-baht notes. Their color suggests that this money is stained with the blood that was shed for it.

protagonist's first night home, then, she must contend with the loss of her arm, her grandfather, and her pet.

The protagonist's grandfather was the only family member who had continued to treat her with empathy and love despite her wealth. Now that he is gone, she abandons all hope of reconstructing the family she once knew. Her family now seems to her, like her body, irreparably marred. In her desperation over this spiral of loss, she decides to flee, leaving behind the blood money and her broken home. In doing so, she subjects herself to one final loss, her home. The story concludes with the protagonist's departure, and although she seems alone and powerless at this point, it is important to note that the narrative follows her beyond the confines of the village. Although she loses many things with migration, she never loses her voice or her story; in the end, she has the final word.[3]

Sunee Namso's short story "The Exemplary Worker" (2006) portrays another migrant protagonist who must grapple with loss due to unsafe factory conditions. When Sunee's protagonist Boonsong moves to Bangkok with her husband, they find jobs in a textile factory and work hard to save money so that they can return to their village to open a small store. Their hard work is duly noted by their manager (who includes them in the factory's list of exemplary workers seven years in a row). In their eighth year at the factory, however, Boonsong falls ill. She begins to cough, has trouble breathing, and tires easily, and although she takes medicine, her symptoms do not subside. When Boonsong eventually begins coughing up blood, she makes a firm decision to visit her doctor the next day—even if this means skipping an overtime shift. The foreman, however, refuses to let her go, saying, "That's impossible. Haven't you seen all of the work we have to send off in time for the Olympics? Don't you realize that your group will have to finish all of the [athletes'] shirts today? If the work isn't done by tomorrow morning, you'll all be docked" (Sunee 2006, 166–67).

---

3. We find a similar rendition of the maimed, vulnerable protagonist in Sridaoruang's "The Hand." Although the protagonist of this text is poor and marginalized (once she loses her fingers through factory work, she is left to wander through garbage dumps collecting plastic bags), she never loses her voice or moral authority. Toward the end of the story, she even addresses the reader directly, implicating us in her oppression and blaming us for her marginality.

Boonsong feels strong pressure to continue working. Although she knows that visiting her doctor is more important than an overtime shift, the foreman has raised the stakes: if Boonsong leaves, all of the workers may be docked. And there is a deeper, unspoken message in the foreman's words: if Boonsong leaves, she will be replaced. "And so Boonsong remained, for no one dared go against the boss's orders. They were all afraid of being fired, especially Boonsong, who was now nearly forty years old. She would have a hard time finding another job at this age. She had no choice but to obey" (167).

That night, Boonsong and the other women sew furiously to meet their deadline. Boonsong continues to cough, and her co-workers suggest she take a short break. She is exhausted, but she is afraid to rest because she knows that the foreman's eyes are always on her. Just before dawn, Boonsong collapses at her sewing machine. The other workers rush in to help, including Boonsong's husband, who works at a nearby station. He runs over, lifts Boonsong up over his shoulders, and carries her to the elevator. As he reaches it, however, the foreman yells out to him, "Don't use the elevator. It is for managers and merchandise only. I'm warning you. . . . If you don't listen, you'll both be fired" (168). Thinking only of his wife, Boonsong's husband ignores the threat. He assumes that his boss will not fault him for using the elevator when he learns that it was a matter of life or death.

When the couple returns to work a few days later, however, they are fired. The personnel officer tells Boonsong,

Boonsong, you are the reason that our factory did not meet our deadline. We experienced significant losses due to your little incident. Moreover, you disregarded the foreman's orders when she told you not to use the elevator. You set a bad example. If we were to let this pass, in no time we would have a factory full of workers trying to pull off stunts like that. (169)

Despite their eight years of work at the factory—seven of which were "exemplary"—the couple is fired for breaking a factory rule. With this action, the factory owner demonstrates his complete authority over the workers, sending a clear message that they must stay in line if they want to keep their jobs. At the same time, Boonsong and her husband know that they are really being fired because Boonsong is now too sick to work, and the factory owner is seizing this opportunity to get rid of her. "'Where's the justice?' Boonsong asks as tears streamed down her face. Boonsong, the exemplary worker, had been fired. Was this her reward for eight years of hard work? When she was strong, the factory needed her. But now that she was ill, they turned on her" (171).

Boonsong's husband insists that they at least be paid the money they are owed. In response, the factory owner tells him, "You're lucky I don't charge you for the losses you've caused. People like you couldn't even afford one of these outfits [you are making]. As soon as you get a little tired, you start going on and on about being sick" (169). The couple leaves the factory without pay, unable to bring about a fair exchange. And when Boonsong's husband demands a just settlement in subsequent meetings, he comes to a violent end.

Widowed and unable to find another job in the city, Boonsong returns to her village. "She had changed so much that the people who used to know her probably would not even recognize her" (162). Boonsong now lies in bed all day, suffering from an advanced-stage lung disease, as her young daughter Kaewda cares for her. Boonsong accepts this condition as her fate, but Kaewda is outraged by the injustice her mother has endured. Any mention of the factory upsets Kaewda, so when Boonsong suggests that they watch the Olympics on television, she is livid.

> The opening ceremony for the Olympics was about to begin. Boonsong told her daughter to turn on the TV, but Kaewda didn't want to. She hated the Olympics. It was because of the Olympics that her mother was fired and now had to lie here sick like this. But Boonsong insisted—she wanted to watch. So, Kaewda turned on the TV.
>
> On TV, all of the athletes gathered on the field, each wearing a beautiful uniform. Boonsong was happy and excited to see them wearing the clothing brand she had sewn herself.
>
> "Look, Kaewda! Those clothes! I was the one who made them! That one there! That one, too!" (174)

Despite the losses Boonsong has suffered, she is excited to see the shirts she made on television. Viewing the results of her labor in this international forum, Boonsong gains a sense of the broader relevance of her work and her connection to a realm beyond her immediate environment. Tragically, her excitement over this vision raises her heart rate dangerously high and leads shortly after to her death. "The Exemplary Worker" ends with Kaewda mourning the death of her mother against the backdrop of the Olympics' opening games.

Interestingly, an earlier unpublished manuscript concludes with a short epilogue in which the author calls for justice for workers like Boonsong and challenges the reader to take up the cause:

> Compensation for the exemplary worker
>> Compensation for the worker who has no choice
>> Who will seek justice for workers like her? Exemplary workers like Boonsong. Or won't anyone?[4]

With this epilogue, Sunee suggests that although Boonsong may have come to terms with her fate, justice has not been served. Boonsong's exploitation has hurt not only her, but also her co-workers and family members, including the young Kaewda who is orphaned as a result of it. By ending the story with the question, "Who will seek justice for workers like her?" Sunee argues that we are all responsible for stopping such exploitation—especially in cases where those who are exploited are not in a position to make a difference themselves. The author notes further that she has worked under exploitative conditions and that the story is based on her personal experiences. Sunee's act of writing, then, is a first step toward stemming such exploitation by advocating for the rights of workers like Boonsong and herself. She leaves the reader with a challenge to continue this process.

OBLIGATION

Sridaoruang's "Plaeng Phanom's Story (1)" and its sequel "Plaeng Phanom's Story (2)" detail a rural-urban migrant's return home to her village with

---

4. Sunee Namso, "The Exemplary Worker," unpublished manuscript.

her young Bangkok-born son, Plaeng Phanom. In the first story, mother and son visit for Songkran, as they do each year; in the second story, they return at a moment's notice for the funeral of the protagonist's grandmother. With these stories, Sridaoruang links the two tropes of return that appear most frequently in Thai literature about migration: return for Songkran and return for a family tragedy, usually the death of a relative.

While these tropes of return differ in specific ways, they share one main characteristic: obligation. It is expected by the migrant's family and by the community at large that the migrant will return on both of these occasions— even if he or she does not return at any other time. The inability or refusal to fulfill this obligation is understood as a major breach of village and family norms[5] and cause for an examination of the severe impacts of migration on the individual, the family, and the village. In cases where the migrant does return, this return sets the stage for a process of self-evaluation, particularly with regard to the migration experience and the impacts of this migration on others. Such personal evaluation can include the ways in which the migrant has changed since leaving the village, the impact of migration on the family and village, the migrant's altered position with respect to the family and community, and the question of whether migration has brought "success."

In grappling with these issues, the migrant must come to terms with the differing systems of value in the rural and urban realms. If migration to the city exposes the migrant to new norms, return throws the issue of cultural relativity into light. With the initial move to the city, migrants confront

---

5. The obligation to return home to honor the death of one's parents is so great that Uthain Phromdaeng figures it as a force that transcends the visible world. In his short story "A Very Long Time," an elderly villager waits day after day on her porch for her children to come home for a visit. Whenever anyone in the village passes her house, she tells them that her children are coming soon; despite these declarations, she cries every night in her loneliness, making all of the villagers uncomfortable. Before any of the woman's children returns, she dies on the front porch where she waits for them. At this point, the villagers assume the old woman will finally be able to rest. Instead, her cries continue after her death, and her body becomes so heavy that she cannot be moved from the porch. She remains stuck, transformed into a howling ghost of an unrequited mother. It is only "a very long time" later, after the woman's body has decomposed, that her youngest son returns. Although she is no longer alive to receive him, his return sets her spirit free. Her howls cease, and mother and village finally find peace.

and adjust to new systems of value, but may not recognize the depth of the transformation they are undergoing because they have no perspective on it. Even when this transformation is extreme, they may simply understand it to be part of life's natural evolution. It is only once these migrants return to the village that the disjunctures between their rural and urban identities become undeniable. With return, migrants come face-to-face with the fact that the rural and urban realms operate on different assumptions and that migration may have launched them on a trajectory that veers away from that of the village.

Return, even more than migration, engenders an awareness of the relativity of value and the multiplicity of value systems that are part of the migrant's own experience. Return evokes a number of questions: how should migrants "appreciate" the changes they have undergone since leaving the village, which system of value should they use in making this determination, and can the rural and urban systems of value be merged? Return induces a "moment of truth" in which migrants must come to terms with the changes they have undergone as a result of migration and the meaning of these changes for themselves, their families, and their communities. While this self-evaluation can be fraught with anxiety, it also represents an important opportunity for the migrant in terms of personal development and self-awareness. In the end, it can lead to a more balanced sense of self, one that more smoothly incorporates the rural and urban aspects of the migrant's identity.

With the return for Songkran or a family tragedy, the migrant's work of reflection and identity-making takes on a communal dimension as well. Because there is an overwhelming expectation that all out-migrants will return on such occasions, the rural family unit and village community are reconstituted at these times. Returning to the village with fellow out-migrants, a migrant begins to evaluate not only the extent to which he or she has changed since leaving the village, but also the extent of this change relative to others in the out-migrant group. This group of returnees comes to be compared moreover with the non-migrants who have remained behind. Return migrants also assess the changes that the village has undergone since their departure—and as a result of it—including rural development through remittances or the decline of the village due to the out-migration of the productive workforce.

While return for Songkran and for a family tragedy engender similar types of reflection on the part of the migrant, there are important differences in these two moments of return. Songkran is a national holiday, so all village out-migrants are expected to return at this time. The village community is reconstituted, and as a result, return migrants' reflections tend to focus on the group. Comparisons are made with friends who left the village under similar circumstances, and the migrant's own experience is evaluated with respect to theirs. In the case of return for family tragedy, the focus is on the kin group.[6]

These tropes of return also differ in the migrant's ability to prepare for the voyage home. The predictability of Songkran return—out-migrants know exactly when Songkran will occur each year and that they are expected to return at that time—enables migrants to prepare themselves emotionally, psychologically, and financially for the visit. They have time to make the transition between urban and rural paradigms, a process that may entail "readapting" to a rural pace or former identity or that may entail solidifying a new urban-based identity that will be projected for the family and village community. With emergency return, no such preparation is possible. Not only is emergency return unexpected, but it is also emotionally charged (as it generally involves the loss of a loved one). For such reasons, return for a family tragedy can engender a profound crisis of identity on the part of the migrant, particularly in cases where the migrant has not returned home for a significant period of time prior to the tragedy. Such trips home can evoke significant feelings of guilt and ungratefulness, as the migrant struggles with questions of who he or she has become and whether the move was worth it.

SONGKRAN

Over the course of the year, I come home very few times, but one of those times is always Songkran. When Songkran comes around, it doesn't

---

6. Of course, there is crossover: if a migrant fails to return for a family funeral, this breach might reverberate beyond the familial realm to cause gossip in the community; similarly, Songkran can engender reflection on the family. Observing a neighbor's children returning for Songkran when one's own do not can cause reflection on the impacts of out-migration on the family.

matter if I'm north, south, near or far, I always come home. I come home because I know that my parents are waiting for me—and not just for me. They're waiting for all of their children who have gotten married, started families of their own, and moved away. (Panumat 1990, in Raks 1999, 61)

Panumat's short story, "Songkran at Home" opens with the protagonist's return to his village on the night before Songkran. He is the first of six siblings to return, and he finds his parents in the midst of busy preparations. His mother is cooking a ceremonial meal for the monks, while his father is preparing each child's favorite dish. His parents excitedly await the return of all their children, and they take turns poking their heads out the front gate to see if anyone else has arrived.

When no one has arrived by the following evening, the protagonist's mother expresses disappointment that her children have missed the first day's celebrations—especially the offerings to monks and ceremonial ablutions in honor of their grandparents. Despite her disappointment, she knows that her children will arrive shortly. The protagonist's father reasons that the other children may be stuck at work.[7] "Today is Friday, right? That's probably why your elder brothers and sisters haven't come yet" (67). Mother nods in agreement, choosing to believe her husband's rationalization. All three understand, however, that Father's words are simply meant to make them feel better. Songkran is a national holiday, so no one works on that day. Over the course of the weekend, the family continues to produce such rationalizations, but as the weekend wears on, they become flimsier. Mother suggests, for example, that her daughters will return on Sunday because "they always like to come on the final day of Songkran" (69). When no one returns on Sunday, however, they are out of excuses. Mother stops watching through the gate, and Father lies down for a nap, acknowledging with sadness that no one else is coming home.

---

7. Significantly, "work" appears repeatedly in Thai migration narratives as an excuse given by migrants for their failure to return home when expected. Although this excuse is often uttered with a faint sense of guilt for the migrant's failure to fulfill the obligation of return, it is a blanket reason that it is widely accepted by family members. Work is, after all, the primary reason for the migrant's move to the city in the first place. By "working" migrants are fulfilling a parallel obligation to their family – especially if this work contributes to the family's income through remittances.

If the parents ultimately accept this situation, the protagonist is irate. He feels intense anger toward his siblings for their failure to return and an increased sense of obligation toward his parents as the only "dutiful child." He decides to perform the Songkran ceremony on his own—even though all of his siblings are supposed to perform it together.

> After asking my parents' permission to perform the ceremonial ablutions, I bathed them and washed their hair so that they felt clean and refreshed. They changed into new clothes, and I applied baby powder for them. I thought back to when I was little and my mother and father used to wash me like this. It made me happy to be able to pay them back in this small way. Although I don't have enough money to buy them new clothes for the New Year, they looked happy [that I performed this ceremony]. I got down on my hands and knees to receive their New Year's blessing with a sense of sadness. Where were my brothers and sisters anyway? Today is Sunday. Civil servants have the day off—especially teachers in the middle of the summer. If anyone were to say that they couldn't be here because they were busy with work, it would be a flimsy excuse. All of us should be home together today . . . if only for an hour. Don't any of them understand that our mother and father were anxiously awaiting their arrival? . . .
>
> That evening father served me bowl after bowl of the special Thai salad he had prepared. And I ate and ate, as much as I possibly could. I ate for all my brothers and sisters who hadn't come home. (69–70)

Here, the protagonist expresses his indignation at his siblings for having failed to fulfill their obligation to return for Songkran. In an effort to lessen the pain they have caused, he attempts to "fill in" for them, not only performing the Songkran ceremony on their behalf, but eating as much food as possible so his siblings' absence will not be materially apparent in leftovers.[8] Although his parents are saddened by their children's failure to return, they gain a bit of comfort from the protagonist. The presence of one

---

8. The decaying food would constitute a vivid symbol of his family's deteriorating relationships.

child effaces the absence of the others to an extent, enabling a continuation of the Songkran tradition and a disavowal that their family unit has fully disintegrated.

While the parents in Panumat's text play down their children's failure to return, parents whose children obediently fulfill this obligation make their pride known to others. In Jamlong Fangchonlajitr's "Those People Have Changed," Simai, the mother of two dutiful daughters, Bunta and Ratri, tells everyone in the village that her daughters regularly return to visit. All of the villagers are impressed by the girls' dedication to their parents and by their careful fulfillment of their duty. When Bunta writes home to say that she has completed her degree and found a job in Bangkok, everyone is proud of her. Over time, this pride deepens into respect, as Bunta balances her urban lifestyle with clear dedication to her rural parents by coming home on important holidays and sending money each month.

> The two daughters left home to go live in Bangkok, but they never forgot their family in the countryside. Whether it was Songkran or the October merit-making festival, the two daughters would come home to visit their parents and younger brothers, and the family would go to the temple together to make merit. All of their neighbors and the people who knew them well would compliment the girls' radiant white skin, their nice figures, and their beauty, saying that Bangkok had treated them well. (Jamlong 2005b, 25)

In this passage, the narrator highlights first and foremost the villagers' admiration for the daughters' ongoing fulfillment of their familial obligations. Moving to the city has not weakened the girls' ties to the village, but has enabled them to fulfill their obligations to a greater extent through financial support to their parents. When the villagers praise Bunta and Ratri in conversations with one another, they note the girls' fulfillment of their filial duty. When they praise the girls directly, they mention the "white skin" and urban style that the girls have acquired through migration.

> Auntie La-ong ran her fingers over Bunta's back and shoulders and touched the fair skin on her arm. "Bangkok is a strange place," she said. "Whoever goes there comes back looking more beautiful than when they

left. I'm not kidding. Everyone's skin looks so soft I just want to touch it. Not at all like the coarse skin of those of us who work in the fields under the hot sun all day."

Having said this, Auntie La-ong smiled with affection for Bunta, as if the girl were one of her own. (25)

In this passage, Auntie La-ong praises the aspects of Bunta's appearance that mark her as different. In particular, she admires the white skin that the villagers view as a sign of urban wealth and beauty—something that is not only out of reach for them, but that is defined in opposition to the "village" identity. It is clear, then, that Auntie La-ong's praise of these "non-village" characteristics is linked to the fact that Bunta and Ratri have maintained the aspects of the "village daughter" identity that are of primary importance to the village social structure and value scheme. Because these young women continue to work hard for their parents and fulfill their obligations of support and return, the "urbanness" that they exude through their appearance is not taken as a threat, but as a bonus. These girls are admired because they keep up their village obligations *and* acquire the much fetishized "white skin" while doing so.

Bunta and Ratri's success in fulfilling their obligations causes some embarrassment and jealousy, however, among villagers whose own children are less conscientious about remittances and return. After praising Bunta, Auntie La-ong turns her attention to her own children.

Auntie La-ong has three children. Her two sons were civil servants, teachers. Her youngest child, a daughter, worked in Bangkok for the Royal Forestry Department. On some years her daughter was able to come home to visit her parents, but on other years she didn't return. When Auntie La-ong saw the two daughters [Bunta and Ratri] return home, she would complain that she felt slighted. So it was a good thing that her sons had built their homes nearby. (25–26)

Bunta and Ratri provide a point of reference, a control group of "perfect" out-migrants who maintain their duty to the village while taking advantage of the benefits that the city has to offer. Their behavior is closely watched because it represents a standard by which other villagers can measure their own migrant kin. At the same time, such model behavior has the power to evoke negative feelings such as "*noi ok noi chai*" (the feeling of being slighted) and "*man sai*" (resentment) as villagers compare their own children negatively with Simai's (26–30).

Such comparisons can lead to cagey behavior on the part of villagers, who, believing that their own children do not measure up, attempt to save face. While Grandmother Sa-ngiam happily compares her children to Bunta and Ratri in terms of academic achievement,[9] she consistently steers the conversation away from the subject of remittances. "Whether Grandmother Sa-ngiam's children sent money home every month like Bunta and Ratri did, she never divulged to anyone in the village. She was probably worried that her successful children would lose face" (29).

If the villagers initially tolerate the uneasy feeling that their children do not measure up, they cannot fault Bunta or Ratri's behavior, so they refrain from saying anything at all. It is only once the girls' parents break village codes of behavior that the villagers find a rallying point for the expression of their jealously and resentment. Simai and Somkrop's behavior changes shortly after Bunta returns for Songkran with a good-looking man in an expensive car. From this point onward, Simai and Somkrop stop chatting with the other villagers and pull away from village activities. The only social interaction they continue are Simai's weekly trips to the village store, where she brags about her daughters to the other villagers.

> Everyone in the village praised the girls' faithful repaying of their filial debt and agreed that they had always been good children. But after their most recent visit [for Songkran] two or three days ago, Bunta's mother went to brag to Somchai [the storeowner] once again. . . . This time [her bragging] made the other villagers who were there to shop or have a beer feel embarrassed, jealous, or laugh so hard they almost fell out of their chairs. . . . [Simai said] that Panthongtae[10] had chatted up her daughter [Ratri] at the mobile phone shop where she worked. She said this with no trace of humility, as if she didn't know who she was. (30)

---

9. The children in Grandmother Sa-ngiam's family have all been successful in school.

10. Panthongtae is the first name of former Prime Minister Thaksin Shinawatra's son.

The villagers praise Bunta and Ratri's success as long as it contributes to the village economy and society, but once this success leads Srimai to put on airs, they start to gossip angrily. Those who overhear Simai's remarks believe that she now considers herself a member of the upper class. In response, the villagers begin to treat them as outsiders—as the "rich people" they pretend to be. So, when Somkrop asks his neighbor, Satit, to cut down some of his mangosteen trees so that Somkrop can build a road to his house—one that would enable his daughter's rich boyfriend to arrive more easily in his car—Satit refuses, remarking, "How can a rich man ask for a poor man's land?" (31). If Somkrop's family really has become part of the upper class, he suggests, they should be able to resolve this issue on their own.

Satit later confesses that jealousy was the basis for his refusal to help Somkrop. This sense of jealously mixed with anxiety about the potentials and meanings of migration—whether moving to the city really can propel one into the upper class—is echoed in the final part of the story when Grandmother Sa-ngiam tells the story of "Panthongtae" to her son. The son, who now lives in Bangkok, does not refute the potential validity of the story and instead asks, "And what if it's true, Mom, [that Panthongtae really is Ratri's boyfriend]? . . . With globalization, anything is possible—as long as the timing is right" (31).

Grandmother Sa-ngiam's son, a migrant himself, seems comfortable with globalization. This is likely because his dual experience of the rural and urban realms has brought him a broader perspective on the hierarchical relations on which this system is based. The uneven distribution of wealth and power between the rural and urban regions of Thailand parallels the uneven power relations between Thailand and developed countries in the world. Migrants who move between Thailand's rural and urban areas thus experience multiple facets of globalization: the rural underside (with Bangkok as a hegemonic power) and Bangkok (both a powerful center in the national hierarchy and a relatively marginal center in the global arena). By inhabiting these diverse positions in the national and global hierarchies, the rural-urban migrant gains a more nuanced perspective on globalization. And yet, this wider perspective does not always bring comfort or a clear understanding of the meaning or implications of globalization at the local level. Because global forces operate beyond the protagonists' direct experience, a thorough understanding remains somewhat out of reach.

In response to her son's suggestion that with globalization anything is possible, Grandmother Sa-ngiam grunts,

> "Globali-strange-tion. Humph!" Grandmother Sa-ngiam said only this much before she suddenly felt as if a hard rock was shooting up from her intestines and crashing into her Adam's apple.
>
> Her son smiled, chuckling. Today his mother's voice and behavior seemed different. (31)

This surreal ending, in which Grandmother Sa-ngiam vomits in response to the word "globalization" (while simultaneously changing into a man, or at least gaining an Adam's apple), suggests the unease with which villagers approach the reality of a globalized world and its unfamiliar logic. Although Grandmother Sa-ngiam initially rejects the idea that someone from her village could change so quickly and thoroughly as to become a member of the upper class, simply hearing the word "globalization" changes her voice, appearance, and behavior.[11] The story thus ends with a mixture of possibility, absurdity, and unpredictability. The reader is left with the sense that neither the rural nor urban worldview holds the key to unlocking the seemingly unpredictable force of globalization. The question of how "those people" could "have changed"—Simai's family (socially) and Grandmother Sa-ngiam (physically)—remains unanswered, but is vaguely attributed to the new globalized reality.

In Tawan Santipaap's "Reaction," the migrant protagonist Ot expresses a deep unease with the relativity and unpredictability of globalization. He feels that the social rules with which he was raised no longer apply, but he is at a loss to pin down the "new rules." He is baffled by the enormous success that Toi, a girl from his village, attains despite her refusal to follow the path of hard work and slow progress that is laid out in the village value

---

11. The very word seems to change mid-sentence. This is partly attributable to Grandmother Sa-ngiam's "*ban nok*" inability to pronounce this term, partly to her refusal to accept it, and partly to a fast-moving force of change that globalization brings, causing the word to metamorphose mid-breath.

system. If Ot tentatively attributes Toi's success to the fact that she has left the village and operates in an urban framework, he is shocked to learn that the villagers unanimously laud her success and praise her as well. It seems to him that this new logic has permeated not only the city, but the village as well, and he fails to grasp it. Toi's fame seems like a fluke to Ot, and the villagers' apotheosis of her as a "villager celebrity" becomes a source of jealousy and consternation.[12]

Ot and Toi grew up in the same village, and although Ot was older than Toi, the two knew each other well. Toi had difficulty in school, so Ot, the top student in his class, tutored her regularly—until his own education took him away from their village, first to the provincial capital, and then to Bangkok. Over the years, Ot became increasingly distanced from the village both physically and emotionally—to the point where he nearly forgot Toi and the other villagers. It is only years later when Ot returns to the village for Songkran that he and Toi meet again. By this time, Ot has established himself in the capital; he has completed a university degree with honors and is anticipating an academic appointment. Toi still lives in the village, but she too has changed.

> Nature had thrown off any hint of backwardness and turned her into a beautiful young woman, one you couldn't stop staring at. Something had changed deep inside her—she neither looked nor thought like the old Toi. There was not a trace of the humble girl who had worked around the house and done odd jobs to help her parents. This new Toi was full of ambition—more than was seemly. (Tawan 1993, 22–23)

When Toi and Ot meet, she tells him that she has decided to become a famous country singer and is determined to reach her goal. Her plans seem unbelievable to Ot: he cannot understand how a village girl with a fourth-grade education could expect such a brilliant future. Her ambition rubs him the wrong way because it seems beyond what is natural, just as

---

12. This story begins with Ot reading Toi's obituary in the newspaper and considering whether to return to the village for her funeral. The news sets up a frame narrative in which Ot meditates on his relationship with Toi and the evolution of their relationship over several years.

Simai's assertion that Panthongtae is dating her daughter leads the villagers to conclude that she "didn't know who she was" (Jamlong 2005b, 30). In Ot's opinion, Toi's "dreams are fantasies without substance, floating like clouds wherever the wind blows" (Tawan 1993, 24). He views his own success, in contrast, as the well-deserved product of hard work. He has spent years depriving himself of luxuries and working conscientiously toward his goals, and he views his academic appointment as the appropriate result.

Despite Ot's dismissal of Toi's chances, she does, in fact, become a hit singer shortly after their meeting. Toi reaches her goal quickly and—it seems to Ot—effortlessly, achieving a level of fame that far surpasses his own. "Her fame spread so much more widely than his that you couldn't even compare the two. His work was printed in only a thousand books, while the news of her stardom spread through newspapers with circulations of over a million" (25).

Toi's enormous success perplexes Ot because it seems impossible to emulate or explain.

> She didn't struggle. . . . She let her life float along as chance took it, without direction, like a cloud in the sky. But in the end, she achieved greater success than the person who sweated all his life. How could he accept that life is led by chance, not hard work, diligence, and intelligence? (26)

It is the impact of Toi's fame on the village—and the impact on Ot's perception of his own place in the village—that he finds hardest to accept. Ot has always defined himself in opposition to the rural realm. Even as a young boy, he treated the village as a place he would eventually leave to find success in the city. As Ot succeeds in school and moves to the capital, he seems to affirm this destiny. And when he completes graduate school, he achieves the highest level of success he envisioned for himself from his village starting point. When he returns to the village, then, he expects to be viewed as a success—and he is, but Toi is treated as a greater success.

Ot engages in a complex relationship with the village—it is at once the underdeveloped place he seeks to flee and the reference point by which he measures his self-worth. Ot cannot deny his village roots because he needs them to ground his "betterment." At the same time, these rural roots lurk inside him, threatening to define him as a villager at heart. The precariousness of this scheme becomes clear when villagers praise Toi's achievements instead of his. When this occurs, Ot falls into an identity crisis; without the villagers' affirmation of his success, he no longer has a frame of reference by which to measure his self worth. He becomes obsessed with proving that he is more successful than Toi, comparing himself to her in a variety of realms (national name recognition, articles published, salary, and others). Unfortunately, he falls short in all of these.

While Ot defines himself in opposition to the village, Toi defines herself through it. She too, has migrated to Bangkok, but her success is based on a rural phenomenon, country music. Moreover, Toi does not use her urban success to distance herself from the village as Ot does, but returns the products of this success to the rural realm. She donates money to build a new village temple and to improve the village school. She even sets up a music facility, encouraging village children to follow in her footsteps (thus illuminating the obscure "path to success" that Ot has failed to see). Because Toi retains close ties to the people and place of her birth, she is respected by the villagers. Ot cannot see the connection between Toi's ongoing relations with the village and the villagers' praise of her, however; he simply feels cheated out of his role of "village celebrity." (It is actually not even clear from the text whether Ot has ever held this role or whether the villagers' apotheosis of Toi forces him to recognize for the first time that his self-esteem is predicated on their vision of him.) Ot remains unable to view himself as a success because he compares his achievements to Toi's, an out-migrant whose migration trajectory has been radically different from his own. Moreover, he has difficulty understanding the shift that village society has undergone since his departure. Ot continues to evaluate himself in terms of a fixed village paradigm that he developed as a child—one that is out of touch with contemporary village norms and perspectives.

Rather than confront the roots of his identity crisis, Ot simply reasserts the "self-evident" nature of his success and defensively argues that his success is underappreciated. He gives a number of examples of this, the most flagrant of which is that people living in "underdeveloped countries" are too ignorant to recognize his importance: "Underdeveloped countries are like that all over the world. The value of a brain sharpened over a whole life is much lower than the value of the soft leg of a beautiful woman" (27). In this passage, Ot extends his vision of the village as an "underdeveloped" realm to Thailand as a whole, suggesting that both have lost a clear system of value. While his nod to Thailand's multiplicity of value systems is valid, Ot himself seems stuck in a particular space of disjuncture. He hearkens back to a nostalgic village, but when he actually visits the village in which his value system is supposedly rooted, he finds that the system he "remembers" no longer applies. His "success" is thus destabilized, and he can find no clear context in which to re-root it. As a result, Ot is left at the end of the narrative without a sense of place in the village or society at large. He is so confused and angry that he continues to feel jealous of Toi even after she has died. Unable to inhabit the roles of co-villager, friend, or teacher, he remains unsure at the end of the narrative if he should even attend her funeral.

FAMILY TRAGEDY

When family tragedy strikes and the rural-urban migrant is forced to return to the village on a moment's notice, he or she must make the sorts of personal and community evaluations described in the previous section without the opportunity to prepare for them. Such return represents a moment of truth, where migrants must stand before their family "as is." For migrants who have avoided returning to the village precisely because they feel that they have not yet attained success in the urban realm, feelings of embarrassment and guilt can accompany this experience. The out-migrant's failure to fulfill this obligation of return for an extended period of time may now reveal itself as an ineffective mask for his or her urban identity (as this identity is now laid bare) as well as a contributing factor to the breakdown of the rural family unit. The guilt that sudden return can engender is particularly pronounced for migrants who return after the death of a loved one. In such cases, the migrant may experience feelings of failure and loss that can never be resolved, as such feelings could only be allayed by the forgiveness of the deceased.

When the Bangkok-based protagonist of Uthain Phromdaeng's "Khao San Seed"[13] learns that his mother has died, he immediately returns to

---

13. The *khao san* tree is known by the Latin name *Raphistemma hooperianum*.

the village with his wife, five-year-old son, and ten-month-old daughter. Although his mother has been in and out of the hospital for some time, her death comes as a surprise. As the protagonist prepares to return for her funeral, he thinks about the time that has passed since his last visit. He and his siblings are generally good about returning home, but in recent years they have become somewhat more lax in fulfilling this obligation. The protagonist notes, "Lately, it seems like one of us children always has business to take care of when the rest of us get together to visit Mother. We come together as a group less and less. Now it's really only at Songkran that we all get together to pay our respects to Mother" (Uthain 2004c, 20).

The protagonist has not returned in over a year, and this year he failed to return for Songkran. He offers a myriad of excuses, including the distance between Bangkok and the village, his need to concentrate on work in order to provide for his family, and the time and energy that his family requires. As for Songkran, he explains that his newborn baby could not make the trip.

If the obligation to return for Songkran was not enough for the family to travel with a small child, however, the death of his mother is. Now, shortly after Songkran, the whole family travels in their car to the village (belying the protagonist's earlier claim that the baby was too small for the trip). His decision to return with his family is immediate, instinctual.

> I sat there dumbstruck for a long while. The most valuable thing in my life was now gone. I cried quietly by myself. Then I pulled myself together, got rid of all work responsibilities, and grabbed a suitcase to bring my wife and children back to the place of my birth.
>
> All six of us brothers and sisters came back together much faster than I ever would have imagined. (21–22)

The family unit that had become increasingly distant is quickly reconstituted on this occasion. And in this regrouping, the protagonist comes to understand a number of things about his family relationships. He recognizes first of all the extent to which he and his siblings have grown apart. Their failure to return home has affected not only their relationships with their mother, but also their relationships with one another. Seeing everyone together now, the protagonist realizes that many of his relatives do not even know one another. "This was the first time I had seen some of my nieces and nephews, and my daughter was meeting her aunts and uncles for the first time, too" (18–19). He also recognizes the relative ease with which his extended family is capable of regrouping when return is a priority, as it is on this occasion. The trip itself is faster and easier than it used to be, since the road to the house has now been paved. The protagonist feels pleased that they have all returned and reconstituted the family unit—it seems to suggest a new beginning and the possibility of closer links in the future.

> It's been a long time since I've seen all of us brothers and sisters working together and helping each other out like this. I felt happy deep down inside that all of us children had come together to pay respects to our mother for the last time. If Mother could see us now, I'm sure she'd be pleased to see all of the children she raised now standing firmly on their own feet, here together to pay their respects to her one last time. (19)

Despite the protagonist's happiness at the regrouping of his family and his new awareness that the maintenance of kin ties is easier than he and his siblings had thought, it is not at all clear by the end of the narrative that the protagonist will continue to maintain these ties. It appears, in fact, that he may quickly slip back into his earlier pattern. In the final part of the story, the protagonist drives away from the village, noting the *khao san* seeds that float in the air above the fields. They, too, spread out from the village, drifting away from their place of birth.

> I turned and looked out the car window. A sea of *khao san* seeds floated over the vast fields, their downy white filaments carrying them higher and higher, wherever the wind took them. No one knew how far they had drifted from their tree—perhaps farther than one might imagine. Nature makes them this way. They break away from the tree in order to take root and grow in faraway places. The mother tree doesn't know where her seeds will scatter or how they will survive in this new place. And the *khao san* flower itself may forget where it came from once it shoots up a stalk in that new place. : I noticed then one *khao san* flower floating in the same direction as I.

My car kept driving farther and farther from the place of my birth. And I asked myself, "Now that I no longer have my mother, how many more months, more years will it be before I and all of my brothers and sisters return home together again as we did on this occasion? (23)

Uthain's story ends on an ambivalent note. Although the protagonist acknowledges his obligation to return and even professes pleasure in his recent return, he now suggests that it is "natural" for children, like *khao san* seeds, to float away and take up root wherever they land, forgetting the "mother" tree that gave them life. Before he returns to the city, then, the protagonist paves the way for another period of forgetting, constructing an argument through which he can settle into a new period of distance.

The Bangkok-based protagonist of Pirot Boonbragop's "If You Can't Do It, Then Come Down!" experiences a similar period of separation from his rural family. Since his move to the city, his bonds with the village have become increasingly tenuous, and he has not returned to visit the aunt who raised him in over ten years. When he receives a letter saying that his aunt will undergo surgery, however, he immediately prepares to return. The letter provokes feelings of guilt and ungratefulness in him, but he quickly pushes these feelings aside, arranges to take three days off work, and travels to the province of his birth.

Pirot's protagonist is determined to be with his aunt in the hospital, but is nervous about the trip home. He feels guilty that he has allowed so much time to elapse since his last visit. "I felt ashamed of myself. My aunt has always been good to me, and how do I repay the favor—by forgetting her!" (Pirot 1993c, 23). He worries moreover that his other relatives will regard him as ungrateful. "The family member who wrote the letter didn't blame me for staying away so long, but I know that he must have been wondering what kind of person I could be to act like this" (23). Imagining his arrival, the protagonist thinks to himself, "It will be Auntie herself who will declare my shame [by the look on her face] without even uttering a word" (23).

In an attempt to convince himself that he does not deserve their censure, the protagonist offers a number of excuses for his failure to return.

It's been ten years since I've seen my aunt. Modern life has turned me into an ungrateful person, or at least one who nearly forgets his elder relatives. It's not just me, though—there are a lot of people like me, and even more who are becoming like me. (11)

The protagonist initially admits that he is "ungrateful," but quickly amends this characterization. If the highly negative word "*nerakhun*"— literally, a child who does not pay back his debt to his elders—describes the protagonist perfectly, the term hits too close to home. He therefore tempers this self-criticism by calling himself a person "who *nearly* forgets his elder relatives" (11). He then ducks this euphemism by spreading the blame over all members of the rural-urban migrant community. Everyone who lives a "modern life" in Bangkok, he tells us, behaves like this.

Allegiance to a community of rural-urban migrants cannot absolve him, however. Others in this community, he admits, feel guilty about their behavior toward their village kin as well.

We're all afraid to look directly into the eyes of anyone who casually asks us about the people who raised us. We usually change the subject and talk about our own children, because that's the only familial responsibility we feel comfortable boasting about. (11)

As these migrants become increasingly absorbed in urban life, their connections to rural kin weaken. The distance is great, as is the social gap between Bangkok and the village. If this gap makes communication across the realms difficult, it does not erode the migrants' sense of obligation to the village. Their duty to show gratefulness towards their parents remains, and this debt accumulates as they fail repeatedly to repay it. The result is a cycle that can be paralyzing for migrants. They feel so guilty about their previous failure to return that they become unable to face a future return; and the longer they remain in the city, the guiltier they feel.

For the protagonist of "If You Can't Do It, Then Come Down!" the defining feature of Bangkok life is work, and work is the primary excuse he offers for not returning to the village. "My job keeps me tied down. I'm like a mouse stuck in a mousetrap—not dead, but not free to go anywhere either" (23–24). Pointing to the high cost of living in the city, he describes his family's struggle to make ends meet and his need to work constantly. "I'm so busy with my life and responsibilities that I hardly have time for

anybody, especially relatives in the village. I barely see anyone at all" (22).
The ease with which the protagonist takes off work when he hears about his
aunt's surgery, however, belies these excuses. The protagonist simply alerts
his boss, boards a bus, and arrives home the following morning.

Contrary to the protagonist's expectation, his aunt does not berate him
for his long absence. Rather, she is happy to see him and excited to hear
about his life in the city.

> On the first day I spent with my aunt, she didn't tell me any stories at all.
> She only wanted to ask about my life and family. I answered her truthfully
> even though I could tell from her sighs that she was disappointed. Auntie
> is part of the old generation who tend to believe that a good education
> will magically change your life. What I told her contradicted this. Over
> and over, she responded to my words with exclamations of surprise and
> disappointment. (24)

The protagonist's aunt had told him that if he studied hard, he would
become an important person (*chao khon nai khon*). In her generation,
few people earned university degrees, and those who did were guaranteed
government positions. She therefore encouraged him to pursue the highest
educational opportunities possible, supporting his move to Bangkok (even
though this meant their separation) and paying for his high school and
university education. Despite this support, the protagonist was ultimately
unable to find the sort of high-status position she had envisioned for him.
When he explains this to her now, she is incredulous: "Do all people who
have studied to a high level live like that?" she asks. "Most," he replies,
"unless they had high status before, or unless they have an 'in.' But most
end up like me" (25). His aunt has trouble believing these words; they
contradict her very worldview. She has always seen education as a clear
path to employment and success; her nephew's diligent pursuit of this path
and subsequent failure to secure employment seem to her unjust.

The protagonist's inability to become a *chao khon nai khon* through
education ultimately confirms another underlying belief of Auntie's— that
villagers are doomed to live a life of struggle and exploitation no matter
how hard they work. Most people from their village, she tells him, have
lost their land; many of them have migrated to the city in search of better

options. When Auntie learns that the protagonist's migration and education have not brought him social mobility, she is dismayed: "I can't believe it. . . . You've struggled to become educated, and they still keep you in debt?" (24). This "they" suggests a large-scale structural force that conspires against villagers, dooming their efforts to improve themselves.

The protagonist corroborates this vision in his reflection on rural-urban migration to Bangkok.

> As I closed my eyes, I could see the stream of people moving toward Bangkok. One after the other, they come from all parts of the country— from my village, too. Their hope lies in Bangkok, but as soon as they take one step into the capital, all of their wishes disappear. It's true that there is lots of money in Bangkok, but it's not for those migrants to send back home to help. (28)

If villagers come to the capital intending to take advantage of high Bangkok salaries and turn them into remittances, this plan, he suggests, is ill-fated. In the end, most migrants will not have the means to support themselves *and* their village kin. This passage suggests that Bangkok offers migrants an alternate home, a place for which village life can be exchanged, but that this exchange must be complete. Few will succeed in maintaining intact financial, social, and emotional relationships with the village. The text implies further that the breakdown of financial connections with the village has the power to damage social and emotional relationships between rural and urban kin. Kerry Richter's demographic study of Isan out-migrants points out that most migrants bring remittances with them when they visit, rather than sending money by mail (1997, 48). There is thus a link between return and remittances. When the behavior of migrant protagonists is examined in light of these findings, it seems quite plausible that the migrants' inability to support their rural family financially is an important factor in their failure to return and in the deterioration of social relations between rural and urban kin.

Uthain's and Pirot's texts make it clear that the migrant's return to the village provides an important opportunity for the reconstitution of these relationships. Once Pirot's protagonist finishes telling his aunt about life in the city, he listens for two days as she updates him on village life. He begins to relax as he reestablishes contact with the people and place of his birth, and he even begins to feel like a kid again. Toward the end of his visit, the protagonist comments, "I'm not sure whether I came to see my aunt or myself" (Pirot 1993c, 26). His unexpected return to the rural realm has led him to "see himself" by breaking down the false barrier between his urban and rural personae. He realizes now that it was not the villagers' rejection of him that was keeping him from home, but his own inability to integrate his rural roots into his ongoing urban reality. He also comes to understand that his fear of being judged by his family was misguided—when he comes clean about his "lack of success" in the city, his aunt does not blame *him*, but rather blames the city and broader social forces beyond their control. The protagonist's return thus reestablishes the social support network, a network that the protagonist—in his distance and fear of return—thought he had lost.

The protagonist of Hoy Loh's "At the Bedside," like Pirot's protagonist, knows that he must return to the village when he hears that his father has become ill. Although Hoy Loh's protagonist does not question his obligation to return, he does not look forward to returning either. He has avoided the village for some time now because he has not attained the level of success that he or his father hoped he would achieve in the city. He was waiting for his situation to improve before returning, but now that he must return at a moment's notice, he can no longer put off this moment of truth.

Years earlier, when the protagonist first expressed a desire to move to Bangkok, his mother tried to dissuade him. She saw the city as a dangerous place and feared that if he moved there he would become tempted by illicit activities.

> Mother couldn't see the point of moving far away. She asked, "Can't you study here, close to home?" I told her that in the city I could work and study at the same time. She didn't dare go against this. Work meant money. Studying meant success. I had an ingenious argument. As for my father, he hid his happiness quietly away. (Hoy Loh 1996, 141)

The protagonist uses "work" as a trump card. For a poor village family, the promise of additional income cannot easily be brushed aside, nor can the opportunity for a more stable future through an urban education. The protagonist's ultimate experience of work and higher education in the city, however, prove less glowing than what he had envisioned. He moves through job after job, quitting his first position as a waiter and then getting fired from his second as a manual laborer. As for school, he has difficulty with the academic material and faces various obstacles in the learning process. In the end, he spends most of his time drinking. His father, however, never loses faith in him, firmly believing he will overcome these difficulties and forge a successful life in the city. "Father never criticized my low-level jobs. He still hoped his son would advance" (143). It is his father's undying faith in his potential that makes it so hard for the protagonist to return home and face his father "as is"—perhaps for the final time. This moment of return seems premature; the protagonist has not yet become the "returnee" he wants to be for his father.

This unexpected trip was now beginning. It was a sad return home. Sadness churned deep in the heart of this dreamer who had once secretly dreamed of moving far away from his home. The life of this dreamer was just beginning. It was still too early to see the results of this dreaming. All he knew was that he wanted to bring the new things he learned [in the urban environment] back to share with his father who was anxiously awaiting him. But alas—the person who was waiting to hear his news was now deathly ill. Now who could he tell his story of migration to? (144)

The protagonist's return is particularly devastating because it signals the loss of the one person who truly supported his migration journey. Although his father did not physically join him in migration, he joined him in spirit, experiencing the city vicariously through him and eagerly awaiting his stories upon return. When the protagonist arrives to find his father on his deathbed, he feels lost. His move to the city has not brought him to his intended destination, and now his connection to home has slipped away as well. As he sits by his father's side in the final part of the story, he waits for the one question he knows his father will ask. The author does not tell us what this question is—only that the protagonist is afraid to hear it. We imagine possibilities ranging from, "Have you gotten a job yet?" to "How are things going in school?" Whatever the question may be, the protagonist is caught between his fear of revealing the truth to his father and his desire to do so. He is about to lose the only person who truly cares about his migration story. And just as Pirot's protagonist comes to "see himself" by sharing this story, Hoy Loh's protagonist risks losing himself when he can no longer share his.

SEARCHING FOR HOME

At the moment that rural-urban migrants depart from the countryside, the village becomes locked in time. No longer the naturally evolving realm in which they live, the village comes to be associated with a set of completed events in their past. The resulting tendency on the part of the migrant to link the village with the past is supported by broader cultural discourses that align Bangkok with modernity and the countryside with an older, more traditional way of life. As a result, many of the Bangkok-based protagonists of Thai migration narratives view their village with a deep sense of nostalgia.

At the same time, migrants invariably view their village as "home." What does it mean, then, for "home" to be this "other" place—a place that urban dwellers rarely, if ever, visit? Does this notion of "home as other" lock the migrants into a sense of irresolvable exile, doomed never to fully integrate into the urban surroundings? Or, does it facilitate the migrants' efforts to make a life for themselves in Bangkok by creating a safety net, an idealized "home" about which they can dream and to which they could theoretically return at any time?

The middle-class protagonist of Warop Worrapa's "Khao Sao by Father's Hand" grew up in a small fishing village, but has lived in the city for many years. He has established a successful life in the urban realm, but is frustrated by many aspects of his family's urban existence. He feels that the mall-based culture of urban Thailand is pulling his family away from the things that are truly important, including close relations with the natural environment and a true sense of home.

> For several Saturdays now, the members of my family have brought me out to eat [at a suki restaurant in the mall]. My children love preparing suki, mixing together the various ingredients in an electric pot so large that it takes a family like ours—father, mother, and three children—two meals to finish it.

[As my children prepare suki] their happy laughter blends with the cheerful chatter from other tables, the booming advertisements from the loudspeakers, and the boisterous shoppers in the mall.

I may be the only one here who isn't enjoying this experience. I come only because my children ask me to—it is for them that I force myself to taste the modern times.

For several Saturdays now, I've felt as if I've been dragged far from home, from my true home, my first home.

My home is on a small island in the Straits of Malacca. (Warop 2005, 140–41)

Despite the fact that the protagonist has lived in the city since his teens, "home" remains the village of his birth. When he thinks of home, he envisions the natural landscape of the Andaman Sea and the simple life of the fishermen who live there. He remembers the fresh fish that his father caught each day and the homemade *khao sao*[14] his father made from it. The freshness of those meals—and the hard work that went into them—seem to the protagonist the antithesis of the fabricated and processed suki that he must endure each weekend in the city.

Suki is, for the protagonist, a symbol of all that is wrong with contemporary urban life. It is instantly available, overabundant, and artificially sweet. The pre-cut ingredients seem to spring forth from the mall ready for consumption with no hint of their origins or the processes that brought them to the table. As the protagonist watches his children drop the pre-cut suki ingredients into the pot, he feels as if he is watching a charade, a simulacrum of the true experience of preparing food for one's family. The setting disturbs him as well, as the family's weekend trips to the mall for suki have replaced their earlier ritual of eating at home. The protagonist worries that the mall may be becoming "the real home of middle-class people like us."

All of the tables [in the suki restaurant] were filled with people—like relatives who had come together in the kitchen. Although these people

---

14. *Khao sao* is a mixture of rice, soy sauce, and fish.

did not have the same ancestors, their souls all issued forth from the same womb of modernity. These souls were identical, and yet they did not connect with one another at all.

My children and others their age have "homes" like this all over the city [in the various malls]. Or are these the real homes of middle-class people like us? (141)

Khao sao, which evokes the village, nature, and home for the protagonist, becomes the key to reclaiming the true home that he fears is slipping away. Just as suki symbolizes urban modernity for the protagonist, his father's *khao sao* evokes the village, nature, and home. "For the last few Saturdays, I've tried to bring my family back to our roots—and the *khao sao* I remember so well is one way I tried to get them there" (144). By preparing this quintessential village meal for his children, the protagonist hopes to give them a true village experience. His efforts to recreate *khao sao* in the city fail, however. His urban *khao sao* looks and tastes different from the meal of his childhood. The aura around the food has changed as well. When he was a child, he would fight with his brother over the *khao sao* until their father chanted a spell over the rice to quiet them down. The protagonist's own children hardly turn their heads from the television set as he prepares the food, and when they do take a bite of the *khao sao*, they scrunch up their faces in disgust. The experience leaves the protagonist feeling sad and dejected, "dried up, like the uneaten rice that stuck to the bottom of the ceramic bowls" (145).

The protagonist tries to figure out what went wrong with his urban *khao sao*. Is the food he made somehow inferior to his father's, and if so, what caused the difference? Could it be his electric rice cooker? His father always used an earthenware pot. Or could the difference lie in their very hands—his father's were coarse and strong from a life of hard work, while his own were "soft as a baby's bottom" from holding expensive pens and tapping on computer keys (148). Perhaps, he thinks, his hands are too weak to knead the rice properly. Or perhaps he has failed to evoke the mystical aura around the meal. Whenever his father prepared *khao sao*, he would chant a spell over the rice and blow on it, telling his children, "You are not eating plain rice" (143). The protagonist now wonders whether he remembered to cast a spell over the rice when making *khao sao* for his children.

As he meditates on the possible reasons that his own children have not embraced the *khao sao* he loved as a child, the protagonist locates the problem in a lack of authenticity: if he could truly reproduce *khao sao* by using the precise ingredients and preparation techniques his father used, his children would appreciate it. With this mission in mind, he decides to bring his family to the village the following weekend so that they can experience the "true" *khao sao* made by his father's hand. The protagonist is sure that once his children try real *khao sao* in its original location, they will understand the authentic "taste of home" he has been trying to convey.

When the protagonist arrives at his father's house to set this plan in motion, however, his village-based family responds with surprise and confusion. His younger brother Pla Rapu exclaims, "You've made it to the city, where there are tons of delicious things to eat, but you don't want to eat them! Instead, you'd rather come back here and eat some rice mixed with a little soy sauce" (151). This description of *khao sao* calls the protagonist's memory and judgment into question. Up to this point in the narrative, the reader has accepted the protagonist's description of *khao sao* as a feast of fresh fish; we must now reconcile the narrator's claim with Pla Rapu's description of *khao sao* as "rice mixed with a little soy sauce." Moreover, Pla Rapu's statement that villagers would rather eat city food than *khao sao* undermines the protagonist's apotheosis of *khao sao* and his suggestion that the village is an unchanged realm where villagers live as they did generations earlier.

The harder the protagonist looks for the unchanged village of his memory, the more this "true village" and its essential meal seems to elude him. The protagonist's father not only wonders why he wants to make *khao sao*, but is surprised that the protagonist can even remember *khao sao*, as he himself has not made this meal in years.

"Dad, remember our special mystical rice?" I asked, turning my head to look at my father from where I lay on the floor.

Father looked confused for a moment, and then a flicker of recognition sparkled in his murky eyes and he chuckled a bit. "There's no one left to make it for. You kids are all grown up now. And anyway, there was nothing special about it—it was just ordinary rice with a few drops of soy sauce."

"The spell, Dad! The spell that Grandpa taught you! We didn't eat plain rice. Right?" I raised my head and sat up a bit.

My words made my father laugh hard.

"Oh, son. That was just a joke to tease children. You still remember that?"

"Dad. Make the mystical rice again," I sat up and spoke seriously now. "I want my three children to eat your mystical rice. Just like my brother and I used to eat." (146)

In this passage, the protagonist's father exposes the relativity inherent in the meaning of *khao sao* even within the village context. Adults in the village know that the "magic" of *khao sao* is simply "a joke to tease children" to get them to behave—not the mystical experience that the protagonist believed it to be. Just as Pla Rapu calls the protagonist's essentialist view of *khao sao* into question by situating it in a wider rural-urban context, father undercuts this view by suggesting it is no more than the vision of a child. Because the protagonist left the village at a young age, he never reinterpreted his understanding of *khao sao*. That vision simply became locked in time.

Now, when father confronts the protagonist with this revised vision, the protagonist becomes uneasy. He responds to his father's rejection of *khao sao*'s mystical power with mounting anxiety and a determination to disavow what his father has said. Over the course of their conversation, the protagonist sits up straighter and speaks more firmly, ending the exchange with a near command, "Dad. Make the mystical rice again. I want my three children to eat your mystical rice. Just like my brother and I used to eat." The mystical *khao sao*, the protagonist insists, is real—one must simply recreate the authentic experience of it.

The protagonist's father agrees to prepare *khao sao* to please his son, but explains that it is not possible to make the same *khao sao* the protagonist ate as a child. The environment and economy of the village have changed so thoroughly that one cannot even obtain the fish or soy sauce they used to use for the meal. The local fishermen, father explains, are indebted to a *taokae* (Chinese male boss) who has taken over the fishing trade, and anyone who wants to buy fresh fish must row out to sea and meet the fishing boats before they come to shore. Father is not even sure if the fishermen will sell to the protagonist, as they owe money to the *taokae* and fear him. Most likely, the protagonist will have to buy fish and soy sauce from the *taokae*'s convenience store and put up with inferior ingredients.

Despite these compromises, the protagonist insists on going through with his plan. He procures the substitute ingredients and brings them to his father. His father begins to prepare the meal, and as the family gathers around, a certain magic *is* created. The feeling only lasts an instant, however, before it is broken by the protagonist's brother and children. Pla Rapu wonders aloud why they are making *khao sao* at all, and his sons chime in with words that unintentionally hurt their grandfather. The youngest yells out, "Grandpa's hands are wrinkly. They're getting all over the food. I don't want to eat it!" The experience deteriorates further as the protagonist's father chants the magical spell and blows on the rice. Instead of being spellbound by this ceremony, one of the children shouts out, "Grandpa's spit went in! Eew!" (151). The protagonist feels horrible. He quickly shoos the children away and tries to make his father feel better. "Don't worry about it," his father tells him. "It's not just your kids—Pla Rapu's kids won't eat it either. There aren't any kids asking me to make *khao sao* anymore" (152). The children nibble at the *khao sao* and then leave the rest in their bowls. The protagonist glances at the dry leftover rice and then dumps the remainder of the *khao sao* into the sea. The grains of rice swell up and float around, and he notices that not even the fish come up to eat it. He wonders to himself, "Is this because the sea too has changed?" (152).

With this failure to recreate the *khao sao* experience, the protagonist ultimately must acknowledge that the village of his memory has changed. His efforts to forcefully recreate the home of his memory have damaged his real home through insults to his father, and he is left with a deep sense of sadness and alienation. The world he remembers no longer exists. Even the sea seems to have changed. No one wants *khao sao* anymore.

In the final scene, the protagonist leaves his father's house to return with his children to the city. "We leave the village near the sea just as the sun is about to touch the water, and we will reach the big city when the bright lights are shining throughout" (152). The story ends in an in-between space. The day is now over, but night has not yet come; the protagonist has left the village, but has not yet arrived in the city. This final setting acts as a metaphor for the protagonist's ultimate psychological position in between two realms. He is now homeless, caught between the urban home of "middle-class people like us" from which he seeks to distance himself and the village "time of *khao sao*" that no longer exists. As he drives toward the city, he must begin the work of reconciling these two identities, now knowing that he cannot fit neatly into either of them. In the final line of the story, the protagonist poses a question: "On future Saturdays, who (myself or the children) will invite whom where?" (152). The story ends ambivalently, with this question unanswered. Will the family go back to the mall or back to the village? Either is possible, but neither offers any firm footing.

Thian, the protagonist of Pira Sudham's "A Food Vendor and a Taxi Driver"[15] experiences similar feelings of "in betweenness," coupled with nostalgia for an idealized village. Although Thian has lived in Bangkok for many years, he has never stopped dreaming of Isan. The ironic twist of Pira's story is that the home Thian longs for does not exist and never has.

Thian was an orphan. He does not know where he was born or who his parents were, but he knows that he comes from Isan. The couple who raised him moved from village to village throughout the northeast, and although "Isan" evokes home for Thian, it also evokes a sense of rootlessness and migrancy. "Throughout the years [growing up in Isan], I hardly felt I belonged to the people and to the land there, so I became a wandering monk, and eventually ended up in a temple in Bangkok" (Pira 1994, 54).

The tenuousness of Thian's connection to his place of birth leads him to move away from Isan, but he never stops missing his "Isan home." His inability to return to his exact place of his birth, in fact, heightens his sense of longing. He expresses jealousy towards rural-urban migrants who "have a village" to return to, as he laments his own fate.

> The difference between you and me is that you have a village, and your people to go back to when you want to, but I haven't. . . . I have been homesick for a home that I don't have, and I envy those who, like yourself, when the time comes, can go back, to escape from the muck, the poisonous fumes, the traffic chaos, and the struggle of city life. (54–55)

---

15. Pira Sudham, a Thai writer born in Isan and now based in Thailand and the United Kingdom, writes in English in order make his literature accessible to a wider international audience. The excerpts included here are passages from the original English text.

In order to "escape from the muck" of the city, Thian attempts to return to the village vicariously through others—by driving them home in his taxicab. He initiates his first vicarious return when he meets a young woman in a Patpong bar. He guesses from her features that she is from Isan, and he is shocked that a woman from his part of the country could expose herself onstage like that; such behavior, he thinks, would never be allowed in her village community. "I could not imagine she would be so blatantly sensual, wearing strings, exposing her body to the eyes of men in a village" (56). Watching her onstage, Thian feels a strong desire to take this woman—and all of the other Isan girls—out of this bar and return them to the village. "There were several very young girls there, with Esarn [Isan] features. I longed to take them away, out of this den of vice, to give them back to their villages and the fresh air of their rice fields" (56).

Thian's desire to bring these young women home is not as innocent as it may seem. It is complicated by the gendered nature of his desire to "save" the women by placing them in a more strictly controlled environment where the "eyes of men" will keep them in check. It is also complicated by Thian's own admission that these women do not want to return home (and his use of coercive tactics to get them to do so).[16] Thian's attempt to bring the dancer back to a "purer" place is subverted, further, by his own actions. He charges her 1,000 baht for the ride home, 500 baht of which he takes out "in kind . . . in the road-side motel at the edge of Korat, just to prove to her that I am not that old" (59). His desire to "save" this woman from a life of impurity is thus tainted by a desire to assert his own virility and masculinity through the role of "savior."

If Thian aims to become this woman's savior, she turns this effort inside out, shifting the meaning of their return to the village and the power relations involved in it. When they arrive in the village, the young woman

---

16. Thian offers to drive the woman onstage home for less money than it costs him for the trip knowing that she will be unable to resist returning to her village in a taxicab. Returning to the village in a taxicab is not only extravagantly expensive, but also suggests a transition in the migrant's *axis mundi* to the urban realm. Taxis are a decidedly urban mode of transportation—one usually kept within the limits of the metropolitan region (as opposed to trains or buses that serve as connections between the rural and urban realms). By returning in a taxi, the migrant positions herself as rooted firmly in the city for the eyes of the villagers she has left behind.

makes no effort to reintegrate into village society, instead retaining her urban persona and acting "like a splendid well-off lady and [treating him] just like any taxi driver who drove her all the way home for her money" (59). To Thian's dismay, the woman insists on going back to Bangkok once she has demonstrated her urban status to her co-villagers. Worse, she brings another girl from the village to the city with them. In the end, Thian fails not only to effect this woman's "return"—he also facilitates the trafficking of another Isan girl into urban prostitution.

Thian makes a second attempt at vicarious return, offering to drive an Isan woman who works in a Bangkok noodle shop back to her village. This woman left her village years earlier in an attempt to escape the stifling environment of the place. Her husband had left her, and she had become known in the village as "the deserted woman"—an identity she could not shake off.

> In our village, people have a way of identifying the unfortunate by their misfortune. So there we have the mute, the lame, the blind, the kratoey, the deserted. And the word: DESERTED was grafted on me like a nasty cake of mud which I could not wash off, while tradition, our village way of life, and my own sense of duty became a heavy steel lid on my life. (39–40)

In an effort to escape this oppressive environment and gain a sense of agency over her life, she migrated to Bangkok. Over time, she distances herself so thoroughly from her rural roots that when the taxi driver asks about her life in Isan, it seems to her like a near-forgotten dream. And although she once felt an almost desperate need to leave the village, years of living in the city have eased these feelings. The "deserted woman" identity that used to feel like "a nasty cake of mud which I could not wash off," now seems more like "a nightmare which could be washed off from memory by being awake" (39–43). The woman acknowledges that she now misses her family. When the taxi driver asks if she would like to return home, she immediately answers, "Yes, of course" (44). He comes to pick her up the next morning.

> Around a corner, the old and battered Toyota was waiting for me. The driver must have known that I wouldn't leave the shop till the coast was

clear. We sped excitedly away from the scene. My head swirled and my
heart beat fast. The streets were quite empty at that hour.

For hours we talked in Lao which sounded more from the heart than
when we had spoken together in Bangkok. I felt free and happy too, with
the wind blowing in my face and through my hair. I was grateful to him
for rescuing me from the maze of the city. (44–45)

As they drive toward Isan, the woman reassumes her northeastern
identity, abandoning Central Thai to speak in her native Isan dialect with
a sense of freedom. The village ahead no longer seems oppressive; it feels
like her true home. When the taxi arrives, villagers crowd around to meet
the car, greeting the woman happily. "It seemed," she says, that "all of us were
tearful and I was forgiven [for leaving the village]" (51). But shortly after,
the return migrant comes to see the challenges of reintegration. The gap
she left behind with her departure has long since been filled by others, and
the relationships among community members and kin have restructured
in her absence. There is no longer a clear place for her. She still inhabits
the roles of "mother" and "daughter," but some reorganization will have
to occur to define the limits of this space, and she is unsure of where this
restructuring will leave her.

It did not take long for me to realize that the house was no longer my
home. It had become the house of my son and his wife who had been
taking care of it, looking after the grandparents all the years I slaved
away in Bangkok. I was so pleased to see my son who had grown into
a fine young man with a good wife who showed me so much respect,
which made me ashamed of my escape. But to live with them would
bring some unhappiness later on, I knew. So before my dear old taxi man
would depart from the village for Bangkok the next day I asked him to
take me back. (51–52)

Neither of the women whom Thian attempts to "give . . . back to their
village" stays there (56). Both the prostitute and the food vendor find greater
freedom in the city, and both value this freedom over the sense of security
that the village provides. If the village offers a familiar environment and
an established social group that includes them, the social structures of

the village also require that the individual submit to an identity that is recognizable (and approved) within that structure. The city, in contrast, offers anonymity—a lack of pre-formed social relations—that can either lead to loneliness or to a sense of freedom (or both). Through this anonymity, these migrant women are free to fashion malleable—and even multiple—identities. Ultimately, they privilege this agency over the village's familiarity.

In the case of the prostitute, it is clear almost from the beginning of the narrative that she will choose urban freedom. She shows no desire to be "saved" from her current surroundings; on the contrary, she makes every effort to define herself as urban and to distance herself from Thian and their shared Isan origins. When Thian speaks to her in their Isan dialect, for example, she responds in Central Thai. She even goes so far as to ask him not to visit her at the bar where she works because she doesn't want her foreign clients to see her with a Thai. It is no surprise, then, that she maintains a staunchly Bangkok-based identity when she returns to the village.

The food vendor's ultimate choice of urban independence takes a more circuitous route, however. Like the prostitute, she refuses to allow the taxi driver to put her in a "protective" situation of his own choosing (although she is more appreciative of his efforts to bring her back to the village than the prostitute is, noting almost wistfully that "he treated me as if I were a young girl needing protection" [47]). Unlike the prostitute, who clearly aligns freedom with the city, the food vendor locates freedom in her ability to determine her own future. When she initially chooses to return to the village, she is confident in her decision (and any negative consequences it may bring, including shame at having abandoned her family). It is only once she arrives in the village and realizes that she will be subjected to the will of others that she feels she must leave. Significantly, upon her return to Bangkok, she decides not to return to the noodle shop where she previously worked and instead to begin a more independent life selling food from her own pushcart.

It is interesting to consider the women's explicit decisions to remain in the city in light of Thian's own assertion that he would return to the village if he could. Because Thian officially has "no home," he is absolved of the need to decide whether to stay or go—a decision that other migrants must make constantly, with each moment they remain in the city. We may wonder, in fact, whether the "loss" of Thian's village is convenient for him. The village of his memory is the only village he has; he can thus idealize it without having to bring his imaginings in line with a real place. He is not subject to the "reality checks" that the women in this narrative or the protagonist of "Khao Sao by Father's Hand" must face. For this reason, "Isan" remains for him a strong antidote to the "muck" of city life. He never has to extricate himself from this muck because he cannot. Given Thian's engagement with urban activities for which he criticizes others (visiting go-go bars, sleeping with prostitutes, etc.) we may question the extent to which he actually wants to return to the purer, idyllic village he imagines. In the end, it seems that experiencing this purity vicariously through others is enough.

Han, the protagonist of Plinda Siripong's "Exchange," attempts to keep the village a pure, untainted realm—not in the nostalgic space of his memory, but in the physical world. This story is set at the historical moment in which migrants begin to stream from Isan into Bangkok, and the headman of Han's village asks him to travel to the city to determine if their own villagers might benefit from such migration. Boon, a return migrant from another village, has spread tempting stories about the wonders of Bangkok—the money to be made and the ease of life there— and the headman's curiosity has been piqued.

Han travels to Bangkok and remains there for several years. The author offers no details about the protagonist's time there; all we learn is that when Han returns, his hair has turned white and he has become almost silent. The villagers are all eager to learn about the big city, but all Han will say is, "The faraway city has nothing good to offer. It is filled with deceit, pain, and emptiness" (Plinda 1993, 54). Whenever anyone asks about Bangkok, Han responds in this way—until the villagers tire of asking and fall back into their earlier routines.

Although Han has observed the benefits of development in the city, he believes that its undersides far outweigh its benefits. In particular, he believes that "development" can destroy communities that experience it too quickly. "If we let it [development] come in before we [the villagers] are fully ready for it, we will fall and there will be nothing left [of our society] to be proud of" (56). In order to shield the villagers from the negative aspects of development, then, he keeps his knowledge of the city to himself and quells the villagers' interest in Bangkok. Han thus undertakes a strange, utopian experiment: he creates an "intact" village by artificially keeping all knowledge of the outside world from the villagers. As a result, the village evolves in extreme isolation for many years. The author describes this utopian village in the nostalgic terms usually reserved for out-migrants' portrayals of their village homes:

> The culture and traditions passed down from the ancestors continued unchanged. It was a simple way of life, where women never tired of bending over looms and stitching fabric together to make clothes and men never minded working hard in the fields in exchange for food to sustain themselves.
>
> Children's laughter filled the place with life. On merit-making days, the sounds of teenagers teasing one another flirtatiously and the red-gummed grins of grandfathers and grandmothers chewing betel were like a fable that spoke to the deep happiness of the village. (54)

Although Han succeeds in maintaining the village's isolation for an extended period of time, urbanization eventually wins out. One day, three strangers arrive, telling stories about the modern things Bangkok has to offer: televisions, fans, refrigerators, air conditioners, cars, and "so many other things they can't even be listed" (55). These men also bring a sample of Bangkok's modernity to show the villagers, a radio. The strangers turn the radio on, and the villagers dance with excitement at the music that flows from this strange machine.

Han looks on in fright as the villagers experience "modernity" for the first time.

> "It" had finally made it to their home—the "it" that he had strived for so many years to keep far from their village. Now, "it" was here.
>
> What was "it" exactly? The people from the faraway city called "it" "development." But, as far as Han was concerned, "it" meant that which was never enough. "It" meant ruin. (55)

The villagers turn on Han, demanding to know why he has kept these wonderful things from them for so long. They accuse him of harming them by keeping them ignorant. As punishment for Han's deception, the village headman sentences him to permanent exile from the village. Although Han firmly believes that he made his decision in the best interest of the village, he knows that he must accept the headman's decree, for the decree itself is village custom, part of the village system Han has striven to uphold.

> The headman's words were like a decree from the heavens that a small person like himself could not oppose.
>
> It was law. It was custom. It was an understanding that had been passed down from the time of their ancestors. It was one part of the culture he was trying to uphold, wasn't it? (53)

Han is forced to leave the village and is cut off from his family and friends. His exile is, in a sense, the ultimate consequence of his migration to the city. With Han's initial move, he sacrifices his home (for a few years) and his youth (permanently) to determine what the city has to offer the villagers. In making his determination that the city has nothing of substance to offer, Han returns home and attempts to reintegrate into village life. But the seeds of exile are already planted. Although he believes he is doing the right thing by lying to the villagers, he also knows that he is violating a village rule by doing so. Han's very contact with the city, then, forces him into an impossible bind: respect village rules and tell the truth, facilitating the demise of the village culture he loves,[17] or break village law by lying, thus defiling the tradition he seeks to preserve. Either choice leads to exile— personal exile from the village, or communal exile from the village way of life. In the end, he is forced to endure both.

Once Han is cast out from the village, development and modernity flood in, including the negative elements he feared. Diang, an old friend of Han's who secretly visits Han in exile, tells him about the changes the village has undergone. The headman now earns money by allowing an outsider to cut down the village's trees, and he has purchased a car and television set with the money he has earned from this venture. The headman has also brought electricity to the village, and villagers are now scrambling to migrate so that they can buy modern things like lights and appliances that require cash. The

---

17. The inexorable push of urbanization is unquestioned here. Han's very logic and motives are based on the assumption that the villagers will want to partake in modernity— whether or not it will have negative consequences for them.

young men all work in the city as day laborers, and the women—some as young as twelve or thirteen—are working in the city as well.[18] Diang tells Han that his own daughter Lao has gone to the city and that he received three thousand baht[19] from an agent upon her departure. Since then, Diang has not heard from his daughter, but the agent has assured him that she is doing well. Han listens to these stories in silence. He feels as if he is watching a growing storm that is about to unleash itself.

Han's granddaughter Chanta comes to visit him in the final scene of the narrative. She too is about to migrate—her father has just received three thousand baht for her (which he has already spent on a radio and motorcycle). She wants to say goodbye to her grandfather before she leaves because she fears that, like her friend Lao, she may not return. She tells Han that her father is planning to send her little sister to Bangkok as well. With two children working in the city, she explains, he will be able to build a new house and "not look inferior to anyone in the village" (60).

As Han listens to these stories, he thinks to himself, "the city sent them many good, new things. But what it wanted in exchange was all too valuable" (59). He closes his eyes as if in pain, and a tear falls down his cheeks. "It," he thinks to himself, "has fully arrived" (59). Han's migration to the city has ultimately brought about not only his own exile, but also the out-migration and exile of many other villagers, including his granddaughter. It is as if his departure sets in motion a series of events that are beyond anyone's control. He now understands that the urbanization of the village and of the villagers was only a matter of time.

---

18. While not explicitly stated, the author implies that these girls are sex workers.

19. Equivalent to 120 dollars at the time this story was written.

CHAPTER 7

CONCLUSION

BOUND BY BANGKOK

Thai literature about rural-urban migration reveals the myriad ways that Bangkok-bound migrants are ultimately (and already) bound *by* Bangkok. The city forges ties that bind, transforming the migrant's sense of self and making it impossible ever to go back to being the person he or she once was. In subtle ways, Bangkok's binding can begin even before the migrant leaves home. The city's wealth, power, and modernity exert a strong attractive force on the migrant; this urban hegemony, coupled with the urbanization of the countryside, makes urban binds all but inescapable. Thus, we find a number of rural-born protagonists who express urban perspectives even as young children in the village. Tawan Santipaap's Ot argues that because he is a strong student, he will one day live and work in Bangkok—expressing a clear alignment of success with the urban realm. Kosol Anusim's protagonist embraces the scientific worldview he has learned in school, despite his family's espousal of traditional rural beliefs. It is ultimately this disjuncture that leads him to move to Bangkok, where he can pursue a career and lifestyle more in line with his modern views.

The city's pull on villagers is clearly depicted in stories where rural individuals engage with modern objects and ideas for the first time. In Plinda Siripong's "Exchange," villagers dance excitedly as music emanates from the first radio they have ever seen, and they buy all of the appliances a salesman from the city offers—even when this means sacrificing the village's natural resources and productive labor in exchange for these goods. The protagonist of Raks Mananya's "Along the Way" is similarly entranced by the money, jewelry, and expensive clothing he has seen other migrants attain in the city: "New clothes, expensive accessories—weren't those the things he wanted, too?" (Raks 1993c, 52). Despite an older migrant's warnings that the undersides of the urban realm far outweigh these tokens of financial success, the new migrant is unable to understand such dangers from his pre-migration standpoint.

A number of Thai writers depict urban hegemony through the symbolism of the train, whose tracks spread out over the countryside and whose cars serve as icons of modernity. In addition to the physical connection the train forges between rural and urban realms, the modern allure of the train forges psychological connections that bind villagers to Bangkok and lure them to the city. When these individuals board the train for the first time, such ties are strengthened, and the train inducts the migrant into a new urban experience. This transformation is depicted in Raks Mananya's "Along the Way" as two migrants discuss the experience of rural-urban migration over the course of their journey. The older migrant explains the transition that the new migrant has begun with his decision to move to the city, detailing the losses and changes in identity that migration entails. And we watch as his predictions are realized when they arrive in the city.

Several narratives describe the process of identity-making that the migrant undergoes on the train. It is in this space that migrants first gain a sense of themselves as non-villagers. Until they arrive in the city, however, they are not yet urbanites. It is during the train journey, then, that a new identity is formed—one linked not to the static realms of country or city, but to an in-between space characterized by movement. The train enables the migrants to see themselves from this new mobile perspective and to imagine themselves as part of a migrant community for the first time. This emerging vision will affect the migrants' sense of self, community, and home from this point forward.

Bangkok's binding of the migrant begins in full force when the migrant arrives in the city. For those who adapt easily to Bangkok, the adoption of urban behaviors and a modern urban lifestyle may seem natural. The female protagonist of Tadsanawadee's "Wall" is conscious of becoming increasingly urbanized and embraces this transition. She argues that because Thailand is on a path toward ever greater urbanization, all Thais should take on an urban way of life and seek success within that framework. The protagonists of Sila Khomchai's "The Family in the Streets" and Suthipong Thamawut's

"The City That is Punished for Consumption" hold similar (if slightly more cynical) views: they adapt to urban rhythms, even as they recognize these as unnatural. They simply feel they have no other choice.

The transformation from rural to urban identity is even more insidious in cases where Bangkok binds the migrant without his knowledge or consent. The protagonist of Yohda Hasaemsaeng's "Trap" delights in the success he has gained as a "setter of traps" in Bangkok—until he realizes that the city has set a trap for *him*. In Kon Krailat's "There Was a Day," Ussiri Dhammachoti's "What's Gone Is Gone," and Sunee Namso's "The Exemplary Worker," migrants find themselves sacrificing more than they are willing to give. As the city robs these individuals of their health, dignity, and humanity, it binds them through trauma they will not be able to shake off—even years after they have returned home.

The migrant's relationship with home is key to understanding the ways in which the city binds the migrant. Most rural-urban migrants move to the city with an expectation that they will achieve some form of success in the urban realm, whether through economic gain, a rise in social status, or educational advancement.[1] The protagonist of Pirot Boonbragop's "If You Can't Do It, Then Come Down!" notes that most migrants move to Bangkok with the goal of supporting their extended families. The migrants' sense of success in the city and relationships with village kin can be quickly complicated by the inability to achieve this goal—a goal that may have seemed reasonable (and eminently achievable) from the pre-migration perspective. Pirot's protagonist notes,

> As I closed my eyes, I could see the stream of people moving toward Bangkok. One after the other, they come from all parts of the country—from my village, too. Their hope lies in Bangkok, but as soon as they take one step into the capital, all of their wishes disappear. It's true that there is lots of money in Bangkok, but it's not for those migrants to send back home to help. (Pirot 1993c, 28)

---

1. The exception is forced migrants, who move to the city because they have no other choice.

When migrants discover that they do not earn enough money to send remittances to their village kin, they may experience deep feelings of guilt or embarrassment. One way to assuage these feelings is to dissociate from the village, thus eliminating the context in which these migrants could be construed as ungrateful (or as failures). In distancing themselves from the village, however, they also dissolve their support network.

The corrected version should read: Their fear and avoidance of return—arising from their inability to support their rural families financially—literally force them to remain in the city, bound to the urban space. Their failure to return weakens their ties to the village and produces anxiety about the possibility of reestablishing links. Bangkok thus binds migrants physically and psychologically, holding them ever more tightly to the urban realm.

This binding of the migrant through a repression of rural linkages can be so subtle that it plays out in everyday interactions with other urbanites. In Uthain Phromdaeng's "A Man," the protagonist Pracha watches a police officer arrest someone who resembles his childhood friend Chamrat. Overcome with guilt and fear that someone from his village could reach such a low, Pracha decides to deny that the man indeed is Chamrat. Instead of helping his co-villager, Pracha hails a cab and distances himself from the scene. It is important to note that the author never reveals whether the man on the street is actually Chamrat; it is equally possible that Pracha has shirked his duties as co-villager or that he has simply imagined a connection to the man. In either case, Pracha's decision to repress his rural connection (despite his empathy for "Chamrat") suggests the tenacity with which Pracha must cling to a constructed urban identity if he is to maintain a sense of normalcy in the city. And if Pracha has in fact projected a village identity onto an urban stranger, the slippage in identity is particularly poignant. In this case, Pracha's unconscious desire to reestablish a connection with the rural realm (which emerges in his imagined vision of a co-villager) is consciously and forcefully suppressed.

We find a similar dynamic in Tarin's "Fake Beggar," where the middle-class protagonist Pimala surmises that an elderly beggar is asking for money to return to "her provincial home—to the place where she once lived. The place she loved" (Tarin 1993, 243). It is Pimala's assumption that the beggar is physically bound to Bangkok that leads her to empathize with her. This moment of empathy serves as a springboard for an exploration of the subtler ways in which Pimala is herself bound to Bangkok, the ways in which she, too, is unable to return home. Pimala's crisis is one of identity: she remains caught between the role of urban professional she now inhabits and an unspoken nostalgia for her earlier rural-based self. Although Pimala feels empathy for the poorer migrants she sees on the street, she refuses to connect with them, and the narrative plays out as a series of renunciations of her former self. As Pimala struggles to suppress her pangs of nostalgia and guilt, she fortifies the city's binds on her.

If Bangkok's binds are subtly apparent during such interactions in the city, the full force of these binds becomes clear when the migrant returns to the village. The moment of return reveals the extent to which the migrant's perspectives, values, and needs have changed. Return not only reveals the personal changes that the migrant has undergone, but it also unveils the altered position that the migrant now holds within his or her family and community groups. The experience of return throws light on Bangkok's binds on the migrants, forcing migrants to come to terms with these changes and reevaluate their sense of self and place.

All of the migrants in these stories learn that they can never go back to being the person they were before they left home. Their experiences in Bangkok have altered them in expected and unexpected ways, and the city's binds on them endure. Stories such as Yohda Hasaemsaeng's "Return from the Battlefield" and Ussiri Dhammachoti's "What's Gone is Gone" depict migrants who return to their villages after a traumatic migration experience in an effort to find safety, peace, and comfort at home. However, the permanent change that migration has wrought makes it impossible for any of these migrants to adequately occupy the role they once did. The physical and emotional trauma they have experienced transform not only them, but also the context in which they relate to their rural kin. In the case of Ussiri's protagonist, who returns with compensation for the loss of her arm, family members forget the human connection they once held with her and focus instead on the future they will forge with her money. In "Return from the Battlefield," the trauma of the migration experience incapacitates and isolates the migrant protagonist upon his return—even though his family desperately attempts to connect with him. Ussiri's title, "What's Gone Is Gone," speaks to the central theme in both of these narratives: once something of the migrant's is lost through migration, it can never be brought back. The transformation is permanent, and the best the migrant can do is come to terms with this loss and adapt to new circumstances.

Migrants who succeed in accommodating the losses of migration and who succeed in bridging the rural and urban elements of their identities display the greatest levels of happiness and psychological well-being. Even when a unified identity can be attained only by renouncing long-held myths about "home" or "the city," or where the migrant must admit that he or she has "failed" in one of these realms, the clear sense of self that emerges makes the struggles worth it. Migrants such as Pirot Boonbragop's and Kosol Anusim's protagonists ultimately find peace and truth through this process, and although Bangkok (and the migration experience in general) continues to bind them, these migrants accept the changes that Bangkok has wrought as an undeniable part of who they are.

This book, in the end, is about identity—about who these migrants are and who they become through their act of migration. The protagonists of these narratives find that migration, like life, is an ever-changing process of becoming, and the more sites involved in this process, the more complex—and revealing—it becomes. As these migrants grapple with the multiple facets of their identity—both rural and urban, bound for Bangkok and yet already bound by it—they must work to understand where they belong in the world and who they truly are. In doing so, they take part in the broader human drama of discovering who we are, even as we constantly change.

REFERENCES

MIGRATION NARRATIVES ANALYZED

Note: First date given is original publication date; parenthetical author and date refer to Thai selected reference list below.

Boreetat Hootangkoon. 1997. "The Witch of the Building." ปริทรรศ หุตางกูร. "แม่มดบนตึก." (Boreetat 2002)

Chamaiporn Saengkrachang. 1992. "The Motorcycle Gangstress." ชมัยพร แสงกระจ่าง. "นางสิงห์มอเตอร์ไซค์." (Chamaiporn 1992)

Chatchawan Kotsongkram. 1994. "The Far Away Person." ชัชวาลย์ โคตรสงคราม. "ผู้ห่างไกล." (Chatchawan 1994)

Eur Unchalee. 1996. "There's No Water Under the Bridge." เอื้อ อัญชลี. "สะพานไม่มีน้ำ." (Eur 1996)

Duanwad Pimwana. 1991. "City of Flowers." เดือนวาด พิมวนา. "เมืองดอกไม้." (Duanwad 1993)

Hoy Loh. 1996. "At the Bedside." ฮอยล้อ. "บนความเปลี่ยนไปของสามัญชน." (Hoy Loh 1996)

Jamlong Fangchonlajitr. 2004. "Those People Have Changed." จำลอง ฝั่งชลจิตร. "พวกเขาเปลี่ยนไป." (Jamlong 2005b)

Kajohnrit Ragsa. 1990. "Cockroaches." ขจรฤทธิ์ รักษา. "แมลงสาบ." (Kajohnrit 1998)

Kon Krailat. 1977. "In the Mirror." กรณ์ ไกรลาศ. "ในกระจกเงา." (Kon 1977; translated in Anderson and Mendiones 1985)

Kon Krailat. 1976. "There Was a Day." กรณ์ ไกรลาศ. "มีอยู่วันหนึ่ง." (Kon 1976)

Kosol Anusim. 1994. "The Marvelous Leaf-Blown Song." โกศล อนุสิม. "เพลงเป่าใบไม้มหัศจรรย์." (Kosol 1994)

Manot Promsingh. 2000. "Kao Pradapdin Night" มาโนช พรหมสิงห์. "คืนข้าวประดับดิน." (Manot 2005a)

Mone Sawasdsri. 1997. "Travelling in Sweden (2): The Train and My Favorite Hat." โมน สวัสดิ์ศรี. "เที่ยวสวีเดน (2): รถไฟกับหมวกใบโปรด." (Mone 2001)

Nirunsak Boonchan. 1992. "Middle Class People, Second-Hand Car, and Mangy Dogs." นิรันศักดิ์ บุญจันทร์. "คนชั้นกลาง รถมือสอง หมาขี้เรื้อน." (Nirunsak 1992)

Paiwarin Khao-Ngam. 1993. "Morning Song." ไพวรินทร์ ขาวงาม. "เพลงยามเช้า." (Paiwarin 1993)

Paiwarin Khao-Ngam. 1995. *Banana Tree Horse.* ไพวรินทร์ ขาวงาม. *ม้าก้านกล้วย.* (Paiwarin 1995; translated by B. Kasemsri)

Panumat. 1990. "Songkran at Home." ภานุมาศ. "สงกรานต์ที่บ้านเกิด." (Raks 1999)

Pira Sudham. 1994. "A Food Vendor and a Taxi Driver." In English. (Pira 1994)

Pirot Boonbragop. 1982. "If You Can't Do It, Then Come Down!" ไพโรจน์ บุญประกอบ. "เป็นไม่ได้ก็ลงมา." (Pirot 1993c)

Plinda Siripong. 1993. "Exchange." พลินดา ศิริพงษ์. "สิ่งแลกเปลี่ยน." (Plinda 1993)

Prachakom Lunachai. 1996. "Rain and Night." ประชาคม ลุนาชัย. "สายฝนและค่ำคืน." (Prachakom 1996d)

Raks Mananya. 1993. "Along the Way." รักษ์ มนัญญา. "ระหว่างการเดินทาง." (Raks 1993c)

Samrung Kampa-oo. 1991. "Oriole." สำเริง คำพะอุ. "นกขมิ้น." (Samrung 2005)

Seinee Saowaphong. 1951. *Wanlaya's Love.* (Seinee 1996; translated by Marcel Barang)

Sila Khomchai. 1988. "Lost Dog." ศิลา โคมฉาย. "เสียหมา." (Sila 1993e)

Sila Khomchai. 1993. "The Family in the Street." ศิลา โคมฉาย. "ครอบครัวกลางถนน." (Sila 1993d; translated by Susan Kepner in Yamada 2002)

Siriworn Kaewkan. 2003. "About a Cell Phone." ศิริวร แก้วกาญจน์. "เกี่ยวกับโทรศัพท์มือถือ." (Siriworn 2003g)

Siriworn Kaewkan. 2003. "About a Letter to the Editor." ศิริวร แก้วกาญจน์. "เกี่ยวกับจดหมายถึงบรรณาธิการ." (Siriworn 2003b)

Siriworn Kaewkan. 2003. "About a One Baht Coin." ศิริวร แก้วกาญจน์. "เกี่ยวกับเหรียญบาท." (Siriworn 2003e)

Siriworn Kaewkan. 2003. "About Animals of All Kinds, Especially Dogs." ศิริวร แก้วกาญจน์. "เกี่ยวกับสัตว์ชนิดต่างๆ โดยเฉพาะหมา." (Siriworn 2003f)

Siriworn Kaewkan. 2003. "About the Person Who Turns off the Lights." ศิริวร แก้วกาญจน์. "เกี่ยวกับนักปิดไฟ." (Siriworn 2003c)

Sridaoruang. "Father." 1975. (Sidaoruang 1994; translated by Rachel Harrison)

Sridaoruang. "The Hand." 1976. (Sidaoruang 1994; translated by Rachel Harrison)

Sridaoruang. 1989. "Plaeng Phanom's Story (1)." ศรีดาวเรือง. "เรื่องเล่าของเพลงพนม (1)." (Sridaoruang 1993c)

Sridaoruang. 1992. "Plaeng Phanom's Story (2)." ศรีดาวเรือง. "เรื่องเล่าของเพลงพนม (2)." (Sridaoruang 1993d)

Sunee Namso. 2006. "The Exemplary Worker." สุนี นามโส. "พนักงานดีเด่น." (Sunee 2006)

Supachai Singyamoot. 1991. "Butterfly." ศุภชัย สิงห์ยะบุศย์. "ผีเสื้อ." (Supachai 1994)

Surachai Janthimathorn. 1967. "On the Third Class Train." สุรชัย จันทิมาธร. "บนรถไฟชั้นสาม." (Surachai 1982a)

Surachai Janthimathorn. 1969. "Train." สุรชัย จันทิมาธร. "รถไฟ." (Surachai 1982b)

Suthipong Thamawuit. 1990. "The City That is Punished for Consumption." สุทธิพงศ์ ธรรมวุฒิ. "นครบริโภคทัณฑ์." (Suthipong 2004)

Tadsanawadee. 1995. "Wall." ทัศนาวดี. "กำแพง." (Tadsanawadee 1995)

Taratip. 1993. "On the Road." ธราธิป. "บนเส้นทาง." (Taratip 1993)

Tarin. 1989. "Fake Beggar." ธาริน. "ขอเทียม." (Tarin 1993)

Tawan Santipaap. 1993. "Reaction." ตะวัน สันติภาพ. "ปฏิกิริยา." (Tawan 1993)

Ussiri Dhammachoti. 1977. "Fifth Time on the Train." อัศศิริ ธรรมโชติ. "รถไฟครั้งที่
ห้า." (Ussiri 2002c)

Ussiri Dhammachoti. 1977. "What's Gone is Gone." อัศศิริ ธรรมโชติ. "เสียแล้วเสียไป."
(Ussiri 1992f)

Ussiri Dhammachoti. 1992. "Angel-Slave." อัศศิริ ธรรมโชติ. "นางฟ้า-ทาสี." (Ussiri 1992c)

Ussiri Dhammachoti. 1992. "The Bountiful Fields." อัศศิริ ธรรมโชติ. "ผืนแผ่นดิน
ตฤณชาติ." (Ussiri 1992e)

Uthain Phromdaeng. 2002. "Khao San Seed." อุเทน พรมแดง. "เมล็ดข้าวสาร." (Uthain
2004c)

Uthain Phromdaeng. 2003. "A Very Long Time." อุเทน พรมแดง. "กัปกัลป์." (Uthain
2003)

Uthain Phromdaeng. 2004. "Desert." อุเทน พรมแดง. "ทะเลทราย." (Uthain 2004d)

Uthain Phromdaeng. 2005. "A Man." อุเทน พรมแดง. "ชายคนหนึ่ง." (Uthain 2005)

Warop Worrapa. 2003. "Khao Sao by Father's Hand." วรภ วรภา. "ข้าวซาวมือพ่อ."
(Warop 2005)

Wat Wanlayangkun. 1975. "Red Hot Morning Glory." วัฒน์ วรรลยางกูร. "ผักบุ้งไฟแดง."
(Wat 1984)

Yohda Hasaemsaeng. 1993. "Return from the Battlefield." ยอดา ฮะเซ็มเซ็ง. "กลับจาก
สมรภูมิ." (Yohda 1999a)

Yohda Hasaemsaeng. 1993. "Trap." ยอดา ฮะเซ็มเซ็ง. "กับดัก." (Yohda 1993)

INTERVIEWS

Chamaiporn Saengkrachang, September 13, 2007

Duanwad Pimwana, October 2, 2007

Eur Unchalee, September 13, 2007

Jamlong Fangchonlajitr, October 31, 2007

Kajohnrit Ragsa, September 13, 2007

Kosol Anusim, September 13, 2007

Niransuk Boonchan, October 2, 2007 (by email)

Nitaya Masavisut, September 21, 2007

Paiwarin Khao-Ngam, November 12, 2007

Prachakom Lunachai, November 12, 2007

Raks Mananya, October 19, 2007

Siriworn Kaewkan, April 29, 2006; May 17, 2007; October 5, 2007

Sridaoruang, September 13, 2007 and September 26, 2007

Suchart Sawasdsri, September 26, 2007

Sunee Namso, November 6, 2007
Surachai Janthimathorn, October 19, 2007
Suthipong Thamawuit, October 4, 2007
Ussiri Dhammachoti, May 22, 2006 and October 19, 2007
Uthain Phromdaeng, September 3, 2005 and September 11, 2007
Vieng Vachirabuason, September 29, 2007
Warop Worrapa, September 20, 2007

SELECTED REFERENCES (ENGLISH)

Note: Thai names are alphabetized by first name.

Abu-Lughod, Lila. 1993. *Writing Women's Worlds: Bedouin Stories*. Berkeley: University of California Press.

Adas, Michael. 1989. *Machines as the Measure of Men: Science, Technology, and Ideologies of Western Dominance*. Ithaca, NY: Cornell University Press.

Afkhami, Mahnaz. 1994. *Women in Exile*. Charlottesville: University Press of Virginia.

Ali, Tariq. 2006. *Conversations with Edward Said*. London: Seagull Books.

Anderson, Benedict R. O'G., and Ruchira Mendiones, eds. and trans. 1985. *In the Mirror: Literature and Politics in Siam in the American Era*. Bangkok: Duang Kamol.

Anuchat Phoungsomlee, and Helen Ross. 1992. *Impacts of Modernisation and Urbanisation in Bangkok: An Integrative Ecological and Biosocial Study*. IPSR Publication 164. Nakhon Pathom, Thailand: Institute for Population and Social Research, Mahidol University.

Aphichat Chamratrithirong. 1985. *Recent Migrants in Bangkok Metropolis: A Follow-up Study of Migrants' Adjustment, Assimilation, and Integration*. Bangkok: Institute of Population and Social Research, Mahidol University, 1985.

———. 1995. *National Migration Survey of Thailand*. IPSR Publication 188. Nakhon Pathom, Thailand: Institute of Population and Social Research, Mahidol University, 1995.

———. 1999. *The Study of Population-Consumption-Environment Link: The Case of Air Pollution in Bangkok*. IPSR Publication 224. Nakhon Pathom, Thailand: Institute for Population and Social Research, Mahidol University, 1999.

Appadurai, Arjun. 1996. *Modernity at Large: Cultural Dimensions of Globalization*. Minneapolis: University of Minnesota Press.

ASEAN COCI [Committee on Culture and Information]. 2000. "Thai Literary Works of the Thonburi and Rattanakosin Periods." Bangkok: ASEAN.

Askew, Marc. 1994. *Interpreting Bangkok: The Urban Question in Thai Studies*. Bangkok: Chulalongkorn University Press.

———. 2002. *Bangkok: Place, Practice and Representation*. London: Routledge.

Aykut, Ebru. 2007. "Constructing Divisions between City and Countryside: *On Fertile Lands* and *Distant*." *Journal of Historical Studies* 5: 69–82.

Banyat Yongyuan. 2001. "Migrant Adjustment in Thailand." PhD diss., Mahidol University.

Barmé, Scot. 2002. *Woman, Man, Bangkok: Love, Sex, and Popular Culture in Thailand*. Lanham, MD: Rowman and Littlefield.

Bello, Walden F., Shea Cunningham, and Kheng Poh Li. 1998. *A Siamese Tragedy: Development and Disintegration in Modern Thailand*. London: Zed Books.

Bishop, Ryan, John Phillips, and Wei-Wei Yeo, eds. 2003. *Postcolonial Urbanism: Southeast Asian Cities and Global Processes*. New York: Routledge.

Boelhower, William Q. 1981. "The Immigrant Novel as Genre." *MELUS* 8 (1): 3–13.

Bongie, Chris. 1991. *Exotic Memories: Literature, Colonialism, and the Fin-de-siècle*. Stanford, CA: Stanford University Press.

Botan. 2002. *Letters from Thailand*. Translated by Susan F. Kepner. Chiang Mai, Thailand: Silkworm Books.

Brummelhuis, Han ten, and Jeremy Kemp, eds. 1984. *Strategies and Structures in Thai Society*. Amsterdam: Antropologisch-Sociologisch Centrum, University of Amsterdam.

Cate, Sandra. 1999. "Cars-Stuck-Together: Tourism and the Bangkok Traffic Jam." In *Converging Interests: Traders, Travelers, and Tourists in Southeast Asia*, edited by Jill Forshee, Christina Fink, and Sandra Cate, 23–50. Berkeley: International and Area Studies, University of California at Berkeley.

Chakchai Sueprasertsitthi. 2004. "Urbanization in Thailand, 1960–2000." Master's thesis, Mahidol University.

Chalongphob Sussangkarn, and Yongyuth Chalamwong. 1994. "Development Strategies and Their Impacts on Labour Markey and Migration: Thai Case Study." Unpub. paper presented at the OECD Development Centre Workshop on Development Strategy, Employment and Migration, Paris, France, 11–13 July.

Chambers, Iain. 1994. *Migrancy, Culture, Identity, Comedia*. London: Routledge.

Chant, Sylvia H. 1992. *Gender and Migration in Developing Countries*. London: Belhaven Press.

Chart Korbjitti. 2001. *The Judgment*. Translated by Phongdeit Jiangphatthana-kit and Marcel Barang. Nakhon Ratchasima: Howling Books.

Chatsumarn Kabilsingh. 1991. *Thai Women in Buddhism*. Berkeley: Parallax Press.

Chetana Nagavajara. 1996. *Comparative Literature from a Thai Perspective: Collected Articles, 1978–1992*. Bangkok: Chulalongkorn University Press.

Chitakasem Manas, ed. 1995. *Thai Literary Traditions*. Bangkok: Institute of Thai Studies, Chulalongkorn University.

Cohen, Erik. 1996. *Thai Tourism: Hill Tribes, Islands and Open-Ended Prostitution: Collected Papers*. Bangkok: White Lotus.

Dawahare, Anthony. 1996. "Review: *Ethnic Passages: Literary Immigrants in Twentieth-Century America* by Thomas J. Ferraro." *MELUS* 21 (2): 182–84.

Drakakis-Smith, D. W. 2000. *Third World Cities*. 2nd ed. London: Routledge.

Ekachai Sanitsuda. 1990. *Behind the Smile: Voices of Thailand*. Bangkok: Thai Development Support Committee.

Eliasova, Vera. 2006. "A Cab of Her Own: Immigration and Mobility in Iva Pekárková's Gimme the Money." *Contemporary Literature* 47 (4): 636-68.

Elson, Robert E. 1999. "International Commerce, the State and Society: Economic and Social Change." In *The Cambridge History of Southeast Asia, Volume Two, Part One, from c. 1800 to the 1930s*, edited by Nicholas Tarling, 127–91. Cambridge: Cambridge University Press.

Forbes, D. K. 1996. *Asian Metropolis: Urbanisation and the Southeast Asian City*. New York: Oxford University Press.

Frank, Soren. 2006. "Transgressive 'Space Travels' and 'Time Travels' in Grass's *Dog Years*." In *Quest* 2. Accessed at http://www.qub.ac.uk/sites/QUEST/FileStore/Filetoupload,52383,en.pdf.

Fried, Istvan. 2004. "Folk Odysseus in History: Migration and Literature in East-Central Europe." *Neohelicon* 31 (1): 69–77.

Fuller, Thomas. 2007. "Bangkok's Template for Breathable Air." *International Herald Tribune*, 24–25 February, A1.

Gabriel, Michelle. 2006. "Youth Migration and Social Advancement: How Young People Manage Emerging Differences between Themselves and Their Hometown." *Journal of Youth Studies* 9 (1): 33–46.

Gaonkar, Dilip Parameshwar. 2001. *Alternative Modernities*. Durham, NC: Duke University Press.

Garrett, Leah. 2001. "Trains and Train Travel in Modern Yiddish Literature." *Jewish Social Studies* 7 (2): 67–88.

Geertz, Clifford. *Negara: The Theatre State in Nineteenth-Century Bali*. Princeton: Princeton University Press, 1980.

Girling, J. L. S. 1996. *Interpreting Development: Capitalism, Democracy, and the Middle Class in Thailand*. Ithaca, NY: Southeast Asia Program, Cornell University.

Gnisci, Armando. 1998. *La letteratura italiana della migrazione*. Roma: Lilith.

Goldstein, Sidney. 1972. *Urbanization in Thailand 1947–1967*. Rev. ed. Bangkok: Institute of Population Studies, Chulalongkorn University.

———. 1979. *Migration and Rural Development: Research Directions on Interrelations*. Rome: FAO.

Goldstein, Sidney, and Alice Goldstein. 1986. *Migration in Thailand: A Twenty-Five-Year Review, Papers of the East-West Population Institute 100*. Honolulu: East-West Center.

Goss, Jon. 2000. "Urbanization." In Leinbach and Ulack, *Southeast Asia*, 110–32.

Green, Sarah, Gerry Hendershot, Laurie McCutcheon, and Penporn Pirasawat. 1978. *Comparative Studies of Migrant Adjustment in Asian Cities*. Providence, RI: Population Studies and Training Center, Brown University.

Greenbaum, Alex. 2002. "Asia and the American Model." *The Globalist*, 1 August.

Islam, Nazrul. 1985. "Rural-Urban Migration in Asia: Its Patterns, Impact and Policy

Implications." *HSD Working Papers*. Bangkok: Human Settlements Division, Asian Institute of Technology.

Jameson, Fredric, and Masao Miyoshi. 1998. *The Cultures of Globalization*. Durham, NC: Duke University Press.

Jeffrey, Leslie Ann. 2002. *Sex and Borders: Gender, National Identity, and Prostitution Policy in Thailand*. Vancouver: UBC Press.

Kain, Geoffrey, ed. 1997. *Ideas of Home: Literature of Asian Migration*. East Lansing: Michigan State University Press.

Kaminsky, Amy K. 1999. *After Exile: Writing the Latin American Diaspora*. Minneapolis: University of Minnesota Press.

Kampoon Boontawee. 1987. *A Child of the Northeast*. Translated by Susan F. Kepner. Bangkok: Duang Kamol.

Kaplan, Caren. 1996. *Questions of Travel: Postmodern Discourses of Displacement*. Durham, NC: Duke University Press.

Kepner, Susan F. 1990. "On a Cloudy Morning." *Tenggara* 29: 90–99.

———, ed. and trans. 1996. *The Lioness in Bloom: Modern Thai Fiction About Women*. Berkeley: University of California Press.

———. 1998. "A Civilized Woman: A Cultural Biography of M.L. Boonlua Tepyasuwan." PhD diss., University of California, Berkeley.

———. 2004. *Married to the Demon King*. Chiang Mai, Thailand: Silkworm Books.

Khonkhai Khamman. 1982. *The Teachers of Mad Dog Swamp*. Translated by Gehan Wijeyewardene. St. Lucia: University of Queensland Press.

King, Russell, John Connell, and Paul White, eds. 1995. *Writing across Worlds: Literature and Migration*. London: Routledge.

Klausner, William. 1997. *Thai Culture in Transition*. Bangkok: Siam Society.

Klima, Alan. 2002. *The Funeral Casino: Meditation, Massacre, and Exchange with the Dead in Thailand*. Princeton: Princeton University Press.

Koret, Peter. 1995. "Whispered So Softly It Resounds through the Forest, Spoken So Loudly It Can Hardly Be Heard: The Art of Parallelism in Lao Literature." In Chitakasem Manas, *Thai Literary Traditions*, 265–98.

Korff, Rudiger. 1986. *Bangkok: Urban System and Everyday Life*. Saarbrucken: Breitenbach.

———. 1996. "An Urban Revolution: Globalisation and Civilisation in the Concrete Jungle?" Working Paper 248. Bielefeld: Sociology of Development Research Centre, Bielefeld University.

Korinek, Kim, Barbara Entwisle, and Aree Jampaklay. 2005. "Through Thick and Thin: Layers of Social Ties and Urban Settlement among Thai Migrants." *American Sociological Review* 70 (5): 779–800.

Kritaya Archavanitkul. 1988. *Migration and Urbanisation in Thailand, 1980: The Urban-Rural Continuum Analysis*. IPSR Publication 122. Nakhon Pathom, Thailand: Institute for Population and Social Research, Mahidol University.

Kukrit Pramoj. 1999. *Many Lives*. Translated by Meredith Borthwick. Chiang Mai, Thailand: Silkworm Books.

Kutsche, Paul. 1994. *Voices of Migrants: Rural-Urban Migration in Costa Rica.* Gainsville: University Press of Florida.

Laroussi, Farid. 2002. "Literature in Migration." *The European Legacy* 7 (6): 709–22.

Lehan, Richard D. 1998. *The City in Literature: An Intellectual and Cultural History.* Berkeley: University of California Press.

Leinbach, Thomas R., and Richard Ulack, eds. 2000. *Southeast Asia: Diversity and Development.* Upper Saddle River, NJ: Prentice Hall, 2000.

Lewis, David, Dennis Rodgers, and Michael Woolcock. 2005. "The Fiction of Development: Literary Representation as a Source of Authoritative Knowledge." *Journal of Development Studies* 44 (2): 198–216.

Light, Ivan H., and Steven J. Gold. 2000. *Ethnic Economies.* San Diego, CA: Academic Press.

Lightfoot, Paul, Theodore Fuller, and Kamnuansilpa Peerasit. 1983. *Circulation and Interpersonal Networks Linking Rural and Urban Areas: The Case of Roi-Et, Northeastern Thailand. Papers of the East-West Population Institute 84.* Honolulu: East-West Population Institute, East-West Center.

Lim, Lin Lean, ed. 1998. *The Sex Sector: The Economic and Social Bases of Prostitution in Southeast Asia.* Geneva: International Labour Office.

Lim, Shirley Geok-lin, and Cheng Lok Chua, eds. 2000. *Tilting the Continent: Southeast Asian American Writing.* Minneapolis, MN: New Rivers Press.

Ling, Richard Seyler. 2004. *The Mobile Connection: The Cell Phone's Impact on Society.* San Francisco: Morgan Kaufmann.

Lo, Fu-chen, and Yue-man Yeung, eds. 1996. *Emerging World Cities in Pacific Asia.* Tokyo: United Nations University Press.

Lockard, Craig A. 1998. *Dance of Life: Popular Music and Politics in Southeast Asia.* Honolulu: University of Hawaii Press.

Loos, Tamara L. 2006. *Subject Siam: Family, Law, and Colonial Modernity in Thailand.* Ithaca, NY: Cornell University Press.

Lutz, Tom. 2005. "Spending Time." In *Consumption in an Age of Information*, edited by Sande Cohen and R. L. Rutsky, 41–60. Oxford: Berg.

MacLean, Gerald M., Donna Landry, and Joseph P. Ward, eds. 1999. *The Country and the City Revisited: England and the Politics of Culture, 1550–1850.* Cambridge: Cambridge University Press.

Maeda, Ai. 2004. *Text and the City: Essays on Japanese Modernity.* Edited by James A. Fujii. Durham, NC: Duke University Press.

Majaj, Lisa Suhair. 1999. "The Hyphenated Author: Emerging Genre of 'Arab-American Literature' Poses Questions of Definition, Ethnicity and Art." *Aljadid* 5 (26).

Masavisut Nitaya, and Matthew Grose. 1996. *The S.E.A. Write Anthology of Thai Short Stories and Poems.* Chiang Mai, Thailand: Silkworm Books.

Mattani Mojdara Rutnin. 1988. *Modern Thai Literature: The Process of Modernization and the Transformation of Values.* Bangkok, Thailand: Thammasat University Press.

McGee, T. G. 1967. *The Southeast Asian City: A Social Geography of the Primate Cities of Southeast Asia*. London: Bell.

―――. 1997. *Five Decades of Urbanization in Southeast Asia: A Personal Encounter*. Hong Kong: Hong Kong Institute of Asia-Pacific Studies, Chinese University of Hong Kong.

McGee, T. G., and Ira M. Robinson, eds. 1995. *The Mega-Urban Regions of Southeast Asia*. Vancouver: UBC Press.

McGrath, Brian. 2006. "Modernities and Memories in Bangkok." *Nakhara: Journal of Oriental Design and Planning* 1: 25–40.

McKenna, Teresa. 1997. *Migrant Song: Politics and Process in Contemporary Chicano Literature*. Austin: University of Texas Press.

Medhi Krongkaew. 1996. "The Changing Urban System in a Fast-Growing City and Economy: The Case of Bangkok and Thailand." In *Emerging World Cities in Pacific Asia*, edited by Fu-chen Lo and Yue-man Yeung, 286–334. Tokyo: United Nations University Press.

Michinobu, Ryoko. 2004. "Configuring an Ideal Self through Maintaining a Family Network: Northern Thai Factory Women in an Industrializing Society." *Southeast Asian Studies* 42 (1): 26–45.

Mills, Mary Beth. 1997. "Contesting the Margins of Modernity: Women, Migration, and Consumption in Thailand." *American Ethnologist* 24 (1): 37–61.

―――. 1999. *Thai Women in the Global Labor Force: Consuming Desires, Contested Selves*. New Brunswick, NJ: Rutgers University Press.

Missingham, Bruce D. 2003. *The Assembly of the Poor in Thailand: From Local Struggles to National Protest Movement*. Chiang Mai, Thailand: Silkworm Books.

Montri Sriyong. "Speech of Montri Sriyong, Thai Awardee." S.E.A. Write Awards Ceremony, 2007.

Montri Umavijani. 1978. *The Domain of Thai Literature*. Bangkok: Prachandra Printing Press.

Moore, Christopher G. 2006. *Heart Talk: Say What You Feel in Thai*. Bangkok: Heaven Lake Press.

Morris, Rosalind C. 2000. *In the Place of Origins: Modernity and Its Mediums in Northern Thailand*. Durham, NC: Duke University Press.

Mosby, Dorothy E. 2003. *Place, Language, and Identity in Afro-Costa Rican Literature*. Columbia: University of Missouri Press.

Muller, Gilbert H. 1999. *New Strangers in Paradise: The Immigrant Experience and Contemporary American Fiction*. Lexington: University Press of Kentucky.

Myers, David. 1994. "Pira Sudham and the Rape of the Esarn People of Northeastern Thailand." *Asian Studies Review* 18 (2): 77–87.

Nithi Eoseewong. 2005. *Pen and Sail: Literature and History in Early Bangkok Including the History of Bangkok in the Chronicles of Ayutthaya*. Edited by Chris Baker, Ben Anderson, and Craig J. Reynolds. Chiang Mai, Thailand: Silkworm Books.

O'Connor, Richard A. 1983. *A Theory of Indigenous Southeast Asian Urbanism. Research Notes and Discussions Paper 38*. Singapore: Institute of Southeast Asian Studies.

Ockey, Jim. 1999. "Creating the Thai Middle Class." In *Culture and Privilege in Capitalist Asia*, edited by Michael Pinches, 231–51. London: Routledge.

Paerregaard, Karsten. 1997. *Linking Separate Worlds: Urban Migrants and Rural Lives in Peru*. Oxford: Berg.

Paiwarin Khao-Ngam. 1995. *Banana Tree Horse and Other Poems*. Translated by B. Kasemsri. Bangkok: Amarin.

Palen, J. John. 1997. *The Urban World*. 5th ed. New York: McGraw-Hill.

Parati, Graziella, ed. 1999. *Mediterranean Crossroads: Migration Literature in Italy*. Madison, NJ: Fairleigh Dickinson University Press.

Pasuk, Phongpaichit, and Chris Baker. 2004. *Thaksin: The Business of Politics in Thailand*. Chiang Mai, Thailand: Silkworm Books.

P. E. N. International. 1984. *Thai P.E.N. Anthology: Short Stories and Poems of Social Consciousness*. Thailand: Amarin Press.

Phillips, Herbert P. 1987. *Modern Thai Literature: With an Ethnographic Interpretation*. Honolulu: University of Hawaii Press.

Pira Sudham. 1988. *Monsoon Country*. Bangkok: Shire Books.

———. 1994. *People of Esarn*. 7th ed. Bangkok: Shire Books.

———. 1996. *Tales of Thailand*. Bangkok: Shire Books.

Platt, Martin B. 2002. "Regionalism and Modern Thai Literature." PhD diss., School of Oriental and African Studies, University of London.

Pongpaiboon Suthiwong. 1995. "Local Literature of Southern Thailand." In Chitakasem Manas, *Thai Literary Traditions*, 218–47.

Ponzanesi, Sandra, and Daniela Merolla. *Migrant Cartographies: New Cultural and Literary Spaces in Post-Colonial Europe*. Lanham, MD: Lexington Books, 2005.

Poonotoke Dhawat. 1995. "A Comparative Study of Isan and Lanna Thai Literature." In Chitakasem Manas, *Thai Literary Traditions*, 248–64.

Pratt, Mary Louise. 1992. *Imperial Eyes: Travel Writing and Transculturation*. London: Routledge.

Procter, James. 2003. *Dwelling Places: Postwar Black British Writing*. New York: Manchester University Press.

Rabibhadana, Akin. 1993. *Social Inequality: A Source of Conflict in the Future*. Bangkok: TDRI.

Reynolds, Craig J., ed. 1991. *National Identity and Its Defenders, Thailand, 1939–1989. Monash Papers on Southeast Asia 25*. Clayton, Victoria: Centre of Southeast Asian Studies, Monash University.

Richter, Kerry. 1997. *Migration and the Rural Family: Sources of Support and Strain in a Mobile Society: Report of the Northeastern Follow-up to the National Migration Survey*. IPSR Publication 190. Nakhon Pathom, Thailand: Institute for Population and Social Research, Mahidol University, 1997.

Roberson, Susan L. 1998. *Women, America, and Movement: Narratives of Relocation.* Columbia: University of Missouri Press.

Rotella, Carlo. 1998. *October Cities: The Redevelopment of Urban Literature.* Berkeley: University of California Press.

Roy, Ananya. 2003. *City Requiem, Calcutta: Gender and the Politics of Poverty.* Minneapolis: University of Minnesota Press.

Roy, Ananya, and Nezar AlSayyad, eds. 2004. *Urban Informality: Transnational Perspectives from the Middle East, Latin America, and South Asia.* Lanham, MD: Lexington Books.

Ruland, Jurgen, ed. 1996. *The Dynamics of Metropolitan Management in Southeast Asia.* Singapore: Institute of Southeast Asian Studies.

Rushdie, Salman. 2002. *Step Across This Line: Collected Nonfiction 1992–2002.* New York: Random House.

Ruskin, John, Edward T. Cook, and Alexander D. Oligvy Wedderburn. 1903. *The Works of John Ruskin.* London: G. Allen.

Said, Edward W. 2000. *Reflections on Exile and Other Essays.* Cambridge, MA: Harvard University Press.

Said, Edward W., and Gauri Viswanathan. 2001. *Power, Politics, and Culture: Interviews with Edward W. Said.* New York: Pantheon Books.

Samruam Singh. 2008 [1998]. *Voices from the Thai Countryside.* Edited and translated by Katherine A. Bowie. Madison: University of Wisconsin Press.

Sarker, Sonita, and Esha Niyogi De. 2002. *Trans-Status Subjects: Gender in the Globalization of South and Southeast Asia.* Durham, NC: Duke University Press.

Sassen, Saskia. 1999. *Guests and Aliens.* New York: New Press.

———. 2001. *The Global City: New York, London, Tokyo.* 2nd ed. Princeton, NJ: Princeton University Press.

Savasdisara Tongchai. 1983. "Qualitative and Quantitative Factors in Rural-Urban Migration in Thailand." PhD diss., University of Michigan.

Scruggs, Charles. 1993. *Sweet Home: Invisible Cities in the Afro-American Novel.* Baltimore, MD: Johns Hopkins University Press.

Seinee, Saowaphong. 1996. *Wanlaya's Love.* Translated by Marcel Barang. Bangkok: Thai Modern Classics.

Siburapha. 1990. *Behind the Painting and Other Stories.* Translated by David Smyth. Singapore: Oxford University Press.

Sidaoruang. 1994. *A Drop of Glass and Other Stories.* Translated by Rachel Harrison. Bangkok: Editions Duang Kamol.

Siddall, William R. 1987. "Transportation and the Experience of Travel." *Geographical Review* 77 (3): 309–17.

Simmel, Georg. 2002. "The Metropolis and Mental Life." In *The City Reader*, edited by Gary Bridge and Sophie Watson, 11–19. Oxford: Blackwell.

Simmons, Alan B., Sergio Diaz-Briquets, and Aprodicio A. Laquian. 1977. *Social Change and Internal Migration: A Review of Research Findings from Africa, Asia and Latin America.* Ottawa: International Development Research Centre.

Skinner, G. William. 1957. *Chinese Society in Thailand: An Analytical History*. Ithaca, NY: Cornell University Press.

Smith, David A. 1996. *Third World Cities in Global Perspective: The Political Economy of Uneven Urbanization*. Boulder, CO: Westview Press.

Social Research Institute. 1986. *Wanakam Lanna = Lan Na Literature: Catalogue of 954 Secular Titles among the 3,700 Palm-Leaf Manuscripts Borrowed from Wats throughout Northern Thailand and Preserved on Microfilm at the Social Research Institute of Chiang Mai University*. Chiang Mai, Thailand: Social Research Institute, Chiang Mai University.

Solnit, Rebecca. 1997. *A Book of Migrations: Some Passages in Ireland*. London: Verso.

Sompop Manarangsan. 1989. *Economic Development of Thailand, 1850–1950: Response to the Challenge of the World Economy*. Bangkok: Institute of Asian Studies, Chulalongkorn University.

Sridaorueang. 2004. *The Citizen's Path*. Bangkok: Neo Way Publishing House.

Srisurang Poolthupya. 2001. *ASEAN Short Stories and Poems*. Bangkok: Thai P.E.N. Centre.

Sternstein, Larry. 1984. *Spatial Aspects of Recent Internal Migration to and from Bangkok: An Exploratory Analysis of Data from the 1980 Population and Housing Census*. Bangkok: Department of Policy and Planning, Bangkok Metropolitan Administration.

Stevenson, Robert Louis. 1892. *Across the Plains, with Other Memories and Essays*. London: Chatto and Windus.

Sulak Sivaraksa. 1989. "Siamese Literature and Social Liberation." Occasional Papers 6. [Bangkok]: Santi Pracha Dhamma Institute, Thai Inter-religious Commission for Development.

Supang Chantavanich, and Gary Risser. 1996. *Intra-Regional Migration in South East and East Asia: Theoretical Overview, Trends of Migratory Flows, Labour Linkages, and Implications for Thailand and Thai Migrant Workers*. Bangkok: Asian Research Center for Migration.

Surangkhanang, K. 1994. *The Prostitute*. Translated by David Smyth. Kuala Lumpur: Oxford University Press.

Sureeporn Punpuing. 1992. *Correlates of Commuting Patterns: A Case Study of Bangkok, Thailand*. IPSR Publication 162. Nakhon Pathom: Institute for Population and Social Research, Mahidol University.

Suvanna Kriengkraipetch, and Larry E. Smith. 1992. *Value Conflicts in Thai Society: Agonies of Change Seen in Short Stories*. [Bangkok]: Social Research Institute, Chulalongkorn University.

Teera Ashakul. 1989. "Migration: Trends and Determinants." In *Annual Seminar of the National Economic and Social Development Board's Project on "Promotion of Analysis and Consideration of Population Consequences of Development Planning and Policy in Thailand."* Thailand Development Research Institute.

Tew Bunnag. 2003. *Fragile Days: Tales from Bangkok*. Singapore: SNP International.

Textor, Robert B. 1961. *From Peasant to Pedicab Driver*. 2nd ed. New Haven, CT: Yale University, Southeast Asia Studies.

Thailand National Statistics Office. 1994. *Report of the Migration Survey 1994*. Bangkok: National Statistics Office, Office of the Prime Minister.

———. 1985. *The Survey of Migration into the Bangkok Metropolis and Vicinity, 1984*. Bangkok: National Statistics Office, Office of the Prime Minister.

Thongchai Winichakul. 1994. *Siam Mapped: A History of the Geo-Body of a Nation*. Honolulu: University of Hawaii Press.

———. 2000. "The Quest for Siwilai: A Geographical Discourse of Civilizational Thinking in Late Nineteenth and Early Twentieth-Century Siam." *Journal of Asian Studies* 59 (3): 528–49.

Thorbek, Susanne. 1994. *Gender and Slum Culture in Urban Asia*. London: Zed Books.

Trager, Lillian. 1988. *The City Connection: Migration and Family Interdependence in the Philippines*. Ann Arbor: University of Michigan Press.

Treasury of Thai Literature: The Modern Period. 1988. Bangkok: National Identity Board, Office of the Prime Minister.

UN DIESA (United Nations Department of International Economic and Social Affairs). 1987. *Population Growth and Policies in Mega-Cities: Bangkok*. Population Policy Paper 72. New York: UN.

———. 1991. *Integrating Development and Population Planning in Thailand*. New York: UN.

UN ESCAP (United Nations Economic and Social Commission for Asia and the Pacific). 1982. *Migration, Urbanization, and Development in Thailand*. Comparative Study on Migration, Urbanization, and Development in the ESCAP Region: Country Reports 5. New York: UN.

———. 1988. *Internal Migration and Structural Changes in the Labour Force, Asian Population Studies Series, No. 90*. Bangkok: UN ESCAP.

———. 1995. *Trends, Patterns, and Implications of Rural-Urban Migration in India, Nepal, and Thailand*. New York: UN.

United Nations Human Settlements Programme. 2003. *The Challenge of Slums: Global Report on Human Settlements, 2003*. London: Earthscan Publications.

Van den Abbeele, Georges. 1992. *Travel as Metaphor: From Montaigne to Rousseau*. Minneapolis: University of Minnesota Press.

Vella, Walter F., and Dorothy B. Vella. 1978. *Chaiyo! King Vajiravudh and the Development of Thai Nationalism*. Honolulu: University Press of Hawaii, 1978.

Voravidh Charoenloet, Amara Soonthorndhada, and Sirinan Saiprasert. 1991. *Factory Management, Skill Formation, and Attitudes of Women Workers in Thailand: A Comparison between an American-Owned Electrical Factory and a Japanese-Owned Electrical Factory*. IPSR Publication 157. Nakhon Pathom: Institute for Population and Social Research, Mahidol University.

Wanich Jarungidanan. 1996. *The Capital*. Translated by M. R. Usnisa Sukhsvasti. Bangkok: Translation Center, Faculty of Arts, Chulalongkorn University.

Wanpen Charoentrakulpeeti, Edsel Sajor, and Willi Zimmermann. 2006. "Middle-Class Travel Patterns, Predispositions and Attitudes, and Present-Day Transport Policy in Bangkok, Thailand." *Transport Reviews* 26 (6): 693–712.

Ward, Colleen, and Antony Kennedy. 1994. "Acculturation Strategies, Psychological Adjustment, and Sociocultural Competence during Cross-Cultural Transitions." *International Journal of Intercultural Relations* 18 (3): 329–43

Ward, Simon. 2003. "Trains." In *The Literature of Travel and Exploration: An Encyclopedia*, edited by Jennifer Speake, 1191. New York: Taylor and Francis.

———. 2005. "The Passenger as *Flâneur*? Railway Networks in German-Language Fiction since 1945." *Modern Language Review* 100 (2): 412–28.

Wathinee Boonchalaksi, and Philip Guest. 1994. *Prostitution in Thailand*. IPSR Publication 171. Nakhon Pathom, Thailand: Institute for Population and Social Research, Mahidol University.

Webster, Douglas. 2000. *Financing City-Building: The Bangkok Case*. Urban Dynamics of East Asia Research Project Working Papers. Stanford, CA: Asia/Pacific Research Center, Stanford University.

———. 2002. *On the Edge: Shaping the Future of Peri-Urban East Asia*. Urban Dynamics of East Asia Research Project Working Papers. Stanford, CA: Asia/Pacific Research Center, Stanford University.

———. 2004. *Urbanization Dynamics and Policy Frameworks in Developing East Asia*. Urban Development Working Papers. Washington: World Bank.

Wenk, Klaus. 1995. *Thai Literature: An Introduction*. Bangkok: White Lotus.

Wibha Senanan Kongkananda. 1975. *The Genesis of the Novel in Thailand*. Bangkok: Thai Watana Panich.

Williams, Raymond. 1973. *The Country and the City*. New York: Oxford University Press.

Wilson, Ara. 2004. *The Intimate Economies of Bangkok: Tomboys, Tycoons, and Avon Ladies in the Global City*. Berkeley: University of California Press.

Wissink, Bart, Renske Dijkwel, and Ronald Meijer. 2006. "Bangkok Boundaries: Social Networks in the City of Mubahnchatsan." *Nakhara: Journal of Environmental Design and Planning* 1: 59–74.

Wyatt, David K. *Thailand: A Short History*. New Haven, CT: Yale University Press, 1984.

Yamada, Teri Shaffer. 2002. *Virtual Lotus: Modern Fiction of Southeast Asia*. Ann Arbor: University of Michigan Press.

Zhang, Li. 2001. *Strangers in the City: Reconfigurations of Space, Power, and Social Networks within China's Floating Population*. Stanford, CA: Stanford University Press.

Zukin, Sharon. 2004. *Point of Purchase: How Shopping Changed American Culture*. New York: Routledge.

SELECTED REFERENCES (THAI)

Amphairat Nilprayun and Charan Inta. 1989. *Maeng si hu ha ta – panha ka lae maengmao – suea tai suea non wanakam chadok lanna*. Edited by Panpen Kruathai. Chiang Mai: Khrongkan sueksa wichai khampi bai lan nai phak nuea sathaban wichai sangkhom Chiang Mai University. อำไพรัตน์ นิลประยูร และ จรัญ อินต๊ะ. 2532. แมงสี่หูห้าตา – ปัญหากาและแมงเม่า – เสือตายเสือนอน วรรณกรรมชาดกล้านนา. พรรณเพ็ญ เครือไทย, บรรณาธิการ. เชียงใหม่: โครงการศึกษาวิจัยคัมภีร์ใบลานในภาคเหนือสถาบันวิจัยสังคม มหาวิทยาลัยเชียงใหม่.

Areeya Hutinta. 1996. "Phaplak sangkhom mueang nai rueang san Thai ruam samai rawang phuttasakarat 2534–2536." Master's thesis, Chulalongkorn University. อารียา หุตินทะ. 2539. "ภาพลักษณ์สังคมเมืองในเรื่องสั้นไทยร่วมสมัยระหว่างพุทธศักราช 2534–2536." วิทยานิพนธ์ปริญญาอักษรศาสตรมหาบัณฑิต สาขาวิชาวรรณคดีเปรียบเทียบ ภาควิชาวรรณคดีเปรียบเทียบ คณะอักษรศาสตร์ จุฬาลงกรณ์มหาวิทยาลัย.

Bantoon Klunkachon. 1979. "Khuen phleng khaen." In *Ruam rueang san witthawat chut thi nueng khan rap pi chaona*. Bangkok: Wittawat. บัณฑูร กลั่นจจร. 2522. "คืนเพลงแคน." รวมเรื่องสั้นวิทวัสชุดที่ ๑ ขานรับปีชาวนา. กรุงเทพฯ: วิทวัส.

Boreetat Hootangkoon. 2002. "Mae mot bon tuek." In *Maemot bon tuek*. Bangkok: Rup Chan. (Orig. pub. 1997) ปริทรรศ หุตางกูร. 2545. "แม่มดบนตึก." แม่มดบนตึก. กรุงเทพฯ: รูปจันทร์.

Chamaiporn Saengkrachang. 1992. "Nang singha motoesai." *Cho Karaket 9* (January–March). Edited by Suchart Sawasdsri. Bangkok: Samnak Chang Wanakam. ชมัยพร แสงกระจ่าง. 2535. "นางสิงห์มอเตอร์ไซค์." ช่อการะเกด 9 (มกราคม-มีนาคม). สุชาติ สวัสดิ์ศรี, บรรณาธิการ. กรุงเทพฯ: สำนักช่างวรรณกรรม.

Chatchawan Kotsongkram. 1994. "Muean rotfai cha ma." In *Muean rotfai cha ma*. Bangkok: Praew Samnakpim. Bangkok: Praew Samnakpim. ชัชวาลย์ โคตรสงคราม. 2537. "เหมือนรถไฟจะมา." เหมือนรถไฟจะมา. กรุงเทพฯ: แพรวสำนักพิมพ์.

———. 1994. "Phu hang klai." In *Muean rotfai cha ma*. Bangkok: Praew Samnakpim. ชัชวาลย์ โคตรสงคราม. 2537. "ผู้ห่างไกล." เหมือนรถไฟจะมา. กรุงเทพฯ: แพรวสำนักพิมพ์.

Duanwad Pimwana. 1993. "Mueang dokmai." In *Mueang dokmai*. Bangkok: Praew. เดือนวาด พิมวนา. 2536. "เมืองดอกไม้." เมืองดอกไม้. กรุงเทพฯ: แพรว.

Eur Unchalee. 1996. "Saphan mai mi nam." *Cho Karaket 27* (May–June). Edited by Suchart Sawasdsri. Bangkok: Samnak Chang Wanakam. เอื้อ อัญชลี. 2539. "สะพานไม่มีน้ำ." ช่อการะเกด 27 (พฤษภาคม-มิถุนายน). สุชาติ สวัสดิ์ศรี, บรรณาธิการ. กรุงเทพฯ: สำนักช่างวรรณกรรม.

Hoy Loh. 1993. "Fao khai." *Cho Karaket 14* (April–June). Edited by Suchart Sawasdsri. Bangkok: Samnak Chang Wanakam. ฮอยล้อ. 2536. "เฝ้าไข่." ช่อการะเกด 14 (เมษายน-มิถุนายน). สุชาติ สวัสดิ์ศรี, บรรณาธิการ. กรุงเทพฯ: สำนักช่างวรรณกรรม.

———. 1996. "Bon khwam plianpai khong saman chon." *Cho Karaket 27* (May–June). Edited by Suchart Sawasdsri. Bangkok: Samnak Chang Wanakam. ฮอยล้อ. 2539. "บนความเปลี่ยนไปของสามัญชน." ช่อการะเกด 27 (พฤษภาคม-มิถุนายน). สุชาติ สวัสดิ์ศรี, บรรณาธิการ. กรุงเทพฯ: สำนักช่างวรรณกรรม.

Isara Chusri. 1993. "Roi charik." In *Cho Karaket* 15 (July–September). Edited by Suchart Sawasdsri. Bangkok: Samnak Chang Wanakam. อิสระ ชูศรี. 2536. "รอยจารึก."ช่อการะเกด 15 (กรกฎาคม–กันยายน). สุชาติ สวัสดิ์ศรี, บรรณาธิการ. กรุงเทพฯ: สำนักช่างวรรณกรรม.

Jamlong Fangchonlajitr. 1996. "Khun yai chai di." In *Khop kap dek*. Pathum Thani: Nakon. จำลอง ฝั่งชลจิตร. 2539. "คุณยายใจดี." คนกับเด็ก. ปทุมธานี: นาคร.

———. 1999. *Mueang na yu*. Bangkok: Praew Samnakpim. จำลอง ฝั่งชลจิตร. 2542. เมืองน่าอยู่. กรุงเทพฯ: แพรวสำนักพิมพ์.

———. 1999a. "Khon mot fai." ["คนหมดไฟ."] In Jamlong 1999.

———. 1999b. "Phu khrong ruean." ["ผู้ครองเรือน."] In Jamlong 1999.

———. 2005. *Ligor phuakkhao plian pai*. Bangkok: Praew Samnakpim จำลอง ฝั่งชลจิตร. 2548. ลิกอร์ พวกเขาเปลี่ยนไป. กรุงเทพฯ: แพรวสำนักพิมพ์.

———. 2005a. "Fang mueang tranom." ["ฝั่งเมืองตระนอม."] In Jamlong 2005.

———. 2005b. "Phuakkhao plian pai." ["พวกเขาเปลี่ยนไป."] In Jamlong 2005.

Kajohnrit Ragsa. 1998. "Malaeng sap." (Orig. pub. 1990). In *Nak tok pla*. Bangkok: Ban Nungsue. ขจรฤทธิ์ รักษา. 2541. "แมลงสาบ." นักตกปลา. กรุงเทพฯ: บ้านหนังสือ.

———. 1999. "Nak muai dang." In Raks 1999.

———. 2003. *Mia khong khon angkrit*. Bangkok: Ban Nangsue. ขจรฤทธิ์ รักษา. 2546. เมียของคนอังกฤษ. กรุงเทพฯ: บ้านหนังสือ.

Kanokpong Songsompan. 1993. "Athit thiang khuen." In *Saphan kat*. Bangkok: Nok Si Lueang. กนกพงศ์ สงสมพันธุ์. 2536. "อาทิตย์เที่ยงคืน." สะพานขาด. กรุงเทพฯ: นกสีเหลือง.

Komsun Pongsutham. 1979. "Phleng phloeng thi ban na." In *Ruam rueang san witthawat chut thi nueng khan rap pi chaona*. Bangkok: Wittawat. คมสัน พงษ์สุธรรม. 2522. "เพลงเพลิงที่บ้านนา." รวมเรื่องสั้นวิทวัสชุดที่ ๑ ขานรับปีชาวนา. กรุงเทพฯ: วิทวัส.

Kon Krailat. 1976. "Mi yu wan nueng." In *Rao maichai dokmai tae rao khue chiwit*. Bangkok: Karawek. กรณ์ ไกรลาศ. 2521. "มือยู่วันหนึ่ง." เราไม่ใช่ดอกไม้ แต่ เราคือชีวิต. กรุงเทพฯ: การเวก.

———. 1977. "Nai krachok ngao." In *Khluen chao phraya*. Bangkok: Karawek. (Published in translation in Anderson and Mendiones 1985, 205–217.) กรณ์ ไกรลาศ. 2520. "ในกระจกเงา." คลื่นเจ้าพระยา. กรุงเทพฯ: การเวก.

———. 1978. "Thuk sing muean cha mai klap ma." In *Rao maichai dokmai tae rao khue chiwit*. Bangkok: Karawek. กรณ์ ไกรลาศ. 2521. "ทุกสิ่งเหมือนจะไม่กลับมา." เราไม่ใช่ดอกไม้ แต่ เราคือชีวิต. กรุงเทพฯ: การเวก.

Korn Siriwattano. 1993. "Ban yat lae phawa waetlom chit." In *Mueang dokmai*. Bangkok: Praew. กร ศิริวัฒโณ. 2536. "บ้าน ญาติ และภาวะแวดล้อมจิต." เมืองดอกไม้. กรุงเทพฯ: แพรว.

Kosol Anusim. 1994. "Phleng pao baimai mahatsachan." *Cho Karaket* 17 (January–March). Edited by Suchart Sawasdsri. Bangkok: Samnak Chang Wanakam. โกศล อนุสิม. 2537. "เพลงเป่าใบไม้มหัศจรรย์." ช่อการะเกด 17 (มกราคม–มีนาคม). สุชาติ สวัสดิ์ศรี, บรรณาธิการ. กรุงเทพฯ: สำนักช่างวรรณกรรม.

Koynut. 2005. *Ma nakhon*. Bangkok: Praew Samnakpim. คอยนุช. 2546. หมานคร. กรุงเทพฯ: แพรวสำนักพิมพ์.

Kritthep Sonsilp. 2005. "Dee Lae D." *A Day* 6 (62): 100. กริชเทพ ศรศิลป์. 2548. "ดี้และ ด." *A Day* 6 (62) (เดือนตุลาคม): 100.

Lamul Chanhom. 1991. *Wanakam thongthin lanna*. Chiang Mai: Witthayalai khru Chiang Mai sahawittayalai lanna Chiang Mai. ลมูล จันทน์หอม. 2534. วรรณกรรมท้อง ถิ่นล้านนา. เชียงใหม่: วิทยาลัยครูเชียงใหม่ สหวิทยาลัยล้านนาเชียงใหม่.

Mahannop Chomchalao. 1995. "Thongtha phu sawaengha langkha khum hua." In *Dekchai sam ta phu bang uen tok long ma bon lok*. Bangkok: Klet Thai. มหรรณพ โฉมเฉลา. 2538. "ทองทาผู้แสวงหาหลังคาคุ้มหัว." เด็กชายสามตา ผู้บังเอิญตกลงมาบนโลก. กรุงเทพฯ: เคล็ดไทย.

Manot Promsingh. 2005. *Sai lom bon thanon boran*. Bangkok: Praew Samnakpim. มาโนช พรหมสิงห์. 2548. สายลมบนถนนโบราณ. กรุงเทพฯ: แพรวสำนักพิมพ์.

———. 2005a. "Khuen khao pradap din." ["คืนข้าวประดับดิน."] In Manot 2005.

———. 2005b. "Khrap chakkachan." ["คราบจักจั่น."] In Manot 2005.

———. 2005c. "Saphan." ["สะพาน."] In Manot 2005.

Mone Sawasdsri. 1996. "Yindi S.E.A.Write." In *Banthuek khong Mone*. Bangkok: Writer Magazine. โมน สวัสดิ์ศรี. 2539. "ยินดีซีไรท์." บันทึกของโมน. กรุงเทพฯ: Writer Magazine.

———. 2001. "Thiao Sweden (2): rotfai kap muak bai prot." In *Chan chala ti song*. Bangkok: Ik Nueang Samnakpim. โมน สวัสดิ์ศรี. 2544. "เที่ยวสวีเดน (2): รถไฟกับหมวก ใบโปรด." ชานชาลาที่สอง. กรุงเทพฯ: อีกหนึ่งสำนักพิมพ์.

Nai San Wittaya. 1978. "Pang man sadung." In *Ruam rueang san chak siamrath sapda wichan*. Bangkok: Siamrath. นายสันต์ วิทยา. 2521. "ปางมารสะดุ้ง." รวมเรื่องสั้น จาก สยามรัฐสัปดาห์วิจารณ์. กรุงเทพฯ: สยามรัฐ.

Nara Komnamool. 2004. *Rabop khonsong satharana nai ko tho mo*. Bangkok: Seven Printing Group. นระ คมนามูล. 2547. ระบบขนส่งสาธารณะในกทม. กรุงเทพฯ: เซเว่น พริ้นติ้ง กรุ๊ป.

Narin Nuanplang. 1993. "Rak khong mae." *Cho Karaket* 13 (January–March). Edited by Suchart Sawasdsri. Bangkok: Samnak Chang Wanakam. นรินทร์ นวลปลั่ง. 2536. "รักของแม่." ช่อการะเกด 13 (มกราคม–มีนาคม). สุชาติ สวัสดิ์ศรี, บรรณาธิการ. กรุงเทพฯ: สำนักช่างวรรณกรรม.

Narong Chanrueang. 1992. "Kwa cha khiao." In *Mit mai mi khom*. ณรงค์ จันทร์เรือง. 2535. "กว่าจะเขียว." มีดไม่มีคม. กรุงเทพฯ: สำนักพิมพ์กำแพง.

———. 2001. "Klap ban." In *Phrung ni*. Bangkok: Dokya. ณรงค์ จันทร์เรือง. 2544. "กลับบ้าน." พรุ่งนี้. กรุงเทพฯ: ดอกหญ้า.

Nattawut Suthisongkram. 1979. *Wanakam pak tai*. Bangkok: Rueangsilp. ณัฐวุฒิ สุทธิสงคราม. 2522. วรรณกรรมปักษ์ใต้. กรุงเทพฯ: เรืองศิลป์.

Ngamphit Satsa-nguan. 2002. *Pruettikam charachon nai khet krungthep maha nakhon*. Bangkok: Text and Journal Publication. งามพิศ สัตย์สงวน. 2545. พฤติกรรม จราจรในเขตกรุงเทพมหานคร. กรุงเทพฯ: เท็กซ์ แอนด์เจอร์นัล พับลิเคชั่น.

Nirunsak Boonchan. 1992. *Sai fon mot-ngam lae phu dueat ron*. Bangkok: Dokya. นิรัน ศักดิ์ บุญจันทร์. 2535. "บ้านของลูกชาย." สายฝน มดง่าม และผู้เดือดร้อน. กรุงเทพฯ: ดอกหญ้า.

———. 1992a. "Ban khong luk chai." ["บ้านของลูกชาย."] In Nirunsak 1992.

———. 1992b. "Khon chan klang rot muesong ma khiruean." ["คนชั้นกลาง รถมือสอง หมาขี้เรื้อน."] In Nirunsak 1992.

Paiwarin Khao-ngam. 1993. "Phleng yam chao." In *Mueang dokmai*. ไพวรินทร์ ขาวงาม. 2536. "เพลงยามเช้า." เมืองดอกไม้. กรุงเทพฯ: แพรว.

———. 2004. *Ma kan kluai*. Bangkok: Praew Samnakpim. Translated by B. Kasemsri in Paiwarin 1995. ไพวรินทร์ ขาวงาม. 2547. ม้าก้านกล้วย. กรุงเทพฯ: แพรวสำนักพิมพ์.

Panumat. 1999. "Songkran thi ban koet." In Raks 1999.

Phenkhae Phukphan. 1992. "Ruedu nam lak." *Cho Karaket* 10 (April–May). Edited by Suchart Sawasdsri. Bangkok: Samnak Chang Wanakam. เพ็ญแข ผูกพัน. 2535. "ฤดู น้ำหลาก." ช่อการะเกด 10 (เมษายน–พฤษภาคม). สุชาติ สวัสดิ์ศรี, บรรณาธิการ. กรุงเทพฯ: สำนักช่างวรรณกรรม.

Phraisan Phromnoi. 1979. "Fan laeng." In *Ruam rueang san witthawat chut thi nueng khan rap pi chaona*. Bangkok: Wittawat. ไพรสันต์ พรหมน้อย. 2522. "ฝันแล้ง." รวม เรื่องสั้นวิทวัสชุดที่ ๑ ขานรับปีชาวนา. กรุงเทพฯ: วิทวัส.

Piboonsak Lakornpol. 1979. "Fai pa." In *Ruam rueang san witthawat chut thi nueng khan rap pi chaona*. Bangkok: Wittawat. พิบูลศักดิ์ ละครพล. 2522. "ไฟป่า." รวมเรื่อง สั้นวิทวัสชุดที่ ๑ ขานรับปีชาวนา. กรุงเทพฯ: วิทวัส.

Pinampai Siripuchaka. 2000. "Phaplack chon klum noi nai nawaniyai Thai: Kan wichan choeng sangkhom." Master's thesis, Chulalongkorn University. พิณอำไพ สิริปูชกะ. 2543. "ภาพลักษณ์ชนกลุ่มน้อยในนวนิยายไทย: การวิจารณ์เชิงสังคม." วิทยานิพนธ์ ปริญญาอักษรศาสตรมหาบัณฑิต สาขาวรรณคดีเปรียบเทียบ ภาควิชาวรรณคดีเปรียบเทียบ คณะอักษรศาสตร์ จุฬาลงกรณ์มหาวิทยาลัย.

Pirot Boonbragop. 1993. *Jintanakan mai mi mai lek*. Bangkok: Duangkamol Wanakam. ไพโรจน์ บุญประกอบ. 2536. จินตนาการไม่มีหมายเลข. กรุงเทพฯ: ดวงกมล วรรณกรรม.

———. 1993a. "Hon thang." ["หนทาง."] In Pirot 1993.

———. 1993b. "Khattakam." ["ฆาตกรรม."] In Pirot 1993.

———. 1993c. "Pen mai dai ko long ma." ["เป็นไม่ได้ก็ลงมา."] In Pirot 1993. (Orig. pub. 1982)

———. 1993d. "Wisai songkhram." ["วิสัยสงคราม."] In Pirot 1993.

Plinda Siripong. 1993. "Sing laek plian." *Cho Karaket* 15 (July–September). Edited by Suchart Sawasdsri. Bangkok: Samnak Chang Wanakam. พลินดา ศิริพงษ์. 2536. "สิ่ง แลกเปลี่ยน." ช่อการะเกด 15 (กรกฎาคม–กันยายน). สุชาติ สวัสดิ์ศรี, บรรณาธิการ. กรุงเทพฯ: สำนักช่างวรรณกรรม.

Prachakom Lunachai. 1996. *Luk kaew samrong lae rueangsan uen uen*. Bangkok: Duangkamol Wanakam. ประชาคม ลุนาชัย. 2539. ลูกแก้วสำรองและเรื่องสั้นอื่น ๆ. กรุงเทพฯ: ดวงกมลวรรณกรรม.

———. 1996a. "Kot lek kho thi ha." ["กฎเหล็กข้อที่ห้า."] In Prachakom 1996.

———. 1996b. "Luk thalay." ["ลูกทะเล."] In Prachakom 1996.

———. 1996c. "Phuying lai chan." ["ผู้หญิงหลายชั้น."] In Prachakom 1996.

———. 1996d. "Sai fon lae kham khuen." ["สายฝนและค่ำคืน."] In Prachakom 1996.

———. 1998. *Tua lakhon tok samai*. Bangkok: Sahakan Kon wanakam. ประชาคม ลุ นาชัย. 2541. ตัวละครตกสมัย. กรุงเทพฯ: สหการคนวรรณกรรม.

———. 1998a. "Klang pa concrete." ["กลางป่าคอนกรีต."] In Prachakom 1998.

———. 1998b. "Ko klang mueang." ["เกาะกลางเมือง."] In Prachakom 1998.

———. 1998c. "Nak chok klap ban." ["นักชกกลับบ้าน."] In Prachakom 1998.

Prai Phailom. 1978. "Rueang ngai ngai khong khon song khon." In *Ruam rueang san chak Siamrath sapda wichan*. Bangkok: Siamrath. ไพร ไผ่ล้อม. 2521. "เรื่องง่าย ง่ายของคน 2 คน." รวมเรื่องสั้นจาก สยามรัฐสัปดาห์วิจารณ์. กรุงเทพฯ: สยามรัฐ.

Prateep Chumphol. 1976. *Wanakam phak tai*. Bangkok: Sueksa Sampan. ประทีป ชุมพล บรรณาธิการ. 2519. วรรณกรรมภาคใต้. กรุงเทพฯ: ศึกษาสัมพันธ์.

Raks Mananya. 1993. *Rawang kan doen thang*. Bangkok: Dokya. รักษ์ มนัญญา. 2536. ระหว่างการเดินทาง. กรุงเทพฯ: ดอกหญ้า.

Raks Mananya. 1993a. "Lai khaen." ["ลายแคน."] In Raks 1993.

———. 1993b. "Phu khuen klap." ["ผู้คืนกลับ."] In Raks 1993.

———. 1993c. "Rawang kan doen thang." ["ระหว่างการเดินทาง."] In Raks 1993.

———. 1994. *Game wisaman*. Bangkok: Dokya. รักษ์ มนัญญา. 2537. เกมวิสามัญ. กรุงเทพฯ: ดอกหญ้า.

———, ed. 1999. *Rueang san lae bot kawi diden pho so 2532–2538 rangwan khatsan samakhom phasa lae nangsue haeng prathet Thai*. Bangkok: Double Nine Printing. รักษ์ มนัญญา, บรรณาธิการ. 2542. เรื่องสั้นและบทกวีดีเด่น พ.ศ. 2532–2538 รางวัลคัดสรร สมาคมภาษาและหนังสือแห่งประเทศไทย. กรุงเทพฯ: ดับเบิ้ลนายน์ พริ้นติ้ง.

———. 2004. *Pen rueang lao thi son hai rao toepto*. Bangkok: Dokya. รักษ์ มนัญญา. 2547. เป็นเรื่องเล่าที่สอนเราให้เติบโต. กรุงเทพฯ: ดอกหญ้า.

Rewat Panpipat. 2004. *Mae nam ramluek*. Bangkok: Rup Chan. เรวัติ พันพิพัฒน์. 2547. แม่น้ำรำลึก. กรุงเทพฯ: รูปจันทร์.

Rom Ratiwam. 1987. *Pui nun kap duangdao*. Bangkok: Silapa Wanakam. รมย์ รติวัน. 2530. ปุยนุ่นกับดวงดาว. กรุงเทพฯ: ศิลปวรรณกรรม.

Saikam Pakai. 1993. "Phi chai." *Cho Karaket* 16 (October–December). Edited by Suchart Sawasdsri. Bangkok: Samnak Chang Wanakam. สายคำ ผกาย. 2536. "พี่ชาย." ช่อการะเกด 16 (ตุลาคม–ธันวาคม). สุชาติ สวัสดิ์ศรี, บรรณาธิการ. กรุงเทพฯ: สำนัก ช่างวรรณกรรม.

Saksiri Meesomsueb. 1994. *Mue nan si khao*. Bangkok: Silp Siam Kampim. ศักดิ์ศิริ มีสมสืบ. 2537. มือนั้นสีขาว. กรุงเทพฯ: ศิลป์สยามการพิมพ์.

Samrung Kampa-oo. 2005. "Nok khamin." In *Kon arun cha rung*. Bangkok: Pirab. สำเริง คำพะออ. "นกขมิ้น." ก่อนอรุณจะรุ่ง. กรุงเทพฯ: พิราบ.

Sasithorn Yakon. 1997. "Tua lakhon wikoncharit nai rueang san khong Thai (pho so 2520–2538)." Master's thesis, Chulalongkorn University. ศศิธร ยากรณ์. 2540. "ตัว ละครวิกลจริตในเรื่องสั้นไทย (พ.ศ. 2520–2538)." วิทยานิพนธ์ปริญญาอักษรศาสตรมหาบัณฑิต สาขาภาษาไทย ภาควิชาภาษาไทย คณะอักษรศาสตร์ จุฬาลงกรณ์มหาวิทยาลัย.

Siaochan Raemprai. 1993. *Khap khan khang nai*. Bangkok: Samnakpim Ban Nangsue. เสี้ยวจันทร์ แรมไพร. 2536. ขับขานข้างใน. กรุงเทพฯ: สำนักพิมพ์บ้านหนังสือ.

———. 1993a. "Ha sahet." ["หาสาเหตุ."] In Siaochan 1993.

———. 1993b. "Khap khan khang nai." ["ขับขานข้างใน."] In Siaochan 1993.

———. 1993c. "Tua prakob." ["ตัวประกอบ."] In Siaochan 1993.

———. 1993d. "Wan phrungni." ["วันพรุ่งนี้."] In Siaochan 1993.

Sila Khomchai. 1993. *Khropkhrua klang thanon*. Bangkok: Mingmitr. ศิลา โคมฉาย. 2536. ครอบครัวกลางถนน. กรุงเทพฯ: มิ่งมิตร.

———. 1993a. "Dek hua khi lueai kap kradat nangsue phim." ["เด็กหัวขี้เลื่อยกับกระดาษหนังสือพิมพ์."] In Sila 1993.

———. 1993b. "Isara phap." ["อิสรภาพ."] In Sila 1993.

———. 1993c. "Kha sai khong mae." ["ขาซ้ายของแม่."] In Sila 1993.

———. 1993d. "Khropkhrua klang thanon." ["ครอบครัวกลางถนน."] In Sila 1993.

———. 1993e. "Sia ma." ["เสียหมา."] In Sila 1993. (Orig. pub.1988)

Siriworn Kaewkan. 2003. *Rueang lao khong khon banthuek rueang lao thi nak lao rueang khon nueng lao hai khao fang*. Bangkok: Ngai Ngam. ศิริวร แก้วกาญจน์. 2546. เรื่องเล่าของคนบันทึกเรื่องเล่าที่นักเล่าเรื่องคนหนึ่งเล่าให้เขาฟัง. กรุงเทพฯ: ง่ายงาม.

———. 2003a. "Kiaokap bai pit prakat" ["เกี่ยวกับใบปิดประกาศ."] In Siriworn 2003.

———. 2003b. "Kiaokap chotmai thueng bannathikan." ["เกี่ยวกับจดหมายถึงบรรณาธิการ."] In Siriworn 2003.

———. 2003c. "Kiaokap nak pit fai." ["เกี่ยวกับนักปิดไฟ."] In Siriworn 2003.

———. 2003d. "Kiaokap phu rob ru rueang dara phapphayon Thai." ["เกี่ยวกับผู้รอบรู้เรื่องดาราภาพยนตร์ไทย."] In Siriworn 2003.

———. 2003e. "Kiaokap rian baht." ["เกี่ยวกับเหรียญบาท."] In Siriworn 2003.

———. 2003f. "Kiaokap sat chanit tang tang doi chapho ma." ["เกี่ยวกับสัตว์ชนิดต่างๆ โดยเฉพาะหมา."] In Siriworn 2003.

———. 2003g. "Kiaokap thorasap mue thue." ["เกี่ยวกับโทรศัพท์มือถือ."] In Siriworn 2003.

Somjai Somkid. 1995. "Thang ok." *Cho Karaket* 22 (April–June). Edited by Suchart Sawasdsri. Bangkok: Samnak Chang Wanakam. สมใจ สมคิด. 2538. "ทางออก." ช่อการะเกด 22 (เมษายน–มิถุนายน). สุชาติ สวัสดิ์ศรี, บรรณาธิการ. กรุงเทพฯ: สำนักช่างวรรณกรรม.

Somnuek Thaipetkul. 1989. "Kham khuen kap tua-eng." *Cho Karaket* 5 (Chut doen kham khuen). Edited by Suchart Sawasdsri. Bangkok: Samoson Thanon Nangsue. สมนึก ไทยเพชร์กุล. 2532. "ค่ำคืนกับตัวเอง." ช่อการะเกด 5 (ชุด เดินข้ามคืน). สุชาติ สวัสดิ์ศรี, บรรณาธิการ. กรุงเทพฯ: สโมสรถนนหนังสือ.

Sridaoruang. 1984. *Bat prachachon*. Bangkok: Nam Aksorn Kanpim. ศรีดาวเรือง. 2527. บัตรประชาชน. กรุงเทพฯ: น้ำอักษรการพิมพ์.

———. 1984a. "Banphaburut khong khrai." ["บรรพบุรุษของใคร."] In Sridaoruang 1984.

———. 1984b. "Bat prachachon." ["บัตรประชาชน."] In Sridaoruang 1984.

———. 1984c. "Krasae samnuek khong yai." ["กระแสสำนึกของยาย."] In Sridaoruang 1984.

———. 1984d. "Lan yai." ["หลานยาย."] In Sridaoruang 1984.

———. 1984e. "Thang sop phan." ["ทางศพผ่าน."] In Sridaoruang 1984.

———. 1993. *Mae Salu*. Bangkok: Duangkamol Wanakam. ศรีดาวเรือง. 2536. แม่สาลู. กรุงเทพฯ: ดวงกมลวรรณกรรม.

———. 1993a. "Dut dang cha khai khuen." ["ดุจดั่งจะคายคืน."] In Sridaoruang 1993.

———.1993b. "Luk kai mai yak pen dao." ["ลูกไก่ไม่อยากเป็นดาว."] In Sridaoruang 1993.

———. 1993c. "Rueang lao khong Phlengphanom (1)." ["เรื่องเล่าของเพลงพนม (1)."] In Sridaoruang 1993. (Orig. pub. 1989)

———. 1993d. "Rueang lao khong Phlengphanom (2)" ["เรื่องเล่าของเพลงพนม (2)."] In Sridaoruang 1993. (Orig. pub. 1992)

———. 1993e. "Thewada-ma khi." ["เทวดา-หมาขี้."] In Sridaoruang 1993.

———. 1997. *Noen mafueang/chao kawao oey.* Bangkok: Duangkamol. ศรีดาวเรือง. 2540. เนินมะเฟือง/เจ้ากาเหว่าเอย. กรุงเทพฯ: ดวงกมล.

———. 1997a. "Chao kawao oei." ["เจ้ากาเหว่าเอย."] In Sridaoruang 1997.

———. 1997b. "Noen mafueang." ["เนินมะเฟือง."] In Sridaoruang 1997.

Sritawan. 1979. "Pi chaona." In *Ruam rueang san witthawat chut thi nueng khan rap pi chaona.* Bangkok: Wittawat. ศรีตะวัน. 2522. "ปีชาวนา." รวมเรื่องสั้นวิทวัสชุดที่ ๑ ขานรับปีชาวนา. กรุงเทพฯ: วิทวัส

Suchitra Jongphitwanna. 2004. "Ma kan kluai nirat raem rang chak fan." In *25 pi sirait ruam bot wichan khatsan.* Bangkok: Samakhom Phasa lae nangsue haeng prathet thai nai phraboromrachupatham. สุจิตรา จงถิตย์วัฒนา. "ม้าก้านกล้วยนิราศ แรมร้างจากฝัน." ใน ๒๕ ปีซีไรต์ รวมบทวิจารณ์คัดสรร. กรุงเทพฯ: สมาคมภาษาและหนังสือ แห่งประเทศไทย ในพระบรมราชูปถัมภ์, ๒๕๔๗.

Suebsakul Saenhsuwan. 2005. "Kampan sang rueang." In *A Day* 6 (62): 63. สืบสกุล แสงสุวรรณ. 2548. "กำปั้นสร้างเรื่อง." *A Day* 6 (62) (เดือนตุลาคม): 63.

Sunee Namso. 2006. "Phanak-ngan di den." In *Khop fai.* Edited by Kan Na Kan. Bangkok: Khrongkan ronarong phuea raeng-ngan Thai. สุนี นามโส. 2549. "พนักงาน ดีเด่น." คบไฟ. กานต์ ณ กานท์, บรรณาธิการ. กรุงเทพฯ: โครงการรณรงค์เพื่อแรงงานไทย.

Supachai Singyabhut. 1994. "Phi suea." In *Khon thuean.* Bangkok: Ton Aor. ศุภชัย สิงห์ยะบุศย์. 2537. "ผีเสื้อ." คนเถื่อน. กรุงเทพฯ: ต้นอ้อ.

Surachai Janthimathorn. 1982. *Kon khluean kharavan.* Bangkok: Malaeng Po. สุรชัย จันทิมาธร. 2525. ก่อนเคลื่อนคาราวาน. กรุงเทพฯ: แมลงปอ.

———. 1982a. "Bon rotfai chan sam." ["บนรถไฟชั้นสาม."] In Surachai 1982.

———. 1982b. "Rotfai." ["รถไฟ."] In Surachai 1982.

Suthipong Thamawut. 1992. "Phu chep puai." In *Rak ngao.* Bangkok: Nok Si Lueang. สุทธิพงษ์ ธรรมวุฒิ. 2535. "ผู้เจ็บป่วย." รากเหง้า. กรุงเทพฯ: นกสีเหลือง.

———. 2004. "Nakhon boriphokhaphan." In Rak ngao. Bangkok: Saman Chon. สุทธิพงษ์ ธรรมวุฒิ. 2547. "นครบริโภคทัณฑ์." รากเหง้า. กรุงเทพฯ: สามัญชน.

Tadsanawadee. 1995. "Kamphaeng." *Cho Karaket* 21 (January–March). Edited by Suchart Sawasdsri. Bangkok: Samnak Chang Wanakam. ทัศนาวดี. 2538. "กำแพง." ช่อการะเกด 21 (มกราคม–มีนาคม). สุชาติ สวัสดิ์ศรี, บรรณาธิการ. กรุงเทพฯ: สำนักช่าง วรรณกรรม.

Taratip. 1993. "Bon sen thang." *Cho Karaket* 16 (October–December). Edited by Suchart Sawasdsri. Bangkok: Samnak Chang Wanakam. ธราธิป. 2536. "บนเส้น ทาง." ช่อการะเกด 16 (ตุลาคม–ธันวาคม). สุชาติ สวัสดิ์ศรี, บรรณาธิการ. กรุงเทพฯ: สำนัก ช่างวรรณกรรม.

Tarin. 1993. "Kho thiam." In *Mueang dokmai.* Bangkok: Praew. ธาริน. 2536. "ขอเทียม." เมืองดอกไม้. กรุงเทพฯ: แพรว.

Tawan Santipaap. 1993. "Patikiriya." *Cho Karaket* 13 (January–March). Edited by Suchart Sawasdsri. Bangkok: Samnak Chang Wanakam. ตะวัน สันติภาพ. 2536. "ปฏิกิริยา." ช่อการะเกด 13 (มกราคม–มีนาคม). สุชาติ สวัสดิ์ศรี, บรรณาธิการ. กรุงเทพฯ: สำนัก ช่างวรรณกรรม.

Tawat Punnotok. 1979. *Wanakam isan.* Bangkok: Odeon Store. ธวัช ปุณโณทก. 2522. วรรณกรรมอีสาน. กรุงเทพฯ: โอเดียนสโตร์.

Thanet Wetphada et al. 2004. *25 pi S.E.A. Write ruam bot wichan khatsan.* Bangkok: Samakhom phasa lae nangsue haeng prathet Thai nai phra boromarachupatham. ๒๕ ปี ซีไรต์ รวมบทวิจารณ์คัดสรร. ๒๕๔๗. กรุงเทพฯ: สมาคมภาษาและหนังสือแห่งประเทศไทย ในพระบรมราชูปถัมภ์.

Udom Rungrueangsri. 1985. *Wanakam lanna.* Chiang Mai: Khrongkan tamra maha witthayalai. อุดม รุ่งเรืองศรี. 2528. วรรณกรรมล้านนา. เชียงใหม่: โครงการตำรามหาวิทยาลัย.

Ussiri Dhammachoti. 1992. *Thale ram lom sok.* Bangkok: Samnakpim Ko Kai. อัศศิริ ธรรมโชติ. 2535. ทะเลร่ำลมโศก. กรุงเทพฯ: สำนักพิมพ์ ก. ไก่.

———. 1992a. "Ok pai kap fung phi suea." ["ออกไปกับฝูงผีเสื้อ."] In Ussiri 1992.

———. 1992b. "Kanlaya(ni)." ["กัลยา(ณี)."] In Ussiri 1992.

———. 1992c. "Nangfa-thasi." ["นางฟ้า-ทาสี."] In Ussiri 1992.

———. 1992d. "Phap khrueng." ["พับครึ่ง."] In Ussiri 1992.

———. 1992e. "Phuen phan din trinachat." ["ผืนแผ่นดินตฤณชาติ."] In Ussiri 1992.

———. 1992f "Sia laeo sia pai." ["เสียแล้วเสียไป.""] In Ussiri 1992. (Orig. pub. 1977)

———. 2002a. *Kham khong ma.* Bangkok: Ming Mitr. อัศศิริ ธรรมโชติ. 2545. ข้าม โขงมา. กรุงเทพฯ: มิ่งมิตร.

———. 2002b. "Mueng khong phom." In *Nuea nep nao lae rao ron.* Bangkok: Ming Mitr. อัศศิริ ธรรมโชติ. 2545. "เมืองของผม." เหนือเหน็บหนาวและเร่าร้อน. กรุงเทพฯ: มิ่งมิตร.

———. 2002c. "Rotfai khrang thi ha." In *Khunthong chao cha klap ma muea fa sang.* Bangkok: Samnakpim Ko Kai. (Orig. pub. 1977) อัศศิริ ธรรมโชติ. 2530. "รถไฟครั้งที่ ห้า." ขุนทองเจ้าจะกลับเมื่อฟ้าสาง. กรุงเทพฯ: สำนักพิมพ์ ก. ไก่.

———. 2005. *Muean thale mi chao khong.* Bangkok: Kon Ru Chai. อัศศิริ ธรรมโชติ. 2548. เหมือนทะเลมีเจ้าของ. กรุงเทพฯ: คนรู้ใจ.

———. 2005a. "Ban khue wiman khong khao." ["บ้านคือ วิมานของเขา."] In Ussiri 2005.

———. 2005b. "Kan duen thang chak thong thung." ["การเดินทางจากท้องทุ่ง."] In Ussiri 2005.

———. 2005c. "Muean thale mi chao khong." ["เหมือนทะเลมีเจ้าของ."] In Ussiri 2005.

———. 2005d. "Nang ram." ["นางรำ."] In Ussiri 2005.

———. 2005e. "Hom klin fang khao muea khuen raem." ["หอมกลิ่นฟางข้าวเมื่อคืน แรม."] In Ussiri 2005.

Uthain Phromdaeng. 2003. "Kap kal." In *Ton mai pralat.* Bangkok: Double Nine. อุเทน พรมแดง. 2546. "กัปกัลป์." ต้นไม้ประหลาด. กรุงเทพฯ: ดับเบิ้ลนายน์.

————. 2004. *Nak lao rueng kohok*. Bangkok: Wasi Creation. อุเทน พรมแดง. 2547. นักเล่าเรื่องโกหก. กรุงเทพฯ: วสีครีเอชั่น.

————. 2004a. "Khwam hang klai." ["ความห่างไกล."] In Uthain 2004.

————. 2004b. "Long." ["หลง."] In Uthain 2004.

————. 2004c. "Malet khaosan." ["เมล็ดข้าวสาร."] In Uthain 2004.

————. 2004d. "Thale sai." ["ทะเลทราย."] In Uthain 2004.

————. 2005. "Chai chara thi suan satharana." In *Fai khwan man mok*. Bangkok: Dokya Group. อุเทน พรมแดง. 2548. "ชายชราที่สวนสาธารณะ." ไฟ ควัน ม่านหมอก. กรุงเทพฯ: ดอกหญ้ากรุ๊ป.

————. 2005. "Chai khon nueng." In *Ying Thai 712*, 150–156. อุเทน พรมแดง. 2548. "ชายคนหนึ่ง." หญิงไทย 712, 150–156.

Uthit Sangkharat. 1996. "Mai mi nam sai nai bo luek." *Cho Karaket* 27 (May–June). Edited by Suchart Sawasdsri. Bangkok: Samnak Chang Wanakam. อุทิศ สังข รัตน์. 2539. "ไม่มีน้ำใสในบ่อลึก." ช่อการะเกด 27 (พฤษภาคม–มิถุนายน). สุชาติ สวัสดิ์ศรี, บรรณาธิการ. กรุงเทพฯ: สำนักช่างวรรณกรรม.

Vip Buraphadeja. 2005. "Klap ma muea fa krachang." *A Day* 6 (62): 66–67. วิภว์ บูรพา เดชะ. 2548. "กลับมาเมื่อฟ้ากระจ่าง." *A Day* 6 (62) (เดือนตุลาคม): 66–67.

Wan Na Chanthan. 2005. "Wat mot ayu." In *Linchak thi loek chai*. Bangkok: Men Wanakam. วัน ณ จันทร์ธาร. 2548. "วัดหมดอายุ." ลิ้นชักที่เลิกใช้. กรุงเทพฯ: เม่นวรรณกรรม.

Warop Worrapa. 2005. "Khaosao mue pho." In *Ubattikan*. Bangkok: Politics. วรภ วรรภา. 2548. "ข้าวซาวมือพ่อ." อุบัติการณ์. กรุงเทพฯ: Politics.

Wat Wanlayangkun. 1984. "Phakbung fai daeng." In *Nakhon haeng duang dao*. Bangkok: Khon Wanakam. (Orig. pub. 1975) วัฒน์ วรรลยางกูร. 2527. "ผักบุ้งไฟแดง." นครแห่งดวงดาว. กรุงเทพฯ: คนวรรณกรรม.

Yiwa Jira-angkoon. 2005. "Potchananukrom kawi." *A Day* 6 (62): 88–89. ยิหวา จิระอังกูร. 2548. "พจนานุกรมกวี." *A Day* 6 (62) (เดือนตุลาคม): 88–89.

Yohda Hasaemsaeng. 1993. "Kapdak." *Cho Karaket* 16 (October–December). Edited by Suchart Sawasdsri. Bangkok: Samnak Chang Wanakam. ยอดา ฮะเซ็มเซ็ง. 2536. "กับดัก." ช่อการะเกด 16 (ตุลาคม–ธันวาคม). สุชาติ สวัสดิ์ศรี, บรรณาธิการ. กรุงเทพฯ: สำนัก ช่างวรรณกรรม.

————. 1999. *Kapdak nai samoraphum*. Bangkok: Klet Thai. ยอดา ฮะเซ็มเซ็ง. 2542. กับดักในสมรภูมิ. กรุงเทพฯ: เคล็ดไทย.

————. 1999a. "Klap chak samoraphum." ["กลับจากสมรภูมิ."] In Yohda 1999.

————. 1999b. "Lom haichai mae nam." ["ลมหายใจแม่น้ำ."] In Yohda 1999.

Yoon Kamolserirat. "Phu sia priap." *Cho Karaket* 15 (July–September). Edited by Suchart Sawasdsri. Bangkok: Samnak Chang Wanakam. ยูร กมลเสรีรัตน์. 2536. "ผู้เสียเปรียบ." ช่อการะเกด 15 (กรกฎาคม–กันยายน). สุชาติ สวัสดิ์ศรี, บรรณาธิการ. กรุงเทพฯ: สำนักช่างวรรณกรรม.

INDEX